THE MODERN BUDDHIST-CHRISTIAN DIALOGUE

Two Universalistic Religions

in Transformation

Paul O. Ingram

Studies in Comparative Religion
Volume 2

The Edwin Mellen Press
Lewiston/Queenston

Library of Congress Cataloging-in-Publication Data

Ingram, Paul O., 1939-
  The Modern Buddhist-Christian Dialogue: Two Universalistic Religions
in Transformation

  (Studies in comparative religion ; v. 2)
  Bibliography: p.
  Includes index.
  1. Christianity and other religions--Buddhism.
2. Buddhism--Relations--Christianity. I. Title.
II. Series: Studies in comparative religion (Lewiston, N.Y.) ; v. 2.
BR128.B8I53   1987   261.2'43   87-14108
ISBN 0-88946-490-1 (alk. paper)

This is volume 2 in the continuing series
Studies in Comparative Religion
Volume 2 ISBN 0-88946-490-1
SCR Series ISBN 0-88946-488-X

The Edwin Mellen Press   The Edwin Mellen Press
Box 450   Box 67
Lewiston, New York   Queenston, Ontario
USA 14092   L0S 1L0 CANADA

Printed in the United States of America

TABLE OF CONTENTS

PREFACE

What we call the beginning is often the end. And to
make an end is to make a beginning. The end is what we
start from.

T. S. Eliot, *Four Quartets*

Historians of religions are an unconventional
lot. Most of us drawn to this field of religious studies are by nature intellectually and emotionally comfortable with cultural and religious diversity even before we become formally trained historians of religions. The social mores and expectations, the political and economic ideologies, the religious and philosophical absolutes structuring most people's lives all
seem so uninteresting compared to the exciting realities of cultural and religious diversity. So one finds
oneself in the unnerving position of being an outsider
to one's own cultural and religious Way. The truth
claims of teachers, pastors, governmental officials,
politicians, journalists, community and business lead-
ers--even one's closest friends--are more often than
not prefaced with the skeptical interrogative phrase,
"but what if"? Gradually, the realization dawns that
one just does not "fit in."

This vague sense of being out of tune, of being on the fringes, of being in one's cultural and religious Way but not of it, can be very uncomfortable.
It becomes easy to identify with the Sesame Street
character, Kermit the Frog: "it's not easy being
green." But being out of step does have joys and ad-
vantages. "Being green" can teach much about the

beauty of solitude. Being on the fringes creates a hunger for the new and joy in its quest--even when the treasure for which one searches is not found. Life can become exciting, sensitivities sharpened, diversity celebrated, loneliness overcome.

When persons having this nature enter formal graduate training in history of religions, a curious process takes place. The negative and positive sides of the not-easy-being-green feeling of living on the edges of conventionality are transformed from a vague suspicion into a sharply disciplined methodological and philosophical point of view. This transformation occurs because of the sorts of questions with which historians of religions are professionally concerned. What is the generic nature of religious experience? Is there a generic feature or set of features common to all historical forms of religious faith and practice? If so, what accounts for the diversity displayed by the numerous religious Ways of humanity? Why are there so many ways of being religious, and what does this fact tell us about human nature? How does religious faith influence politics, art, economics, literature, ethics, and history? How do political, economic, aesthetic, literary, technological, scientific, institutional, sociological, psychological, biological, and historical factors influence religious faith? Is it possible to understand religious experience *sui generis*, in its own terms, apart from the intellectual reductionism of most contemporary social-scientific explanations of religious faith and practice? Are human beings "naturally religious?" What are the "origins" of religious experience? Are questions of origins meaningful questions?

One common factor underlies these sorts of questions that also provides a clue for understanding the professional concerns of historians of religions. Stated negatively, historians of religions are not interested in theological and philosophical questions. They are not concerned with normative issues about the truth, falsehood, or value of the forms of religious faith and practice constituting the topics of their individual research. A working historian of religions is not concerned with what *ought* to be believed or practiced, but with *what there is to be* believed or practiced. In other words, whether the faith and practice of religious persons represents a true expression of reality, "the way things really are," is of no concern to the historian of religions. The intellectual task of this academic discipline is to descriptively set out what religious persons do, not evaluate the truth, beauty, or goodness of what they do—questions which are supposedly the professional prerogative of theologians and philosophers.

Of course, many historians of religions are passionately grasped by theological and philosophical commitments. But while performing the tasks of teaching, research, and writing they try to set their normative commitments aside in order to allow them as little operational influence on their work as possible. "Objective description" of "religious matters of fact," has been the goal of historians of religions since the nineteenth century beginnings of this discipline in the writings of Max Müller.

Professionally, therefore, historians of religions are let off a number of difficult intellectual hooks. Issues of the truth, value, and falsehood of a religious Way's particular forms of faith and practice can be safely ignored. *That* the Buddhist Way, for example, teaches that all things and events are constituted as "nonselves" (Pāli: *anattā* or "nonself"), and describing what this teaching implies about how Buddhists view the world, is different from having to make normative value judgments about whether the doctrine of nonself accurately represents reality. Freedom from personally struggling with the existential meaning and value of the diverse forms of religious faith and practice allows historians of religions freedom to confront the cultural diversity of religious experience. Freedom from bothering about the "truth" of "religious matters of fact" places the scholar in a powerful methodological position for determining what the "religious matters of facts are." Because historians of religions are not supposed to allow their own existential faith commitments to influence their work, they are, among all religious scholars, intellectually best situated for accurate description of the nature of religious experience and the diversity of religious faith and practice.

But historians of religions must pay a heavy price for this intellectual freedom. Ignoring normative questions about religious faith and practice does not make these questions go away. Leaving them alone, setting them aside to be cleaned up by theologians and philosophers, is also an intellectual cop out. Merely settling on abstract descriptive accounts of religious experience divorces faith and practice from the experience of religious human beings. One winds up falsifying the "religious matters of fact" one so conscientiously tries to describe because one winds up telling only half the story. In the "real" world, religious faith and practice cannot be rationally understood when divorced from the experience of religious persons-- human beings searching for normative meanings and values as they practice their religious faith.

Nevertheless, the methodological tensions between descriptive accounts of religious experience, and normative questions about what the facts of religious experience mean, are real. They are also difficult to balance against one another, especially when historians of religions confront students, particularly undergraduate students. Experience with students, engaging in research, publishing, attending academic conferences-- often create existential tensions that drag historians of religions kicking and screaming into confrontation with normative religious questions. These questions also force the realities of modern religious and secular pluralism to the forefront of conscious awareness.

In my case, twenty years of teaching courses in "world religions" has been the most potent force pulling me out of total immmersion in the descriptive commitments of history of religions. While students, particularly undergraduate students, are often interested in abstract, factual accounts of *what*

religious persons "do and believe," they refuse to
remain satisfied with merely analytical summations of
religious faith and practice. Indeed, most students
understand the importance of knowing something of the
pluralism of "what there is to be believed and
practiced" because they seek a context for wrestling
with their own religiously normative concerns.
Nevertheless, they remain most interested in "what-
ought-I-believe-and-practice" types of issues. "Which
religion is best for me, or for anyone"? they often
ask. "What can the religious Ways of other cultures
teach me about my own religious commitments and
cultural traditions?" "Should religious persons learn
from religious Ways other than their own, and if so,
what and how?" "Is any one religious Way the only
means to personal salvation, and if so, how do I know
it." "In a religiously and culturally plural world,
can any religious teaching be truer than any other?"
"Are we stuck in a debilitating relativity in which no
religious claims and no religious practices are in
principle better than any others?" "Are all religious
Ways equally true, or are they all equally ignorant, in
their portrayal of realities more truthfully and
honestly disclosed by the natural sciences?" In a
religiously plural world, do any religious commitments
make sense?" "Is it necessary, or even possible, to
remain exclusively loyal to the Christian or the Muslim
or the Buddhist Ways?"

The questions keep coming--all questions of
meaning and truth, all in an astonishing variety of
forms, all wrapped in varying levels of intellectual

and emotional intensity. So as a teacher who is also an historian of religions, I earn my living by placing my students in dialogue with the religious Ways of humanity. Not only this. The methodological pluralism of history of religions is itself a mirror image of the realities of the modern religious and secular pluralism with which I daily confront my students. But even though history of religions is a powerful collection of methods for exposing students to these realities--and placing them in dialogue with them--the discipline fails to help students solve the normative questions that constantly arise in their dialogue with the diversities of religious experience. In fact, at least as defined since the nineteenth century, history of religions is not even supposed to try to help students with such questions.

But I am also a teacher, as well as a historian of religions. Not assisting my students to learn how to seek their own solutions to the normative questions which arise as I confront them with modern religious and secular pluralism is a professional failure. Even if I wanted to, I cannot avoid issues of truth and value; no historian of religions should try. Besides, in my case, the normative questions which grasp so many of my students's imaginations are also my own.

Experiences beyond the demands of classroom instruction and academic research often force historians of religions into confrontation with normative theological and philosophical questions. For me, one such event occurred in 1980 during a clear June morning on a beautiful strip of palm tree lined beach in

Kailua, Hawaii. I was attending the First International Conference on Buddhist-Christian Encounter, sponsored by the Department of Religious Studies of the University of Hawaii. Buddhist and Christian scholars, as well as teachers, clergy, and laity representing all parts of the Buddhist and Christian world, met in daily, intense, dialogical encounter. Part of the conference schedule entailed bussing the participants out of the noisy distractions of Honolulu to a secluded Methodist Church camp on the windward side of Oahu to discuss--and participate in--forms of Buddhist and Christian meditative "practice" (*praxis*). An extraordinary event occurred here that, as it turned out, became the main motivation for writing this book.

The Conference had been intense, and there was much to think about. I arose early one morning after a very restless night--about 4:30 a.m.--and took a walk on the quiet beach. I felt intellectually and emotionally drained, and I thought watching the sunrise would improve my perspective on the scheduled events of the new day. I also wanted solitude--something not easy to find at an academic conference. I only got my wish about the sunrise.

As I walked, absorbed with whatever it was that was on my mind, a shadow-form abruptly jumped into my field of awareness--a female figure sitting quietly under a palm tree in the lotus posture, her presence barely outlined in the dim light of approaching dawn. I was startled for a moment, but then I recognized her. She was a Chinese T'ien T'ai Buddhist nun, sitting in deep meditative concentration, rooted in the special practice which anchored her so impressively in the Buddhist Way. Head shaven, eyes half closed and focused on a spot somewhere in front of her crossed legs, dressed in the dark gray robes of her order, she looked like one of those standardized images of the Buddha gracing the numberless altars dotting East Asia.

As I stared at this meditating figure, a movement to my left caught my attention: a Franciscan monk slowly walking back and forth between two palm trees, contemplatively whispering his morning vespers. He too was focused, attentive, balanced in the self-discipline he practiced which opened him to the depths of his Roman Catholic Christian Way. I had never seen anyone sit so naturally, so noncompulsively as the Buddhist nun. Nor had I ever seen anyone walk so naturally, so gracefully as the Franciscan monk.

The Chinese nun and the Franciscan monk were discussion leaders of the main topic of this period of the Conference--Buddhist and Christian "practice". Both were scholarly, articulate, and conversant with the major traditions of the Buddhist and Christian Ways. Because each existentially dwelled so completely within their own religious Way, they could apprehend the authenticity of the other's religious faith and practice. Neither was a religious imperialist who preached the "one Way" chauvinism of the sort characterizing the lives of so many contemporary Western religious persons. They learned from one another, appropriated insights from one another, and yet remained fully Buddhist and Christian in their faith and practice.

What I saw on that shadowy dawn morning was
the source of their faith and their openness to one another's religious Way: their practice. Because each
was centered in a particular religious Way, each was
open to dimensions of reality most persons lack the
imagination to think possible. What were these realities? In spite of religious and cultural differences,
what had this Buddhist nun discovered in the Franciscan
monk's faith and practice that helped her become more
authentically Buddhist and human? What did the Franciscan monk discover, through his encounter with the
Buddhist nun, that helped him become more authentically
Christian and human? What was going on?

This book is an attempt to discover some answers to this question which the methodological pluralism of history of religions has forced me to encounter,
but which has not helped me--or any one else--to resolve. Facing up to this question requires that an
historian of religions also function as philosopher and
theologian. I have attempted to do this in the present
study. While this book is about contemporary Buddhist-
Christian dialogical encounter, and the normative issues this encounter raises for both Buddhists and
Christians, I also contend that principles similar to
the ones I have followed here apply equally to dialogical encounter with any religious Way. The essential
point to notice, however, is that I have approached
this study as an historian of religions, who happens to
specialize in Japanese Buddhist studies, interested in
discovering possible solutions to theological and
philosophical issues engendered by the "facts" of mod-

ern Buddhist-Christian encounter. In other words, I intend to write as an historian of religions functioning as theologian-philosopher of religion.

The first nine chapters follow a similar format. Each is devoted to an analysis of some of the important issues which have emerged from contemporary Buddhist-Christian dialogical encounter. The main methodological approach has been to compare how Buddhists and Christians have responded to these issues. I have ended each of the first nine chapters with a section entitled "concluding observations," in which I have tried (1) to clearly describe how Buddhists and Christians ought to respond to the issues arising out of their mutual encounter; (2) to set up the themes of the following chapter; and (3) to identify those questions to which I have responded most completely in chapter ten, entitled "Conclusions in Process."

Chapter one, "Dialogue As A Process of Creative Transformation," identifies the specific issues with which this study is concerned. It also attempts to justify using process philosophy and theology as the interpretive framework from which I have approached this study. Modern religious and secular pluralism, the relativity of belief, and the nature and function of dialogue are the topics of this chapter. A slightly different version of this chapter was published in 1981 under the title, "Interfaith Dialogue as a Source of Buddhist-Christian Renewal" in *Dialogue*, 7, (January-December 1981): 6-23.

Chapter two, "The Christian Encounter with Non-Christian Religious Ways," was published in 1984 by

University Press of America in *Tradition As Openness to
the Future, Essays in Honor of Willis W. Fisher*,
edited by Fred 0. Francis. This chapter describes the
general history of Christian encounter with non-Christian religious Ways, while Chapter three, "The Buddhist
Encounter with Non-Buddhist Religious Ways," describes
the history and dynamics of Buddhist encounter with
non-Buddhist religious Ways.

Chapter four, "Buddhist and Christian Experience of Faith," seeks to set forth the "faith
paradigms" of Buddhist and Christian practice. Chapter
five, "Faith as Practice: The Buddhist Way," and chapter six, "Faith as Practice: The Christian Way," specify, compare, and contrast the meaning of "practice"
and the relationship between faith and practice in Buddhist and Christian experience. The experience of
self-identity through time and Buddhist and Christian
conceptualizations of this experience are compared and
contrasted in chapter seven, "Buddhist and Christian
Paradigms of Selfhood."

Since Buddhists and Christians are so sharply
opposed in their traditional understandings of human
selfhood, chapter seven is especially relevant for the
topic of chapter eight, "The Question of God." It is in
these two chapters that I try to overcome the conceptual differences between Buddhist and Christian understandings of selfhood and God by developing a selfhood
paradigm based on the process philosophy of Alfred
North Whitehead. I argue that this process selfhood
paradigm is faithful to both Buddhist and Christian
experience of self-identity through time. Chapter nine,

"Buddhist and Christian Universalism," is a continuation of the discussions of chapters seven and eight. In this chapter, I confront the source of Christian universalism, faith in Christ, with the source of Buddhist universalism, faith in the Dharma. My thesis is that even though faith in Christ and faith in the Dharma are different, they need not be contradictory.

The most pleasant experience for an author occurs when he or she reflects on the numerous friends who have rendered assistance and encouragement during the times of research and writing. In my case, the list is long, and I hope I can further indulge any friend I inadvertently fail to acknowledge to forgive my oversight.

I am especially grateful to John B. Cobb, Jr. for gently, yet rigorously leading me into my first encounter with the process philosophy of Alfred North Whitehead. He was my first teacher in the study of process philosophy and theology. In many ways, most of which he is not aware, his work continues to influence my own research, writing, and developing world view. Cobb's work in Buddhist-Christian dialogue has also had more influence upon my own than any other author, as one can easily see upon reading this book.

Frederick J. Streng, whom I first met in Hawaii in 1980 at the First International Conference on Buddhist-Christian Encounter, and whose scholarship in the general field of history of religions and in Buddhist studies I have admired long before we met, has also contributed much to my understanding of the dynamics and issues of Buddhist-Christian dialogue. The collection of essays we coedited, *Buddhist-Christian Dialogue: Mutual Renewal and Transformation* (Honolulu: University of Hawaii Press, 1986), was the main source motivating me to write my own book on this topic. I wanted to resolve some important issues raised by the contributors to *Buddhist-Christian Dialogue*. To those contributors, and especially to Fred Streng, I remain grateful.

Several colleagues at Pacific Lutheran University were also instrumental in encouraging me to write this book. University President William O. Rieke found money when money was difficult to find that allowed me to attend the First and Second International Conference on Buddhist-Christian Dialogue in Hawaii. He continues to support my interest in this topic, and his encouragement is gratefully acknowledged. Provost Richard Jungkuntz read several chapters and offered valuable suggestions, and much encouragement, during various stages of the book's production. It pleases me to publicly recognize his support of my work as teacher and writer. My colleagues in the Department of Religion read every chapter in various stages of production. They offered invaluable criticism, insight, advice, and support.

One is indeed fortunate to have "three good friends," as the Chinese knew. I am very fortunate to have three good friends and colleagues in the English Department of Pacific Lutheran University, without whose encouragement and willing assistance I would never have completed this book. Audrey S. Eyler, currently Chair of the Department of English, read and edited the entire manuscript. Audrey's gracefully rigorous criticisms about matters of composition and style, her demand that I write with clarity, and her discussions with me about the book's methodology and content were so important that I doubt that I could have completed the writing process without her. Lesley Hazleton, freelance writer, journalist, and Distinguished Writer in Residence during the spring semester 1986 taught me much about the writing process through her public lectures and in private conversation. Finally Jack Cady and his friend, "Rufus Jones," finished off the lessons I received from Audrey and Lesley. Jack is a novelist, one of the finest fiction writers and creative writing teachers I have ever known. His instruction, especially during the summer of 1986 when I "sat in" on his course in fiction writing, also contributed to the creation of this book. "Rufus Jones" did not help me put this book together, except indirectly by being Jack's friend. He also provided the answer to the Chinese Ch'an Buddhist master Chou Cho's question, "Does a dog have the Buddha Nature"? To anyone knowing Rufus, the answer is obvious: "Of course!"

Special thanks must be given to the staff of my university's Computer Center because of the technical assistance they gave me during the final editing of this book. Howard Bandy, Dean of Academic Computing, provided technical assistance and computer and printing equipment when I needed it. He also assigned four skillful--and patient--staff members to guide me through the technical mysteries of word processing. I am particularly grateful to Sally Hilberg for her knowledge of Microsoft Word and her willingness to share this knowledge with me at the drop of a phone call. Liz Moore undertook the difficult process of reformating the preliminary drafts of this book, written in a word processing program called Wordstar, through a text editor, into Microsoft Word format. Paul Petterson and Michille Thibault, both of whom are senior student employees of the Computer Center, were very charitable, if not down right indulgent, in steering me through the mysteries of operating an IBM Personal Computer.

I must also acknowledge the work of Megan Benton, Adjunct Professor of English, and her students in her course, "The Writing Process." Megan and her students proofread every word of the preliminary drafts of this book for technical problems. I cannot speak for her students with any certainty, but I certainly received an education about the preparation of manuscripts. I imagine they did too.

As usual, my wife, Regina, and my two children, Gail and Robert, were always patient with me during those times my research and writing took up so much mental and emotional energy, that I had little left for them. Their support, humor, love, and understanding are the real center of my life and work, so much so that even saying "I'am grateful" fails to capture the reality they always create for me.

Finally, I wish to dedicate this book to two people. My father, Gail O. Ingram, whose way of molding his sons has taken me years to understand, continues exerting the strength of character in everything I have ever undertaken. Whenever I have succeeded in anything, I suspect the degree of success is due primarily to his influence. I am also very fortunate because I have a second father figure. Willis W. Fisher, professor emeritus of Old Testament at the School of Theology at Claremont, California--as well as professor emeritus of religion at Chapman College, Orange, California--was the single most important teacher I had during my student days. The remarkable thing about this fact is that he was not an instructor in my major fields of study. But his demand, backed up when necessary with tough discipline, that I integrate my academic interests into as many fields of inquiry as possible, has served me well as a teacher and scholar. He also gave me my first lessons in combating religious imperialism, including forms that have taken place in my own work. So this one's for you, my father, Gail O. Ingram, car painter emeritus of Joshua Tree, California; and for you too, Willis W. Fisher, father figure, teacher, critic, and friend. I hope this book is worthy of the influence both of you continue exerting upon me.

Paul O. Ingram
Pacific Lutheran University.

CHAPTER ONE
Dialogue as a Process of Creative Transformation

If I had but little knowledge I should, in walking on a broad way fear getting off the road. Broad ways are extremely even, but people are fond of by-paths.

Tao Te Ching, 53

THE PROBLEM OF RELIGIOUS AND SECULAR PLURALISM

Whatever else might be said about the nature of human existence, it seems empirically evident we human beings have a profound need to believe that the truths we apprehend are rooted in, and thereby correspond to, the fundamental structures of the universe. If this were not the case, could any of these "truths," which guide, motivate, give understanding, perhaps even pleasure to our lives, be really important? And yet how can we be sure that the "truths" we believe correspond to the structures of reality, when we have always experienced, apprehended, and propositionally formulated "truth" so differently in spite of sharing the same planet. Primal humankind, wrapped up in limited geographical dwelling spaces and surrounded by tribal mythology, did not have to struggle with questions of pluralism to any significant degree. For at this state of human history, questions of pluralism remain largely isolated in humanity's prereflective consciousness. But even contemporary human beings have been spared the pain of wrestling with this problem, for until very recently the civilizations of the world have been culturally, and therefore intellectually and experientially,

self-contained. It is the individual whom C. G. Jung
called "modern" who encounters the problems of pluralism most acutely--the problem of discovering a unified
sense of meaning within the context of contemporary religious and secular pluralism. For the "modern" person
is

> by no means the average man. He is rather
> the man who stands upon a peak, or at least
> the very edge of the world, the abyss of the
> future before him, above him the heavens and
> below him the whole of mankind with a history
> that disappears in the primal mists. The
> modern man, or let us say the man in the im-
> mediate present is rarely met with. . . Since
> to be wholly in the present means to be fully
> conscious of one's existence as a man, it re-
> quires the most intensive and extensive con-
> sciousness. It must be be clearly understood
> that the mere fact of living in the present
> does not make a man modern. . . . He alone is
> modern who is fully conscious of the pre-
> sent.[1]

"Modernity," then, is a frame of mind, a psychological attitude, a mind-set radically separating an
individual from the normally accepted conventional traditions and attitudes of one's culture. A modern person existentially stands on the fringes of a culture's
"given" values and conventions, and in so standing is
"in" but not "of" the traditional world-view of that
culture. In this sense, "modern persons" have always
existed, some classical examples being the Buddha, Je-

sus, Socrates, Mohammed, Marx, Gandhi, or Martin Luther King, Jr.

The psychological dynamics of modernity noted by Jung over forty years ago have also been recently analyzed by Peter L. Berger from the perspective of the sociology of knowledge. Because contemporary modernity is situated within the context of immense technological power, contemporary modern human existence is marked by a nearly inconceivable expansion of the areas of choice. Wherever modernization occurs, the individual

> lives in a world of choice, in sharp contrast
> to the world of fate inhabited by traditional
> man. He must choose in innumerable situa-
> tions in everyday life, but this necessity of
> choosing reaches into the areas of life be-
> liefs, values, and worldviews. To decide,
> however, means to reflect. The modern indi-
> vidual must stop and pause where premodern
> men could act in unresponsive spontaneity.
> Quite simply, the modern individual must en-
> gage in more deliberate thinking--not because
> he is more intelligent, not because he is on
> some sort of higher level of consciousness,
> but because the necessity to choose, and
> ipso facto the necessity of pausing to re-
> flect before choosing, on various levels of
> life. Ordinary, everyday life is full of
> choices, from the most trivial choices be-
> tween competing consumer commodities to far-
> reaching alternatives in life styles. . . .
> In a historically unprecedented manner the

modern individual plans his own life, and that of his family, as modern societies plan their collective future. And to repeat, this necessity to choose bridges the pretheoretical levels of conscious experience.[2]

Modern self-consciousness is grounded in the necessity of choice, and this necessity Berger labels "the heretical imperative," from the Greek verb *harein*, "to choose." Modernity pluralizes both institutions and world views in a way utterly unimagined by premodern human beings. The modern individual must be a "heretic" because modern self-understanding is radically pluralized by the experience of having to choose among not only the competing gadgets of consumer technology, but more profoundly among different religious and secular social systems and beliefs, none of which can claim a self-evident market on "truth."

Of course, not all contemporary persons experience the relativism and pluralism of modernity in the same way or even as a problem. But modern individuals, wherever they exist, experience the relativity and necessity of choice as absolutely basic to human growth and development. The implication of this situation for modern religious persons, Christian and non-Christian, is the necessity of reformulating religious faith and practice through interreligious dialogue as a means of renewal and growth, often referred to as "creative transformation."

The problem of religious and secular pluralism involves many interrelated issues. Most generally and fundamentally, it involves metaphysical and epistemological issues: how can we really know we possess knowledge corresponding to "the way things really are?" The point is wonderfully illustrated by a conversation between the Taoist sage, Chuang Tzu (between 399-295 B.C.E.), and his friend Hui Tzu

> Chuang Tzu and Hui Tzu were taking a leisurely walk along the Hao River. Chuang Tzu said, "The fish are swimming at ease. This is the happiness of the fish."
>
> "You are not a fish," said Hui Tzu. "How do you know its happiness?
>
> "You are not I," Chuang Tzu said. "How do you know that I do not know the happiness of the fish?"
>
> Hui Tzu said, "Of course I do not know, since I am not you. But you are not a fish, and it is perfectly clear that you do not know the happiness of the fish."
>
> "Let us get at the bottom of the matter," said Chuang Tzu. "When you asked how I knew the happiness of the fish, you already knew that I knew the happiness of the fish, but asked how. I knew it along the river.[3]

Hui Tzu's problem is our problem, for he raised the real question of modern pluralism: how do we know that we know? Here we encounter the religious, theological, and philosophical problems posed by modern religious and secular pluralism most radically, for at this point we are, like Hui Tzu, most directly confronted by differing and often competing visions of reality. Just how can we determine whether our specific beliefs about the more specialized forms of human knowledge, for example, our scientific, social, political, aesthetic, historical, ethical, or religious beliefs--possess any validity?

Accordingly, the remainder of this chapter will specify the interpretive framework governing the thesis I defend throughout this study: dialogue between the religious traditions of the world, as illustrated by contemporary Buddhist-Christian dialogue, is the most appropriate means of confronting and understanding the religious and philosophical issues posed by modern religious and secular pluralism. I begin by briefly describing the conceptual framework underlying my reflections as these bear on the issue of the relativity of belief. I then argue for a specific theoretical understanding of the nature and function of dialogue, after which I conclude with several observations which I hope will establish coherent points of transition to the topics of subsequent chapters of this study.

PROCESS PHILOSOPHY AND THE RELATIVITY OF BELIEF

A conceptual framework is, among other things, a means by which disciplined scholars in any field of inquiry, in this case comparative religions, interpret the nature and meaning of whatever they investigate. Or in the words of the philosopher-scientist Michael Polanyi, "the power of our conceptions lies in identifying new instances of certain things we know. The function of our conceptual framework is akin to our perceptive framework which enables us to see ever-new objects as such, or to that of our appetites

which enables us to recognize ever-new things as satis-
fying to them."[4] Among other things, this means that a
conceptual framework tacitly and implicitly expresses a
wider and more general vision of reality. My own conceptual framework is deeply influenced by a tradition
of thought known as "process philosophy," especially as
expressed through the writings of Alfred North Whitehead, Charles Hartshorne, and John B. Cobb, Jr. While
there is no need to spell out the complete details of
Whitehead's system,[5] a consideration of the meaning of
"process" will help clarify what is to follow.

Process philosophy assumes process is fundamental to existence. But it does not assume everything
is in process or is a process, for this would mean even
the fact of process is subject to change. There are
unchanging principles as well as unchanging, though abstract, forms of process. However, anything that is
not a process is an abstraction, not a fullfledged actuality. In other words, "to be actual" means to be in
process of becoming.

Whitehead's rather detailed and technical account of the structure of process had its own distinctive character. The temporal process, he believed, is
a "transition" from one "actual entity" or "actual occasion of experience" to another. An actual entity is
a momentary experiencing event that immediately perishes upon coming into existence, a state that he
called "objective immortality." However, perished actualities mark the transition to succeeding actualities,
for they become part of the total past which becoming
actual entities must incorporate into themselves

(through "positive" and "negative," "physical" and
"mental," and "hybrid prehensions") in their own internal subjective processes of reaching "satisfaction" or
completeness, at which moment they too become ob-
jectvely immortal, perish, and become incorporated into
the becoming of future actual entities, *ad infinitum*,
or in Whitehead's words, "till the crack of doom." True
"individuals" are momentary experiences, implying that
what we normally call "individuals"--for example, particular things like persons or the sorts of objects we
perceive as remaining self-identical through time--are
not true individuals but "societies" composed of continually becoming, actual entities. There are several
varieties of "societies" in Whitehead's speculative
scheme, and all are involved in this temporal process
of becoming. This process includes human existence,
which he characterized as a "serially ordered society"
of actual occasions of experience.[6]

But interdependent with the transition from
actual entity to actual entity constituting the temporal process, Whitehead wrote about another type of process that is identical to every actual entity. The actual entities comprising the temporal process are themselves processes of their own momentary becoming.
Whitehead called this form of becoming "concrescence,"
meaning "becoming concrete." In other words, the individual, actual occasions of experience constituting the
world of things and events (societies of actual occasions), are themselves dynamically concrete acts of becoming.[7]

The specific details of Whitehead's analysis of these processes are, of course, much more technical and complex than I have outlined. But for the purposes of this chapter it is only necessary to note the essentials of his vision of a universe in which all the elements composing it at any single moment of space-time are what they are because of their interrelation and interdependency with everything else at this moment. In his view, the universe is not a collection of "pill-like atoms," insulated bodies, and isolated minds. Whitehead's vision of reality expressed his interpretation of the picture of the universe emerging within the natural sciences of his day. That is, his thought represents an interpretation of Einstein's general and special theories of relativity.

He therefore believed all forms of organizational relatedness--biological, social, and even space-time--are open systems of interdependent relations interpenetrated by other systems. In his opinion, we neither live in nor experience an amorphous, static universe, but a dynamic universe of open forms and interrelated possibilities. And as the natural sciences are increasingly demonstrating, Whitehead believed the principle of relativity, in the sense of interdependently relational, to be at the heart of things.[8]

If Whitehead's philosophy is an adequate account of human experience, and if the natural sciences are indeed experimentally confirming Einstein's general and special theories of relativity, then religious pluralism should be regarded as one element of our general metaphysical situation. No one need be surprised, therefore, that human beings have perceived the Sacred, however it is named, from culturally, biologically, and historically limited standpoints, because everything must be perceived and understood this way. We "see through a glass darkly," and we shall continue doing so. Once more, it would be surprising if this were not the case in our present "cosmic epoch," to borrow again a phrase from Whitehead. But at the same time, human beings will continue believing that what they have encountered and apprehended from a particular standpoint truly corresponds to the "way things really are" apart from the limitations of standpoint and frame of reference. Again, this should not astonish anyone, since all experience either originates within the regional perspective of the experiencer or there is no experience at all. Nor should anyone be astonished by the resulting epistemological problem of the relativity of not only our religious beliefs, but the relativity of everything we believe about the universe.

At this juncture, however, precision is necessary regarding the meaning of the word belief. Originally, belief meant more than the assertion of knowledge about something directly or indirectly experienced; its meaning included the assertion of knowledge plus the resolve to live in accordance with this knowledge.[9] But in contemporary popular usage, belief connotes "less than knowledge," for we habitually attach to this word ideas the truth of which we are not sure of ourselves, as well as assertions that we know to be wrong, such as the belief that the world is flat. In opposition to contemporary popular usage, I shall

consciously employ the term "belief" to mean "an assertion of knowledge coupled with the resolve to enact
this knowledge." Thus, whenever I really believe something to be true, even if in fact I am in error, I will
always act according to the truth I believe. To a very
great extent, then, I agree with the Chinese philosopher Wang Yang-ming's (1472-1529) teaching of an ontological correlation between what an individual regards
as knowledge and how an individual behaves. I have
also been instructed by a number of John Cobb's highly
suggestive propositions concerning universal relativity
which prevent it from becoming debilitating.[10]

First of all, there can exist no standpoint
from which to think or experience other than the radically particular regional standpoint of oneself, here
and now. Every aspect of this particular here-now
standpoint is interdependent with, because it is relative to, every other here-now standpoint. This is why
no standpoint, and for this reason no belief, is free
from the influences of biology, biography, culture, or
history. At the same time, however, none of these influences remains unaffected by whatever rational, critical, and creative activity we may or may not bring to
the particular here-now regional standpoint we occupy.

Second, our very awareness of the limitations
imposed by our standpoints can only be partial since we
ourselves are participants in them. Regarding this aspect of the relativity of belief, Cobb has noted an important methodological implication:

Sociologists of knowledge rarely reflect
deeply on the sociology of knowledge. Those

who explain belief psychologically rarely reflect deeply on the psychoanalytic explanation of their psychoanalytic explanation of
the sociology of knowledge, or psychoanalysts
sufficiently consider activity.[11]

Our knowledge in any field of inquiry will
always remain incomplete because any methodological
procedure can in principle be pursued endlessly.

Third, any analysis of the relativity of belief, including this analysis, is itself relative, as
is the judgment "it is relative." Indeed this might be
a vicious regress, but it is one to which finitude con-
demns us. There may exist an absolute reality in which
universal relativity is ontologically grounded. Even
so, whatever knowledge we can possess of this reality
must always remain regionally conditioned by the standpoint we occupy at any given moment, and hence be relative.

Finally, the relativity of the here-now moment of our standpoints presupposes there are, have
been, and will be future here-now moments. Universal
relativity presupposes philosophical realism. That is,
the objects of our knowledge are not simply mind dependent, but independently and interdependently existing
entities. It is our beliefs about these entities that
are relative to the particular here-now standpoints we
occupy.[12] The alternative is "solipsism of the present
moment," which is a way of absolutizing the present
here-now moment as all that exists. As a realist I
cannot absolutize even the present here-now moment.

Against solipsism I am a convinced realist who recognizes that this conviction, too, is relative.

The foregoing discussion of the relativity of belief assumes the cosmological perspective of contemporary scientific theory as conceptualized through the categories of Whiteheadian process philosophy. If the principle of relativity is indeed at the heart of existence, several rather perplexing issues concerning the nature of religious faith, practice, and interreligious dialogue require immediate clarification. Before concluding this section, I wish to confront more directly these issues, not to "solve" them, because I do not think I can, but to shed more explicit light on the issue of universal relativity as Whitehead helps me to understand it.

Few Western philosophers so clearly recognized the relativity of their own philosophical perspectives as did Whitehead. But this recognition was not debilitating for him because he thought philosophical relativism analogous to the relativism of scientific theory.[13] The methodological principles governing all contemporary scientific theory are quite remote from the principles governing Newtonian physics. However, contemporary science continues recognizing many areas to which Newtonian physics can be applied. For instance, so long as physicists focus attention upon bodies of moderate mass and velocity, Newton's laws of motion adequately describe natural phenomena. They possess, therefore, real scientific validity. Newtonian physics did not cease being true when the scientific community began accepting Einstein's theories of relativity, along with quantum theory, as these proved experimentally superior in the investigation of natural phenomena to which Newtonian laws had no application. Thus when the limitations of the truth of the Newtonian worldview became evident to the scientific community, Newton's laws did not thereby simply become false, for centuries of experimental verification had also proven the truth of much of Newtonian physics. This truth has not been discredited either by contemporary relativity theory or by quantum theory.

Whitehead believed the situation in philosophy is similar. No philosophical perspective is simply false, because every serious tradition in philosophy has illumined significant portions of human experience. But every philosophical system can only illumine some portion of human experience at the expense of failing to take notice of others. Meanwhile, science and history continue providing new data of which the philosopher must take account. The philosopher's task is, consequently, similar to that of the scientist. Philosophers should not merely refute past and present philosophical theory in order to establish the superiority of their own perspectives. They should instead learn from one another, as well as from the past, while appropriating what has been learned into their own individual perspectives. Whatever various philosophers have demonstrated about human experience is there to be seen. A new philosophy striving for comprehensiveness and coherence must incorporate these insights into itself. Where there are obvious contradictions between philosophers, the goal must be the attainment of a wider vision within which the essential truths of each view can be displayed in its limited clarity[14]

Of course, errors exist in the work of any philosopher, or in the work of any scientist or historian for that matter. Error can and should be detected and rooted out. But error has nothing to do with the question of universal relativity, for no enduring philosophical perspective has ever been built upon complete error. The serious problems of philosophy, or of any form of disciplined inquiry, arise when particular philosophers assume the universal validity of their own systematic points of view. Such inferences always prove erroneous because, given universal relativity, no system of thought can claim finality. All will require modification and enlargement in the future.

If Whitehead's application of the principle of universal relativity to philosophy, including his own system, is valid, several important implications regarding the relativity of belief emerge that bear on the question of interreligious dialogue. First, the relativity of belief does not mean beliefs are unimportant. Indeed, some beliefs are trivial, and there are no reasons for attending to them. But recognizing this also implies the ability to distinguish between trivial beliefs and important beliefs. In other words, the relativity of our beliefs is compatible with concern about whether our beliefs adequately and coherently approximate reality.

Second, the relativity of belief does not falsify particular beliefs. Most likely, human beings are incapable of seriously believing totally false propositions. Even the distorted beliefs of insane persons probably possess varying degrees of truth. In all likelihood, therefore, the important beliefs that have grasped the human imagination most profoundly display varying degrees of positive correspondence to reality. Universal relativity implies this should be the case.

Third, the relativity of belief is compatible with decisive action. Indeed, cognitive uncertainty and the either/or of action always remain in tension with one another. For since nonaction is a form of action, as the *Bhagavad-gītā* tells us, there exists no escape from the necessity to act. It would be foolish as well to contrast this situation with some other conceived ideal situation while lamenting its nonexistence. Universal relativity implies constant readiness to alter the course of action as beliefs are reformed. But there are no reasons for not acting decisively as such.

Fourth, all beliefs are reformable. Since there can be no unconditioned beliefs, there is no justification for thinking we either possess one or are able to find one. The quest for propositional certainty should be abandoned, along with the notion that any tradition or system of belief has cornered the market on truth. In principle, we cannot possess certain knowledge in a universe of relativity and process.

Finally, encountering systems of beliefs other than our own provides us an opportunity for reformation. Since beliefs, religious or nonreligious, are never merely true or false, but are more or less adequate, clear, and free from distortion, encountering divergent systems of beliefs should not be viewed as an either/or confrontation. Such an encounter represents an opportunity for achieving clearer, more adequate, less distorted beliefs. For this reason, dialogue between different religious Ways becomes a source of personal renewal. From the perspective of universal relativity, dialogue is not only the "key to understanding"[15] and increasing tolerance of other religious Ways, but is itself a means of gaining knowledge and insight.

THE STRUCTURE OF DIALOGUE

That interreligious dialogue now seems to be emerging as a significant means of establishing personal and social renewal within the conditions of modern existence can be easily demonstrated. But identifying the nature and goals of dialogue, especially interreligious dialogue, is not so easy. In a rather poetic way, however, an observation by the Roman Catholic theologian, John S. Dunne, provides an excellent point of departure:

> The holy man of our time, it seems, is not a figure like Gotama or Jesus or Mohammed, or a man who would found a new religion, but a figure like Gandhi; a man who passes over by sympathetic understanding from his own religion to other religions and comes back again with new insight into his own. Passing over and coming back, it seems, is the spiritual adventure of our time.[16]

According to Dunne, the structure of any form of dialogue is "socratic" because it involves a two-fold realization by at least one of the participants that she or he does not know the truth and is thereby taking the first steps on the path to wisdom. Awareness of ignorance as the beginning of wisdom energizes dialogical encounter. Once so energized, dialogue involves two movements, which Dunne calls "passing over" and "returning." Thus any dialogue, but particularly interreligious dialogue, is an "adventure" beginning with a departure from the conditioned "homeland" of our own religious standpoint and ending with a return to the "reconditioned home" of our religious standpoint. All dialogue is, in Dunne's language, an "odyssey."

Much, however, depends upon the religious perspective where the odyssey begins and ends. Normally, a Christian begins and ends with the Christian Way, a Muslim with Islam, a Buddhist with Buddhist faith and practice. More deeply understood, however, the starting point and ending point of dialogue as "passing over" and "returning" remain our own lives. Interreligious dialogue is not a means of passing over into abstract, static entities or things called "religions," for religions are not things.[17] Rather, in dialogue we pass over into the lives of persons whose experiences of the Sacred are other than our own in the hope of appropriating what we can into our own lives, thereby enriching our own religious standpoints. In the process we renew, stretch, deepen, or, in the language of process philosophy, "creatively transform" our lives. And since the whole purpose of interreli-

gious dialogue, or of any sort of dialogue for that
matter, is the renewal of our own living standpoints
(otherwise why engage in dialogue at all?), at least
four conditions must be present before passing over
into another human being's religious perspective can
occur and the creative transformation of one's own religious faith and practice result.[18]

No ulterior motives of any kind should motivate dialogue. This is perhaps the most important condition of dialogue. Approaching another person's religious standpoint in this way provides only limited results, usually more negative than positive. For example, studying Buddhist faith and practice merely with
the intention of comparing it with Christian faith and
practice in order to increase Christian awareness of
the elements peculiar to the Christian Way undermines
the integrity of the Buddhist Way. Likewise, studying
the Buddhist Way to demonstrate the superiority of the
Christian Way undermines the integrity of Christian
faith.

Second, being engaged by the faith and practice of persons dwelling in religious standpoints other
than our own enriches our faith and practice. Nothing
can emerge from any dialogue unless our perspectives
are genuinely challenged, tested, and stretched by the
faith and practice of our dialogical partner. Approaching persons of other religious standpoints merely
as advocates of our own faith, or absolutizing our own
religious Way as the only true or most valid religious
standpoint, replaces genuine dialogue with a series of

monologues. Truth is not found, and religious imperialism replaces creative transformation.

Third, interreligious dialogue demands adequate, critical, and articulate understanding of our
own religious standpoint. For part of the openness of
being engaged by the truth claims of others involves
being engaged by the truth claims of our own religious
Way. Without a point of view, dialogue with others is
a formless sharing of ideas in which one person states
what he or she believes and another reciprocates in
kind. Nothing is achieved. But individuals who understand and are open to their own religious Way are more
likely to be open to the truth claims of other perspectives; thereby they become better able to pass over to
these claims and appropriate what they can into their
own transformed religious Way when they return to it.
Having made his own commitments and experienced the
"music" of his own faith, it becomes possible for him
to hear the "music" of his partner's faith and practice. For as a friend can understand the experience of
love or suffering of another human being because of his
own experiences of these realities, so the religious
person may experience to a significant degree the meaning of the faith and practice of a friend because of
his own particular experiences of religsious faith and
practice.

Finally, truth must be explicitly understood
as relational in structure. For those of us who find
ourselves in varying degrees influenced by the Christian Way, this is especially crucial. The Christian
understanding of God's involvement in human history as

witnessed to by the Bible more often than not has been reduced to a set of unchanging doctrinal propositions serving the needs of the institutional church and its bureaucrats more than of Christian persons. The truth that cannot be named became circumscribed by the creeds and confessional statements of the church and by the limited understanding and compassion of individual Christians. But this represents, in fact, a Christian form of *māyā* (delusion). Truth can have no institutional or confessional boundaries in a universe governed by the principle of universal relativity. Therefore, Christians in dialogue can share their faith without having to believe that the truth of their, for example, Buddhist colleagues is inferior or less true. For the opposite is most likely. In dialogue, Christians may possibly discover that the perfection of the faith and practice of non-Christians represents a genuine challenge to their own self-awareness as religious persons. In short, interreligious dialogue becomes possible and meaningful as it grows out of our common humanity as persons whose sense of what it means to be human expresses itself through different yet valid and real encounters with the Sacred, however the Sacred is named. Dialogue cannot happen and truth becomes half-truth when we relate to one another merely through absolutized and abstract labels such as "Christian," "Buddhist," "Hindu," or "Muslim."

CONCLUDING OBSERVATIONS

My conclusions concerning modernity, the relativity of belief, religious and secular pluralism, and the nature and desirability of interreligious dialogue are clearly grounded in Whiteheadian assumptions about the nature of reality. But this does not imply that Whitehead, or any other process thinker, would agree with my conclusions. And even though I pledge a large degree of intellectual allegiance to the camp of process philosophy, I am not a camp follower. Consequently, several summary observations about the process of interreligious dialogue pointing to further possibilities, as well as to real but not insoluble problems, require fuller discussion.

If Whitehead's worldview accurately portrays the picture of the universe now emerging within the natural sciences, as I believe it does--things are what they are because of how they interrelate and interpenetrate every other thing in the universe at any moment of space-time--then the process of creative transformation is an expression of the very structure of the universe itself. That is, creative transformation is the way the universe operates regardless of human knowledge and cooperation. But if we understand this process and cooperate with it, then our imagination and freedom to structure human existence around centers of meaning can be transformed by a lucidity of vision and a new openness to what we see. "Creative transformation" names a natural process that may be consciously mirrored in human thought and action if we so desire. Interreligious dialogue may in turn be an important means of expressing this process because it provides a point of focal unity within which the many centers of meaning and existence grasping the human imagination can be encouraged, understood, appreciated, and integrated. This is why openness to the great religious Ways of humanity can deepen Christian faith. But it can also deepen Buddhist, Confucian, Jewish, or Muslim faith as well. It is this sort of renewal we should be seeking, and which I have called "creative transformation."

My second observation is a negative one. The goal of interreligious dialogue should never be understood as discovering which insights of the different religious traditions of the world can be mixed together to create a new, more universal religious Way. In opposition to the Hindu sage, Śri Ramakrishna, the historical evidence suggests that all paths do not lead to the same summit. Thinking otherwise plays fast and loose with the historical facts and creates a rather subtle form of religious imperialism. For after all, it becomes very easy to posit the unity of all religious Ways when all religious Ways look like your own, as they apparently did to Ramakrishna, who perceived them as versions of his own form of Advaita Vedanta. The point is, creative transformation is likely to occur only when it is carried out in a critical spirit that recognizes the differences, along with the similarities, between the religious Ways of humanity. Uncritical syncretism should be avoided, for not all religious ideas and practices are of equal value. Some are in fact quite pathologically destructive, as the terrible events surrounding the People's Church in Jonestown so tragically demonstrated in 1977.

Third, as matters now stand, Buddhist-Christian dialogue appears quite one-sided. At least in

Japan, the initiative for interreligious dialogue almost completely originates from the Christian side, even though Buddhists are usually pictured as extremely open and tolerant in their attitudes towards other religious Ways.[19] But in reality, Buddhist-Christian dialogue remains primarily a "liberal" Christian monologue. Certainly, some Buddhist study centers occasionally arrange lectures and discussions with Christian thinkers. There are also important circles of interest in studying and learning from the Christian Way. However, apart from the Eastern Buddhist Society, no Buddhist center appears to be stressing dialogue with the Christian Way as a matter of ultimate importance. Individual Buddhists are presently expressing interest and admiration for Christian ethical and social thought, and some Buddhists stress the need to learn from Christians at this point. But at the moment there exists little Buddhist interest in dialogue with the Christian Way that challenges Buddhist faith and practice. And even though Christians are usually represented as more doctrinally intolerant than Buddhists, Christians have in fact more openly and systematically responded to the challenge of Buddhist religious experience. The process of creative transformation appears more evident in at least the "liberal" spectrum of the Christian Way than in the Buddhist Way. But this observation is not meant as an indictment of the Buddhist Way. Interreligious dialogue can never be forced. Even so, surely creative transformation is as necessary and important for Buddhists as it is for Christians in an age of secular and religious pluralism.

A related point must be made on the Christian side of the encounter. Christian dialogue with the Buddhist Way mostly focuses on Japanese Zen tradition and somewhat on Pure Land teachings and practice. More concerted efforts should be made to encounter other forms of Japanese Buddhism, such as Shingon and Tendai, as well as more in-depth encounter with Pure Land faith. Along with this, Christians should seek out non-Japanese forms of Buddhist faith and practice, especially the Theravada and the Tibetan traditions. The Buddhist Way, like the Christian Way, is a highly complex religious Way, the whole of which needs dialogical confrontation.

Fourth, interreligious dialogue poses risks for at least two reasons. Sociologically, Buddhist-Christian dialogue is mostly an elite enterprise led by the more liberal professionals of both Ways. Very little interreligious dialogue occurs at the grass roots levels of Buddhist and Christian religious life. The problem involves whether people are capable of preserving a sense of identity when the boundaries of their religious faith become weakened by the process of creative transformation. Interreligious dialogue could become "dysfunctional" because persons need "discernible identity boundaries."[20] By weakening the boundaries between humanity's religious Ways, interreligious dialogue may cause many individuals to lose those limits from which they derive their self-identities and sense of meaning. If we are insensitive to this, the whole enterprise may become quite harmful and not worth the effort.

On the other hand, precisely because interreligious dialogue changes us, there are no guarantees we will or can or should remain labeled "Christian" or "Buddhist." Here lies the greatest risk and adventure of the process of creative transformation through interreligious dialogue. After passing over to religious Ways other than our own, we may find ourselves returning to a completely different point from where we started. And if Whitehead's understanding of the processive interrelational and interdependent becoming of things is correct, Christians or Buddhists or Jews or Muslims in dialogue with other religious Ways may find themselves so completely transformed as to be totally outside the pale of their original religious Way altogether. In fact, all of the religious Ways that have grasped the human imagination may end up becoming so creatively transformed as to become "objectively immortal" and replaced by novel, more inclusive and universal religious Ways. I do not offer this observation as a prediction of the future. But in a universe of process, relativity, and finitude nothing is permanent while it is alive, including the religious Ways of humanity. Historically, religious Ways have died and been replaced by more inclusive religious visions, just as the Christian Way replaced while including much of the Hellenistic mystery religions, or as the Buddhist Way replaced while including the ancient Bon religion of Tibet. There is no reason to suppose contemporary religious Ways do not face the same future.

An ultimate temptation remains, finally, which process thinkers must avoid at all costs. It is very tempting to perceive the affinities between the Buddhist world-view and process philosophy, along with the obvious Christian interests forming part of the background of Whitehead's philosophy, as a verification of his philosophical vision. As a philosophical judgment this conclusion might be valid, although I doubt it, and I suspect Whitehead doubted it as well. But if we are searching for interreligious understanding and creative transformation through the process of dialogue, absolutizing Whitehead's or any other world view becomes a distortion of the Buddhist and Christian Ways, as well as a distortion of Whitehead's philosophy. Whitehead's philosophy is a highly technical *Western* philosophy, based on a scientific world view expressed in a language meant to explicate his understanding of what this world view means. Using this technical language--terms such as "actual entity," "prehension," "causal efficacy," "presentational immediacy," the "primal"and "consequent natures of God"-- ought to be kept to the barest minimum. Otherwise, Buddhist and Christian faith may too easily become an inferior form of process philosophy articulated more coherently by Whitehead. If this occurs, dialogue between Christians and Buddhists becomes a series of Whiteheadian monologues. Process theologians and philosophers need more sensitivity about this problem than they normally exhibit. A theoretical vision such as Whitehead's should never be confused with an existential religious Way. But if we are careful, Whitehead's process vision may become an important heuristic means of opening us up to the insights of both the Buddhist and the Christian Ways that will not falsify either, but will allow for the creative transformation of both.

NOTES

[1]C. G. Jung, *Modern Man in Search of a Soul* (New York: Harcourt, Brace and World, 1933), 196-97.

[2]Peter L. Berger, *The Heretical Imperative* (Garden City, N.J.: Anchor Books, 1979), 19-20.

[3]Wing-tzit Chan, trans., *A Source Book in Chinese Philosophy* (Princeton: Princeton University Press, 1963), 209-210.

[4]Michael Polanyi, *Personal Knowledge* (New York: Harper and Row, 1964), 103.

[5]The best descriptive account of Whitehead's philosophical system is still William S. Christian's *An Interpretation of Whitehead's Metaphysics* (New Haven: Yale University Press, 1969). Also see John B. Cobb, Jr., *A Christian Natural Theology* (Philadelphia: Westminster Press, 1965), chapters 1-4 for a good summary of Whitehead's system.

[6]Alfred North Whitehead, *Process and Reality* (New York: Macmillan Company, 1929), 136-67.

[7]Ibid., 165.

[8]"The principle of relativity directly transverses Aristotle's dictum, '[a substance] is not present in a subject.' On the contrary, according to this principle an actual entity *is* present in other actual entities. In fact if we allow for deeper relevance, and for negligible relevance, we must say that every actual entity is present in every other actual entity. The philosophy of organism is mainly devoted to the task of making clear the notion of 'being present in another entity.'" Ibid., 78-79. Also see 224-36 and 532.

[9]See Wilfred Cantwell Smith's study of the word "belief" in *Belief and History* (Charlottesville: University Press of Virginia, 1977). All of my remarks concerning the relativity of belief assume the conclusions of Smith's studies.

[10]John B. Cobb, Jr., "Further Reflections on the Relativity of Belief," *John Cobb's Theology in Process*,

ed. David Ray Griffin and Thomas J. J. Altizer, (Philadelphia: The Westminster Press, 1977), 165-70. Also see *A Christian Natural Theology*, pp. 270-77.

[11]Cobb, "Further Reflections," 165.

[12]Whitehead, *Process and Reality*, 62-89.

[13]Ibid., 20-21.

[14]Ibid., 11-16.

[15]See Donald K. Swearer, *Dialogue: The Key to Understanding Other Religions* (Philadelphia: Westminster Press, 1977).

[16]John S. Dunne, *The Way of All the Earth* (South Bend: University of Notre Dame Press, 1978), iv.

[17]The thrust of Smith's argument is that religions are not "things" capable of definition in the same way nouns indicate "things" capable of definition. He is certainly correct in pointing out the possibility of living according to a religious vision without the benefit of a definition of a "thing" called "religion." In reality, this seems to be the normal state of affairs among religious persons. Wilfred Cantwell Smith, *The Meaning and End of Religion* (New York: New American Library, 1966), 7-8. I remain in agreement with Smith's entire statement in this book. Therefore, I understand what is usually meant by the term "religion," but which I personally prefer calling "religious faith" or "religious experience," stressing the verbal nature of what is involved in this label, as that which significantly binds together for individuals their values. Religious faith is a vision or, in Cobb's terminology, a "structure of existence," according to which individuals link themselves to those basic resources both within and without that authenticate a sense of ultimate worth and meaning. Religious faith is a comprehensive Life orientation, a way of achieving personal self-transformation.

[18]Similar points have been made by Swearer, *Dialogue*, 40-50.

[19]Natto R. Thelle, "Prospects and Problems of Buddhist-Christian Dialogue," *Japanese Religions* 10, (July 1979): 53.

[20]Jan Swyngedouw, "Interfaith Dialogue: A Sociological Reflection," *Japanese Religions* 10 (July 1979): 7-26.

CHAPTER TWO
The Christian Encounter with Non-Christian Religious Ways

What, then, are we to say about Abraham, our ancestor in the natural line? If Abraham was justified by anything he had done, then he has a ground for pride. But he has not such ground before God, for what does Scripture say? "Abraham put his faith in God, and that faith was counted to him as righteousness."

Romans 4:1-3, *New English Bible*

INTRODUCTION

The paradigm of interreligious dialogue described in chapter one assumed the perspective of Whiteheadian process philosophy. For the modern person experiencing contemporary religious and secular pluralism, with its relativist values and truth claims, the reformulation of religious images and practices through interreligious dialogue can result in a renewal of our own religious faith. At the same time such reformulation contributes to the creative transformation of our own particular religious community. For, as the history of religions teaches us, no religious Way has ever existed in cultural isolation unaffected by other religious ways.[1] Accordingly, this chapter presents the basic historical pattern of Christian theological reflection on its encounter with non-Christian religious Ways. The following chapter presents a similar overview of the traditional Buddhist response to non-Buddhist religious Ways. This procedure will provide, I hope, sufficient historical perspective on the Buddhist-Christian dialogue as well as offer my own particular interpretations and conclusions concerning this dialogue.

THE EARLY CHURCH

Being a Christian has never been simply a matter of participating in a few ceremonies, or of accepting particular doctrinal formulations, or of acknowledging the significance of the historical Jesus who is also the Christ. Nor for that matter has being a Buddhist simply meant participating in the rituals, disciplines, and ethical lifestyles peculiar to Buddhism, or acknowledging specific doctrinal understandings about the significance of the historical Buddha. In the case of the Christian Way, the glue holding Christian faith together in all of its amazing varieties and ancillary forms is the faith that while God is the God of all that exists in this universe, it is through Jesus as the Christ that God has once and for all effected the salvation of all human beings. This confession not only places the "Jesus of history" and the "Christ of faith" at the center of world history, but also establishes the standard by which Christians measure the validity of all other religious claims. The Christian Way is foremost a matter of faith, meaning "trust," in Christ as the center of one's life because he is the center of all meaningful existence. This affirmation forms the fundamental idiosyncrasy of the Christian Way. Although non-Christians may hold the historical Jesus in highest regard as a teacher, prophet, or sage, only Christians will declare Jesus as the Christ, the central agent through whom God has encountered and continues encountering human beings within the conditions of historical existence in order to effect the salvation of all persons. That is, it is usual for Christians to confess there is no God apart from God's self-revelation through Jesus as the Christ.

These convictions have forced Christian thinkers to reflect on the meaning and value of non-Christian religious Ways from the earliest days of Christianity's origins, especially when non-Christian traditions or practices appeared virtuous and capable of positively transforming human life. The primary motivation energizing this imperative, apart from the historical necessity involved in Christian faith's connection with the Jewish Way and Hellenistic culture of the first and second centuries, was the universalism of the Christian claim itself. The earliest expressions of Christian universalism did not, however, imply God was inaccessible in other religious Ways; it was assumed that by confessing that God is really present and active in the Christ event, Christians could simultaneously grasp something of God's universal love for all creatures.[2]

The earliest Christian encounter with a non-Christian religious Way involved Jewish faith and practice. Christian relations with the Jewish Way were quite difficult and unsettled in the beginning. At first, Christians regarded themselves as perfected Jews and accepted all of the ethical, legal, and cultic obligations of the Torah that any practicing Jew would have accepted. But their faith that a man whom the Romans executed as a criminal on a cross was really God's "anointed one" made the earliest Christians an unacceptable minority within the Jewish Way. In other words, the Christian affirmation of Christ ran counter to all Jewish messianic and apocalyptic expectations. How could a condemned and executed criminal be an authentic announcer of the Kingdom of God? The Christian claim was, however, essentially a reinterpretation of Jewish messianic expectations, so that all of the events of Jesus' life, including his crucifixion by the Romans, were understood as pieces of God's plan for the redemption of humanity. The Kingdom of God was now being established and would be completed at the time of Jesus' soon-to-happen second coming. Consequently, all persons, including Jews, must renounce all other religious claims and turn to Jesus as the Christ.

From the traditional Jewish point of view, Christian claims regarding Jesus were blasphemous. And in spite of the early Christian appeal that they were really Jews who had correctly apprehended and confessed what all other Jews refused to apprehend and confess, the earliest Christian hope was that the "old Israel" would join with the "new Israel" before the final consummation of God's kingdom.

It was Saint Paul who first saw that the Christian claim about the centrality of the Christ event was more universal than this. He proclaimed that Christian faith was not merely a new form of Judaism, but an essentially radical departure from the Jewish Way. Three themes of Pauline theology are of special importance in this regard: the centrality of faith as trust in God's saving action for humanity through the

Christ event, coupled with nontrust of one's own attempts to achieve a saving relationship with God; the
occurrence of salvation apart from and in spite of anything an individual can do alone to achieve it himself;
and the evincing of universal sinfulness in works.
Paul's theology thus transformed the Christian Way from
a minor sectarian movement within the Jewish Way to a
universal world religion.   In this sense, he is the
real "founder" of Christianity, for after him Christians understood their faith as the fulfillment of, not
the extension of, the Jewish Way.   The Church is the
"new Israel" to which the "Old Israel," separated by
God's action in history through Jesus as the Christ,
would eventually join itself.

Once the early church's developing theology
and preaching began following Paul's line of thought,
the religious Ways of the gentiles, meaning non-Jews
and other non-Christians, became objects of reflection.
Essentially, the New Testament views the popular religious traditions and practices of the gentiles quite
negatively as expressions of idolatry. Objects of special criticism were the various mystery religions and
gnostic movements, which were powerfully influential
competitors with the Christian movement during the
first and second centuries.

At the same time, the writers of the New Testament were also positively influenced by Platonic and
Stoic traditions of philosophy, as were the Church Fa-
thers, who also appropriated, although not uncritically, much from the the work of the Greek philosophers
in their doctrinal formulations of Christian faith.

This aspect of Hellenistic tradition could not be easily dismissed as idolatrous. After all, how else could the Christian message be made intelligible to both sophisticated and unsophisticated persons living outside of Palestine in a world governed and established on Hellenistic cultural styles and traditions? The church had to adapt itself to its environment in order to survive. But so doing created tensions within the Christian community with which the Christian Way continues struggling even today, for exactly how should Christian faith adapt itself to its environing world without compromising its distinctive character?

OUTSIDE THE CHURCH THERE IS NO SALVATION

Clearly, Christians have understood the Christian Way as the only way of salvation from the beginning. But this has not always implied the absence of God's saving action for non-Christians, or the inability or unwillingness to incorporate truth and value from other religious Ways into Christian faith. From the time of Constantine the Great (380?-337), however, during whose reign as emperor of Rome the Christian Way not only received legal recognition for the first time, but was also declared to be the "state religion" of the Roman Empire, the original understanding of the nature of the church began to change. In the New Testament the church is generally pictured as a community of believers awaiting the immanent second coming of Christ. But from Constantine's time on the church began transforming itself into a sacred institution claiming both religious and secular authority over the lives of peo-

it has not been good, to judge it. . . .
Whosoever, therefore, resists this power thus
ordained of God resists the ordinances of
God, unless, like Manichaeus, thou dreamest
that there are two principles. . . .
Moreover, to every human creature we declare,
defend and pronounce, that to be subject to
the Roman pontiff is absolutely necessary to
salvation.[3]

  This declaration was reaffirmed in the Decree
of the Council of Florence of 1438-45:

no one outside the catholic church, not just
pagans, but also Jews or heretics or schima-
tics, can become partakers of eternal life;
but they will go to the "everlasting fire
which was prepared for the devil and his an-
gels," unless before the end of life they are
joined to the church.[4]

  Protestants traditionally assert an equivalent of the doctrine of no salvation outside the church
(the Roman Catholic Church): outside of some form of
personal Christian belief and faith there is no salvation, although this has not been formally stated in any
of the articles of the major Lutheran, Reformed, or An-
glican confessional statements. But as John Hick has
noted, the belief that salvation is impossible apart
from Christian faith has been part of the theological
tradition of mainline Protestant teaching since Martin
Luther's day.[5] More recently, it has been included in
the major declarations of most fundamentalist-evangelical groups within Protestant tradition. The Frankfort

Declaration of 1970, for example, challenged "all non-Christians, who belong to God on the basis of creation, to believe in him [Jesus Christ] and to be baptized in his name, for in him alone is eternal salvation promised to them. Thus, "adherents of the non-Christian religions and worldviews . . . must let themselves be freed from their former ties and false hopes in order to be admitted by belief and baptism into the body of Christ."[6]

Therefore, even though most of the New Testament supports the likelihood that God has acted in the world to bring about its final redemption, including those persons who have never heard of Christ, this element of New Testament teaching has either been ignored or deemphasized in the classical doctrinal positions and practices of Catholic and Protestant tradition. This is also the situation in the practices and teachings of the fundamentalist-evangelical subgroups of Protestantism. For the most part, the majority opinion in Christian teaching regarding the non-Christian religious Ways holds they are all forms of spiritual darkness within which there is no salvation. This is hardly an assertion conducive to interreligious dialogue. It is, in fact, a theological monologue best characterized as religious imperialism.

CONTEMPORARY CATHOLIC INTERPRETATIONS

There are, of course, historical reasons behind the development of Christian exclusiveness and intolerance toward non-Christian beliefs and practices. I am not aware, however, that the development and ramifications of the doctrine of no-salvation-outside-the-church or Christian faith have ever been fully researched by any church historian. But it is certain the degree of harshness by which this doctrine was applied to non-Christians varied according to the particular historical situation and from theologian to theologian. Be this as it may, both Roman Catholic and Protestant thought viewed non-Chrisians as candidates for proselytization.

While the intolerant attitude toward non-Christians that this doctrine fosters might have made some sense or have possessed some positive value for Christian faith during the Middle Ages, the doctrine of no salvation outside the church has come to be seen as quite implausible and unrealistic to some theologians.[7] Consequently, strenuous efforts are now being made by numerous Christian thinkers, usually labeled "liberal," to escape the more negative and unacceptable conclusions of this doctrine. No contemporary Roman Catholic theologians have explicitly renounced the doctrine of no-salvation-outside-the-church, because technically no Catholic theologian can publicly declare a formerly proclaimed dogma wrong. But they can reinterpret it to mean something very different from its original meaning and intention. In all probability, this process of reinterpretation began as long ago as 1850 with Pope Pius IX. He did not cease maintaining the original doctrine, but he added a subsidiary theory to it that began changing its practical effect. In an Allocution, Pius IX stated:

It must, of course, be held as a matter of faith that outside the apostolic Roman Church no one can be saved, that the Church is the only ark of salvation, and that whoever does not enter it will perish in the flood. On the other hand, it must likewise be held as certain that those who are affected by ignorance of the true religion, if it is invincible ignorance, are not subject to any guilt in this matter before the eyes of the Lord.[8]

Consequently a non-Catholic, meaning either a Christian of another tradition or an adherent of a non-Christian religious Way, may be saved even though he dies outside the church, provided such a person is "invincibly ignorant" of the truth of Catholic teaching and practice. Once more, only God knows to whom this doctrine applies.

An application of the notion of invincible ignorance involves the two interrelated theories of "implied faith" and "baptism of desire." According to these ideas, there are individuals who may be consciously outside the Roman Catholic Church, but who are nevertheless "unconsciously" within it. Such individuals may be said to possess "implicit faith" in the form of an unconscious but sincere desire to do God's will. They are not baptized members of the church and they do not participate in its other sacraments. Nevertheless, they are "in" the church by a "baptism of desire," meaning they have received God's recognition of their sincere desire for the truth even though they do not fully know what the truth is.

These reinterpretations of the doctrine of no salvation outside the church were the main guides for Roman Catholic relations with non-Christians and non-Catholic Christians until the Second Vatican Council of 1963-1965. As such they were only interim measures. That is, as officially formulated, they either did not go far enough for some theologians, or else they went too far for others. Presumably, only monotheists could sincerely desire to do God's will, so that the notion of implicit desire was not extended to adherents of nontheistic religious Ways such as the Buddhist Way and important segments of Hindu tradition. But if salvation is understood as the right relationship to the divine reality, as variously known and named in the different religious Ways of the world, rather than as incorporation into the Catholic Church, then the original teaching is, in fact, abandoned altogether.

There was not much improvement in this situation when Vatican II began addressing the problem that the sheer fact of the existence of the non-Christian religious Ways presents to the doctrine of no-salvation-outside-the-church. For example, in the "Dogmatic Constitution of the Church," promulgated in 1964, the Council stated:

> Those also can attain to everlasting salvation who through no fault of their own do not know the gospel of Christ or of His Church, yet sincerely seek God and, moved by grace, strive by their deeds to do His will as it is

known to them by the dictates of conscience.
Nor does divine Providence deny the help necessary for salvation to those who, without
blame on their part, have not yet arrived at
an explicit knowledge of God, but who strive
to live a good life thanks to His grace.
Whatever goodness or truth is found among
them is looked upon by the Church as a preparation for the gospel.   She regards such
qualities as given by Him who enlightens all
men so that they may finally have life.[9]

The intention of this passage was later interpreted in the "Declaration on the Relationship of
the Church to Non-Christian Religions," published after
the final session of the Council in 1965:

The Catholic Church rejects nothing which is
true and holy in these religions.   She looks
with sincere respect upon those ways of conduct and of life, those rules and teachings
which, though differing in many particulars
from what she holds and sets forth, nevertheless often reflect a ray of that Truth which
enlightens all men.   Indeed, she proclaims
and must ever proclaim Christ, "the way, the
truth, and the life" (John 14:6), in whom God
has reconciled all things to himself. (Cf.2
Cor. 5:18-19).[10]

In comparison with past history, tradition,
and former dogmatic statements, these declarations are
remarkably open and tolerant.   They reflect the profound change within the emotional and theological cli-

mate of Roman Catholicism, so much so that today Roman Catholic theology and practice are more open to serious interreligious dialogue than most Protestant denominations and theological movements. That Vatican II represents a major change from previous interpretations of the doctrine of no salvation outside the church cannot be questioned. But it is also true that Vatican II reaffirmed the traditional attitude that salvation is still made available to human beings only through Christ and through the believer's incorporation into his mystical body, the Roman Catholic Church. This incorporation is possible because of the non-Christian's sincere efforts to follow whatever goodness and truth are available through his own religious Way. But as such, this is only "preparation for the gospel," suggesting that faithful followers of non-Christian religious Ways are still required by God to arrive eventually at explicit Catholic Christian faith. The older religious imperialism still remains, even though in a subtle and more compassionate form, and dialogue is ultimately excluded from Catholic relations with non-Christians.

Before considering the contemporary Protestant version of the doctrine of no-salvation-apart-from-explicit-Christian faith, some brief reflection on the work of two important Catholic theologians should prove very instructive. Karl Rähner and Hans Küng not only worked for the inclusion of the declarations I have cited in the final pronouncements of Vatican II, but have written far beyond the original intentions of these declarations. Both Rähner and Küng represent "liberal" Catholic positions in their treatment of non-Christian religious Ways. Their theological perspectives have also been influential in stimulating Protestant reflection on interreligious dialogue, essentially because their thought advances a new twist to the doctrine of no-salvation-outside-the-church.

Rähner's understanding of religious pluralism centers on his notion of "anonymous Christianity." In his view, Christians encounter non-Christians as human beings who must be regarded and respected as anonymous Christians. "The devout Muslim," he says, "or Hindu, or Sikh, or Jew can be regarded as an anonymous Christian, this being an honorary status granted unilaterally to people who have not expressed any desire for it."[11] In this way Rähner believes seriously practicing and faithful non-Christians are in reality Christians without knowing it. In other words, non-Christians operate within the sphere of divine grace available within their own religious Ways, even if they do not realize the real source of this grace is God as revealed through Jesus Christ.

Rähner has indeed made a serious effort to do justice to the realities of religious faith and experience outside the Catholic Christian Way, but it is equally certain he has not squarely faced the reality of non-Christian religious Ways as authentic challenges to Christian self-understanding in a religiously plural world. In short, his position provides no support for interreligious dialogue, for the monologue inherent in the older doctrine of no salvation outside the church remains the guiding assumption of his perspective.

By far the boldest Catholic attempt to meet realistically the challenges posed to Christian faith by modern religious pluralism is that of Hans Küng.[12] Küng believes that the world religions, by which he means all religious Ways other than Roman Catholicism, should be viewed as "extraordinary ways of human salvation." The Catholic Church, however, is the "ordinary way." Therefore, individuals may attain salvation through the particular Way which is available to them in their historical and cultural circumstances, since God, whose fullest self-revelation is through Christ, is also at work in the extraordinary ways of non-Christian teachings and practices. A person should seek God within whatever religious Way is available because *all* religious Ways are "ways of salvation in universal salvation history." But compared with the extraordinary ways of salvation, the salvation offered by the church seems, in Küng's view, to be something quite special. For what is only generally offered to human beings through non-Christian teachings and practices becomes most fully available through conscious participation in the faith and sacramental system of the Roman Catholic Church. Hence, the church should engage in missionary efforts to convert the world to Christian faith while at the same time recognizing the profound truths of the non-Christian religious Ways.

If "extraordinary" in this perspective simply means "majority," Küng's understanding of religious pluralism entails little more than that most people are saved outside of incorporation in Catholic Christian faith since most human beings, either living or dead,

are not Roman Catholics. But Küng means much more than
this, for he also understands the "extraordinary ways"
of salvation as merely an interim state of affairs
existing only until the adherents of these Ways arrive
at explicit Catholic Christian faith. The non-
Christian's "right and duty" to seek God within his own
religious Way is valid only until he or she is directly
and existentially confronted with the revelation of God
through Jesus Christ. Participants in other religious
Ways, he believes, "are pre-Christian, directed towards
Christ. . . . The men of the world religions are not
professing Christians, but, by the grace of God, they
are called and marked out to be Christians."
Consequently, non-Christians must sooner or later
become Christians, if Catholic missionaries perform
their task effectively and compassionately. But in the
meantime, non-Christians should not be condemned, for
the gospel has not yet reached them in a form capable
of overcoming their existential ignorance of the full
truth of salvation offered in Roman Catholicism.

Küng's interpretation of modern religious
pluralism is Ptolemaic, for he places Catholic Christian faith and practice in the center of a universe of
religious Ways around which all other religious Ways
must of necessity revolve. Thereby, his interpretation
of religious pluralism leaves no more room for dialogical encounter than Karl Rähner's notion of anonymous
Christianity. Actually, both Küng's and Rähner's understanding of the non-Christian religious Ways are
governed by the traditional dogma of no-salvation-(at
least ultimately)-outside-the-church. The non-Chris-

tian religious Ways are not accepted yet *as different* expressions of valid religious faith and practice in their own right, but only as "preparations for the gospel" or as the religious perspectives of "anonymous Christians." Thus it is possible for non-Christians to attain salvation through their own religious Ways only when their faith and practice do not contradict Roman Catholic teaching.

Though Rähner and Küng explicitly reject the religious imperialism inherent in the doctrine of no-salvation-outside-the-church, even they are unable to escape the negative consequences of this doctrine. As long as this doctrine remains operative in any form, authentic interreligious dialogue cannot be established. If there is really no-salvation-outside-the-church, in principle no non-Christian religious Way can be a valid though different form of saving truth and practice. What will at first glance be called a dialogue will in fact end up a monologue.

CONTEMPORARY PROTESTANT INTERPRETATIONS

The situation is no different in modern Protestant theological reflection on the non-Christian religious Ways, which actually began in the final half of the eighteenth century with Hegel (1770-1831) and Schleiermacher (1768-1834). Each investigated the Eastern religious Ways primarily to demonstrate the superiority of the Christian Way, although not of any particular institutional or denominational form of Christian faith. For this reason the Protestant variation of the Catholic doctrine of no-salvation-outside the-church is best labeled as "no-salvation-outside-of-Christian-faith." An equally important goal of Hegel's and Schleiermacher's studies of Eastern religious Ways was their desire to establish a distinctively religious "essence" that all concrete religious Ways share, but which is most completely expressed and experienced in the Christian Way. They therefore had little interest in interreligious dialogue because of their common apologetic concerns.

Hegel wrote about the "human spirit" arising in the East and moving on to the West, evolving into its final expression in the Prussian state with its distinctive form of Protestant faith. Schleiermacher's reflections were more typological in style, but his thought was also governed by the explicit goal of demonstrating how Protestant belief, teaching, and practice, mostly in its Reformed expression, was the apex of human religious development.

Toward the end of the nineteenth century and the beginning of the twentieth century the most important Protestant theologian reflecting on the question of the relation of Christian faith to the non-Christian religious Ways was Earnst Troeltsch (1866-1923). He began his inquiries with many of the same assumptions guiding Hegel's and Schleiermacher's thought, including their concern for demonstrating the superiority of the Christian Way. His essential approach to religious pluralism was "confessional," while his epistemological orientation might best be described as "pragmatic." That is, he assumed the validity and truth of any religious tradition rest upon the believing

participant's personal convictions, so that what is
required to test the truth of a religious belief is the
broader, objective foundation of empirical fact, the
model for which, he assumed, was the natural sciences
of his time.   He believed the Christian Way alone
possessed such an empirical foundation because the
Christian claim to universal validity and truth is
grounded in the actual experience of revelation.   Now
even though other religious Ways also claim the
absolute validity of their unique teachings and
practices, they do so "quite naively" and in a very
different manner than Christian faith:

> Their claims are always naive--simple and di-
> rect.   They are not the outcome of an apolo-
> getic reasoning, and the differences they ex-
> hibit in their naive claims to absolute va-
> lidity as they really mean and intend are
> within their own minds.[13]

Opposed to this, Troeltsch believed, is the
Christian claim to absolute validity.   It excludes all
cultural and historical limitations *in principle,* because the Christian Way is the creation of God and a
gift to humanity through revelation.   Christian faith
is not, in other words, the creation of the human imagination or of historical necessity, as are the non-
Christian religious Ways.   Only the Christian Way has
empirical objectivity because only it is a revelation
given to humanity prior to and apart from any kind of
human action or response.

> Hence we may simply leave aside the question
> of the measure of the validity possessed by

other religions. Nor need we trouble ourselves with the question of the possible further development of religion itself. . . . In
Christianity is the loftiest and most spiritual revelation we know at all. It has the
highest validity. Let that suffice.[14]

    This was the main point of view of
Troeltsch's earliest statements about religious pluralism, in an essay entitled "The Absolute Validity of
Christianity." But this conclusion did not stand up
for him when, toward the end of his life, he began
studying the major Ways. In fact, he modified this position to the point of renouncing it in an essay entitled "The Place of Christianity Among the World Religions,"[15] written just after World War I. In this
later essay he wrote that just as Christian faith is
bound up with Western culture and the "Western spirit,"
and therefore for Western people is the fullest and final form of religious truth, so the great Asian religious Ways are bound up with their respective cultures
and are the final forms of religious truth and practice
for Asian people. In Troeltsch's words:

    If we wish to determine their relative value,
    it is not the religion alone that we must
    compare, but always only the civilization of
    which the religion in each case constitutes a
    part incapable of severance from the rest.
    But who will presume to make a really final
    pronouncement here? Only God himself, who
    has determined these differences, can do
    that.[16]

Obviously, Troeltsch has introduced a pluralistic understanding of the great religious traditions
of the world. Each religious Way possesses its own validity and truth for its adherents, but none can claim
absolute validity, including the Christian Way. This
was the first time a major Christian thinker, Protestant or Catholic, ever drew this conclusion. Beginning
as a Christian monologue, Troeltsch's theological perspective became thoroughly dialogical.

Perhaps the source of this turn-around was
Troeltsch's involvement in the "history of religion
school" (*Religionsgeschichtliche Schule*). This tradition of theological inquiry was the first to comprehend
fully how the discipline of modern historical inquiry
raises serious problems for all traditional Christian
belief, problems that Troeltsch believed would force a
basic reappraisal of most of the fundamental assumptions of Christian theology.[17] His own thought about
the issues of religious pluralism is a reflection of
this; his earlier essay, "The Absoluteness of Christianity," and his later essay, "The Place of Christianity Among the World Religions," mark a sharp division
between the main styles of Protestant reflection about
religious pluralism that emerged after his death.

Karl Barth's understanding of religious pluralism pushes the conclusions of Troeltsch's first
essay to their furthest extreme. For him, Christian
faith was not a religion at all because "religion is
unbelief," meaning "man's attempt to justify and
sanctify himself before a capricious and arbitrary
picture of God."[18] As such no religion has any truth

value that can lead to salvation because all religions are inventions of sinful persons seeking to establish a positive relationship with God by means of their own contrivances. Understood in these terms, the question of the superiority of one religious Way over another, or questions pertaining to the creative transformation of any religious Way through interreligious dialogue, do not even arise. No particular religious Way can lead to the salvation of humanity.

Opposite to religion is "authentic" Christian faith, which is not a religion but a "witness" to a different reality, namely, God's "condescension to us." Christian faith rests on the event of God's action of breaking into the conditions of historical existence through the life, death, and resurrection of Jesus Christ. Christian faith always rests upon God's prior initiative, and is always experienced by Christian individuals as an objective reality given as a gift to which an individual can only respond. It occurs in spite of our religious efforts and beliefs, and therefore Christian faith is utterly opposed to the human quest for God via any of the specific religious Ways of the world. This finally meant, according to Barth, that no salvation is possible outside of Christian faith, not because it is the superior form of religion, but because authentic Christian faith is not a religion at all. Once more, it is an act of unfaith when Christians become "religious" in any manner.

Barth's position is, of course, completely nondialogical. It is also the most extreme contemporary form of the Protestant assumption of no-salvation-outside-of-Christian-faith. For if religion is defined as a system of unbelief cutting us off from God, there is not much sense in attempting to encounter another person's religious perspective in the hope of creatively transforming our own faith and practice.

The problem with Barth's perspective is not so much that he made it one of the central points of his theology, which he did, but that it has been powerfully influential in later Protestant theological reflection. As a result, very little critical attention was given to thoughtful encounter with non-Christian religious Ways until about ten years after World War II. However, there are voices in contemporary Protestant theology that are now engaging in serious interreligious dialogue as a primary means of doing theology. The two most important transitional figures in this regard are Paul Tillich and Jürgen Moltmann, whose ideas seem to reflect, although perhaps unintentionally, the conclusions of Troeltsch's second essay.

After the publication of *Christianity and the Encounter With the World Religions* and shortly after his now well-known encounter with Buddhist teachers and philosophers in Japan, Tillich concluded that his earlier "method of correlation" was inadequate for judging the value and truth of non-Christian faith and practice. That is, while he previously believed the universal existential questions about the meaning and value of existence are most fully "answered" by the Christian revelation, he later concluded this assertion may have been premature. According to the method of correlation, Tillich had earlier declared the closest correspondents to the structures of reality pointed to by these questions were provided by the "answers" of Christian faith. Accordingly, while Christians could enrich their own faith through dialogue with non-Christians, Tillich did not seriously entertain the possibility there might be more adequate non-Christian answers to these same questions.[19] But after his encounter with Japanese Buddhists, especially within the Zen tradition, he realized there might indeed be some questions and answers in the Buddhist Way correlating more adequately to the structures of reality than specifically Christian answers, at least for Buddhists.[20] Tillich had begun to encounter the fact of religious pluralism, and he concluded that all of the religious Ways of the world need to encounter one another in order to deepen their own faith and practice as authentic responses to the Sacred. Unfortunately, Tillich died before he could work these insights out in any systematic presentation.

In a similar vein, Jürgen Moltmann as recently as 1977 wrote of the need for Christian dialogical encounter with non-Christian religious Ways as a means to not only Christian renewal, but also the renewal of the non-Christian Ways. In a world generally hostile to any form of religious value and insight, his position seems to be that religious persons are "all in this together."

> The only religions that will be able to present themselves and to maintain their ground as "world religions" in the future will be

the ones that accept the "single world" that
is coming into being and the common world
history which will be created today for the
first time. This is the new situation for
the religions, including Christianity.[21]

But before Christians can enter into dialogue
with non-Christians, the two historic prejudices
governing Christian interaction with non-Christians
will have to be explicitly renounced: the absolutism of
the church and the absolutism of Christianity, the two
respective Catholic and Protestant forms of the
doctrine of no-salvation-outside-of-the-Christian Way.
In Moltmann's words:

> Fruitful dialogue involves clear knowledge
> about the identity of one's own faith on the
> one hand, but on the other it requires a
> feeling of one's own incompleteness and a
> real sense of need for fellowship with the
> other.[22]

It is faith as trust in God, not faith as
trust in institutions or doctrinal systems, that makes
dialogical encounter with non-Christians not only possible, but also a theological necessity. Moltmann's
understanding of religious pluralism is significant because he has returned to a New Testament understanding
of Christian interaction with non-Christians. His theology remains authentically Christian while affirming,
although not uncritically, that the reality Christians
name God has probably encountered human beings in non-
Christian religious Ways.

PROCESS THEOLOGY

The most radical and coherent Christian movement now engaging in interreligious dialogue of the sort called for by Moltmann, and to some degree by Tillich before his untimely death, is process theology. The philosophical underpinnings of process theology are largely grounded in the thought of Alfred North Whitehead, and by far the most important theologian of this movement is John B. Cobb, Jr. However, process theology is neither a Protestant nor a Catholic movement, although it did originate within liberal Protestant circles. As a movement excluding nothing from theological reflection, process thought has cut across traditional denominational boundaries.

Most process theologians assume that each of the major religious Ways of the world express real, valid, and yet different human encounters with the Sacred. Therefore, no particular religious Way, or particular expression of any religious Way, can claim superiority over another, for all possess truth and insight missing from the others. In other words, process theology is explicitly dialogical in structure and methodology because it has rejected the traditional Catholic-Protestant doctrine of no-salvation-outside-the-Christian Way.[23] It may be the only movement within modern Christian thought to have done so.

Consequently, process theologians have consistently operated under the conviction that the Christian Way needs to undergo continual creative transformation by not only assimilating whatever emerging aspects of Western scientific culture it authentically can, but also by opening itself to even more radical transformation through dialogue with non-Christian religious Ways. Dialogue with the Buddhist Way has been given special emphasis and seems to be the model for encountering other religious Ways such as Confucian, Hindu, and Jewish traditions. There are good reasons for this. Whitehead's philosophy, which he solidly built on Western scientific thought, was also informed by the Christian religious perspective, even though Whitehead himself was not a confessing Christian. At the same time, his thought is quite congenial with some forms of Asian philosophy and religion, particularly with the Buddhist world view.[24] This congeniality has aided process theologians in their appropriation of Whitehead's philosophical categories as a hermeneutical tool by which to translate Buddhist insights into language understandable to Christians. Likewise, process theologians also employ these categories to translate Christian experience and practice into language more easily grasped by Buddhists to foster their critical understanding of the Christian Way. In this context, Buddhist-Christian discussion and encounter involve many interrelated themes, but the most difficult and perhaps most controversial issue is the question of God. Process thought's encounter with the Buddhist Way has forced process theologians to apprehend more clearly the extent to which Whitehead's philosophy was influenced by specifically Christian interests. That is, when a Buddhist analyzes human experience in a distinctively Buddhist way, informed through the discipline of meditation and unencumbered by Whiteheadian categories, different experiential and cognitive results occur. As Cobb explains it:

> The two sets of results need not be contra-
> dictory. Everything the Buddhist finds may
> be there to be found, and everything White-
> head finds may be there to be found. For
> this reason the encounter with Buddhism can
> lead to a creative transformation of process
> theology that does not deny its insights but
> incorporates them into a larger whole.[25]

The problem is that Buddhist philosophy re-jects all notions of God. This rejection, a conse-quence of Buddhist rejection of all notions of per-sonal, separate, substantial selfhood, means Buddhist teaching and practice do not normally concern them-selves with those experiences that lead Christians (as well as Jews and Muslims) to emphasize purpose, ac-countability, qualitative novelty, and gradations of value as attributes of the Sacred.[26] But there are also degrees of difference in this regard among Bud-dhist schools. For example, the Pure Land tradition of Shinran (1173-1261) called in Japanese *jōdo shinshū* or "True Pure Land School," places great importance on just these very experiences while remaining unconcerned about the question of God.[27] Even so, Buddhists are not usually led by their experiences, informed by the practice of meditation, to belief in either Whitehead's God or in any of the traditional Christian affirmations of God.

Nevertheless, Cobb and other process thinkers believe it is an overstatement to say the Buddhist Way categorically denies the existence of God, since by "God" Buddhists normally understand either an ultimate ground of being or substance underlying the flux of events and things, or a static substantial being transcending the flux of concrete space-time. Process theologians, following Whitehead and the biblical images of God, have also denied the existence of God in these two senses.

Rather than conceiving of God as an ultimate ground of being, Whitehead wrote of "creativity" as categorically ultimate. In his words:

Creativity is the universal of universals characterizing ultimate matters of fact. It is that ultimate principle by which the many, which are the universe disjunctively, become the one actual occasion, which is the universe conjunctively. It lies in the nature of things that the many enter into complex unity.[28]

Because "creativity" is part of the categorical scheme through which Whitehead understood Einstein's theories of special and general relativity, creativity does not exist independently of actual things and events. That is, creativity has no existence in itself. It is found only in actual instances of the "many becoming one and increased by one." In this sense, creativity as Whitehead conceived it is very similar to the Buddhist teaching of "dependent co-origination" (*pratītya-samutpāda*).

Process theology's reflections on God have faithfully followed Whitehead's notions. Instead of a substantial, static being underlying and transcending the flux of the temporal process, process thought conceives of God as a formative element, indeed the chief example, of this flux. Thus, although Whitehead spoke of an eternal "primordial nature" of God (God as God is in God's own self-nature), this is an abstraction from the actual process of what God is in his becoming "consequent nature" (God as God effects and is effected by the multiplicity of past, present, and future "things" and events in the entire universe at any given moment of space-time).

In following Whitehead's lead, process theologians generally conclude that because the questions to which God is the answer in Christian experience are not normally Buddhist questions, Whitehead's God is not explicitly found in Buddhist teaching. Tacitly, however, the possibility of affirming the existence of God might remain metaphysically open because of the presence of beings called *bodhisattvas*[29] that play somewhat analogous cosmological and religious functions in Mahayana teaching and practice. Whether Buddhists will actually affirm this possibility for themselves remains an open question.

Conversation with Buddhists has also led process theologians to reflect on how adequately they have understood the nonsubstantial character of God in relation to Christian experience. At this point process thought has been illumined by what it has incorporated form the Buddhist Way. For example, the Mahayana Buddhist doctrine of "emptiness" (śūnyatā) has played a key role. The question is, what does Buddhist philosophy mean when it teaches an event, for example, a moment of human experience, is "empty"? According to Cobb, who seems to have interpreted quite accurately the meaning of this teaching,[30] it means first of all that the experience is empty of substance. That is, the separate moments of a person's experience are not unified by an enduring self or an "I" remaining self-identical through time. There is no "subject," even in a single moment, to which the experience "happens" or "belongs." For a moment of human experience represents only an event or a happening at a particular moment of space-time. Second, this means an experience lacks all possession, for whatever constitutes it does not belong to it. The particular elements of the experience, in Buddhist language its *dharmas*, are a coming together of what is other than the experience. Third, the experience does not possess a form that it imposes on its constituting elements. In other words, it is empty of form because the form of an experience results from what constitutes it. Finally, an experience is empty of permanent being. The constituting elements of an experience are not the "being" of that experience. Instead, the constituting elements *become* the new experience, or better, this becoming *is* the experience. This also means the constituting elements of an experience do not have being either, for they too are empty. Hence, Mahayana Buddhist philosophy concludes that because there is no being, there are "no-things." There is only "emptiness."

Consequently, some schools of Mahayana Buddhist philosophy teach we should meditatively experience the self as "empty" or void of permanent self-definition to allow whatever exists to fill it. We should seek to achieve maximum fulfillment by imposing no particular principle of selection. In Whiteheadian language, the seeker of enlightenment should meditatively experience the self as a void imposing nothing on the many constituting it as one, and increasing the many by one.

There are remarkable affinities between Whitehead's account of the consequent nature of God and the Buddhist notion of Emptiness. Because the consequent nature of God (God in his relation to the temporal process in its entirety) is his aim at the concrete realization of all possibilities in their proper season, God imposes no principle of selection upon himself. As Whitehead formulated this:

the consequent nature of God is composed of a multiplicity of elements with individual self-realization. It is just as much a multiplicity as it is a unity; it is just as much an immediate fact as it is an unresting advance beyond itself.[31]

Or as Cobb has interpreted Whitehead on this point:

That is, God is "empty" of "self" insofar as "self" is understood as an essence that can be preserved only by excluding "other" things, or at least not allowing them to be received as they are.[32]

And what applies to God's consequent nature applies to all things and events in their becoming, since God, for Whitehead, was not an exception to the principles of process and creativity constituting the becoming of everything in the universe. Indeed, God is the chief example of these principles.

Conceiving God in this way in dialogue with the Buddhist Way has led to a creative transformation of process theology that is not foreign to Christian experience. And while the idea of God does not generally concern Buddhist thinkers, a Whiteheadian notion of God may not be foreign to Buddhist experience. Therefore, Buddhist appropriation of a process understanding of God in a way that does not erode the basic religious integrity of Buddhist experience can lead to its creative transformation. But the specific direction and outcome of this dialogical process cannot be foretold because process thought is still in process. In all probability, the result will not be some final synthesis, but the emergence of new processes of creative transformation within both the Buddhist and Christian Ways.

CONCLUDING OBSERVATIONS

I have described the traditional Catholic and Protestant response to the non-Christian religious Ways in terms of the doctrine of no-salvation-outside-the-church and the Christian faith respectively. The roots of this traditional understanding lie in the New Testament, although this position is not, in my opinion, the dominant scriptural one. The twin doctrines of no-salvation-outside-the-church, the Catholic version, or no-salvation-outside-the-Christian-faith, the Protestant version, are simply not conducive to interreligious dialogue. In principle, there can be no dialogue between Christians and non-Christians until the doctrine of no-salvation-outside-the-church or the Christian faith is explicitly renounced. Until then, any Christian encounter with non-Christians will remain a Christian monologue, preventing the process of creative transformation from even beginning.

However, there is more than one way to interpret the New Testament, as is evident in Moltmann's theology and most radically in process theology. Cobb's version of process thought is particularly dialogical in structure; at the same time it is fully and consciously Christian. Once more, his openness to the creative transformation of the Christian Way through dialogical encounter with non-Christian faith and practice is grounded in the New Testament's understanding of authentic Christian response to non-Christian faith. Because Cobb has renounced the traditional doctrine of no-salvation-outside-of-the-Christian Way, he discovered that being a Christian does not imply non-Christians are cut off from a saving relation with God. Therefore, he is able to conclude that non-Christian religious Ways are authentic, valid, and yet different ways in which the Sacred, however it is named, has been encountered, responded to, and understood within the limitations of historical existence. Accordingly, every religious Way embodies truth about the Sacred, but not completely, and no religious Way is exclusively

valid and universal. Each needs to creatively transform itself through dialogical appropriation of what it
can from others. Or, as Cobb has expressed it, the
Christian can even be a Buddhist while remaining Christian.[33]

There are historical and theological precedents internal to Christian faith upon which dialogical
forms of theological reflection can and should be created. A dialogical style of Christian self-understanding would, in the context of modern religious pluralism, be authentically Christian precisely because it
would begin by rejecting all forms of the doctrine of
no-salvation-outside-the-Christian Way. I do not base
these assertions upon any particular model for theological reflection that I would like to defend or see established as the predominant mode of Christian faith
and practice, although I think Cobb's process model is
as good as any at present. Such a task is better left
to theologians whose job it is to articulate the meaning of the Christian "circle of faith" in the modern
world. But as a historian of religions I can suggest
resources internal to the Christian Way upon which theologians might further reflect in the interest of
creating more dialogical modes of Christian self-
understanding.

Let me point first to an ancient precedent of
Christian history. I do not have in mind the encounter
of the medieval church with Islam or Judaism, but
rather the encounter of the early church with the Hellenistic cultural environment that created the context
for the Christian Way's evolution into a "world reli-

gion." As I have already indicated, the earliest phases of this encounter were utterly negative. The New Testament evolved at a time at which Christians experienced the popular teachings and practices of their Hellenistic environment as superstitious, idolatrous, and immoral. This aspect of popular Hellenistic culture, mostly associated with the mystery religions and gnostic movements of the time, were simply denounced as opposite to the reality Christians experienced in Jesus as the Christ. And indeed, this was probably the appropriate response.

But as thoughtful Christians began encountering the more profound and sophisticated dimensions of their Hellenistic environment--art, law, literature, and especially Greek philosophical wisdom--they encountered something that could not be written off simply as pagan and idolatrous. There was much wisdom in the writings of Plato, Aristotle, the Stoics, the Epicureans, and others. It could not be dismissed as the early Christians had dismissed, say, Diana of Ephesus and the manner in which she was worshipped. The theological issue was how *should* the Christian Way appropriate Greek philosophical wisdom. Centuries were spent in reflection upon this problem, and a number of answers emerged.

One answer involved attitudes quite similar to those encouraged by the doctrine of no-salvation-outside-the-Christian Way. This response is best epitomized the Latin church Father Tertullian's (160-230) question, "What has Jerusalem to do with Athens?"--a question that might be expected from a theologian who confessed, "I believe because it's absurd." No goodness or truth can be discovered apart from the Christian Way, argued Tertullian. In reality, however, his theory was strongly influenced by the very Greek philosophy he detested. But he, at least, did not want it to be; he desired to maintain his distance and purity from all aspects of Hellenistic philosophy and culture.

Another response was to interpret Greek philosophical tradition from the perspective of the Bible. Much wisdom and truth could be found in Greek philosophy, but only because of its origins in the Bible. Moses was older than Plato, Aristotle, and the Stoics, so their wisdom must have derived from biblical sources. And of course where biblical wisdom and Greek philosophy differed, biblical wisdom was to be the Christian's standard of truth. This response at least allowed a positive response to what was discovered apart from the Bible, but historically it was a very questionable approach. After all, concluding that Plato received his major ideas from the Old Testament, for example, rings a bit oddly. It also strained historical credulity in ways not even the early church could allow.

A third possibility suggested God had not left himself without witnesses anywhere in the world, so that Greek philosophy functioned as preparation for Hellenistic reception of the Christian gospel, just as the Old Testament was a preparation for receiving the gospel among the Jews. Whether there was any truth to this approach, many sensitive non-Christians saw it, quite accurately I think, as a not-too-subtle form of Christian arrogance.

The final attitude of Christian theological opinion concerning Greek philosophical thought recognized its autonomy by declaring it different from biblical teachings yet embodying truths not explicitly found in the Bible. This "truth" could then be appropriated into Christian teaching and practice. Admittedly, this approach involved many risks, but it was thoroughly dialogical. For example, some who engaged in it became more Greek than Christian. The power of Greek philosophy is such that once becoming involved with it, one risks being totally absorbed by it. Accepting Plato and Aristotle, for instance, could reduce Christian faith to a form of Platonism or Aristotelianism.

But what if dialogical involvement with Greek philosophy had not occurred in the first four hundred years of Christian history? What if Christian teaching and practice had followed Tertullian? In all probability the Christian movement would have remained an isolated subsect within the Jewish Way. Fortunately, the Christian Way went in the other direction and took a dialogical approach to Hellenistic culture generally and to Greek philosophy particularly. Augustine is the major figure in the encounter of the early church with Greek philosophy. While he appropriated much from Greek philosophy, especially in its Platonic and Neoplatonic forms, his own Christian faith remained the unifying principle of all of his theologizing.

Had the early church simply ignored Greek philosophy or followed Tertullian's aggressive rejection of it, many of the most sensitive, thoughtful people of the Hellenistic world who had committed themselves to the Christian Way would have, with much justification, found it impossible to become Christians. An intelligent and sensitive person is unlikely to be wholeheartedly committed to a religious Way that insists on leaving out whatever goodness, truth, and beauty can be found outside it. For doing so is, in Christian language, a form of idolatry. The Christian Way had no choice but to take serious account of Greek philosophical wisdom by appropriating what it could from it. There may have been much risk in this, but to have failed to have taken it would have been disastrous.

The early church's response to Greek philosophy might well serve as a model for theological interaction with non-Christian religious Ways in the present age of religious pluralism. Just as Greek philosophical wisdom was more than mere "preparation for the gospel" for Hellenistic Christians, so the teaching and practices of non-Christians may offer much truth, beauty, and wisdom to modern Christians. When truth, beauty, and wisdom are found anywhere, they ought to be appropriated by Christians as fundamental for their faith. Doing so engenders the creative transformation of not only individual Christians but also of the Christian Way. Of course this is risky business, just as love is risky business. But the risk of interreligious dialogue, like risk in loving, is also necessary business, now for us, as it was for the early church during its encounter with Greek philosophy in an age of Hellenistic culture.

Finally, the theological precedent that guided the early church's encounter with Greek philosophy might be considered. Had this precedent been consistently followed, the doctrine of no-salvation-outside-the-Christian Way and the resulting religious imperialism this teaching created could have been avoided. What I mean is this: all genuinely Christian teaching and practice in all its amazing variation begins with the awareness that whatever "salvation" means, it is not an event initiated by any human being, either through ethical self-discipline, or belief in doctrinal assertions and confessional statements, or participation within particular religious institutions, or involvement in particular formal or informal patterns of worship. In other words, the Christian trusts God's actions on humanity's behalf through the life, death, and resurrection of Jesus as the Christ. Surely, this experience cannot be reduced to simple belief in creeds or completely enclosed by any form of ecclesiastical institutionalization.

I do not mean that what a person believes or how an individual worships God are unimportant; belief, worship, and institutional organizations are forms of faith seeking understanding. But they are *expressions* of faith, not faith itself. Accordingly, they are not ultimate. I also do not mean that non-Christians have not encountered a sacred reality that Christians name "God" or that "salvation" has not occurred in non-

Christian religious Ways. Indeed, if the Christian experience of God as love has any truth to it, it would
surprise me to learn non-Christians had not been
"saved" through their own religious Ways. But it does
seem to me that the specifically Christian point, one
first made by Saint Paul, and afterwards by Augustine,
Thomas Aquinas, and even Martin Luther, is that Christians are not related to God because of any human contrivance. In other words, a person does not "get
faith" and then have a positive relation with God.
Rather, an individual's relation with God is first established by God, after which faith evolves as a trusting response to what God has done through Christ. Belief and institutional commitments are certainly necessary for understanding the implications of faith, and
occasionally may even express faith seeking understanding. But they are neither identical with faith nor do
they produce faith.

Now if it is true that "faith" as trust in
God's action on humanity's behalf through Christ cannot
be reduced to trust in belief systems, institutional
structures, and liturgical forms, then Christians are
free to take on the risks of exploring the ways in
which non-Christians have authentically encountered and
understood the sacred reality that Christians name God.
Christians are also free not only to appropriate what
can be appropriated in the hope of experiencing the reality of God more fully, but also to make errors of
judgment and belief. For the truth to which faith in
God's manifestation of self through the life, death,
and resurrection of Jesus as the Christ points is a

truth that cannot be reduced to any particular doctrinal formulation, institutional organization, or indeed
any particular experience. The freedom of Christian
faith is freedom from bondage to any form of "law," including forms of law bearing the name "Christian."
Stated most simply, the Christian experience of God is
that God does not care at all about "religions," but
does care very much about people.[34]

In this sense, then, not only are Christians
free to be scientists, carpenters, lawyers, truck
drivers, philosophers, theologians, historians of religions, English teachers, social workers, or psycholo-
gists; Christians are also free to become Buddhists,
Hindus, Muslims, or Taoists. In fact, doing so may be
the single most imortant theological imperative for
contemporary Christian faith. It is also a most exciting and interesting theological adventure because, as
William Temple once expressed it, "Unless all existence
is a medium of revelation, no Particular revelation is
possible. . . ."

NOTES

[1]Peter L. Berger, *The Heretical Imperative* (Garden City, N.J.: Anchor Books, 1979), 19-20.

[2]See Romans 9-11 for Saint Paul's understanding of this. Also, this theme runs throughout all four of the Gospels, as well as throughout Paul's other epistles.

[3]Reinhold Seeberg, *Textbook on the History of Doctrine* (Grand Rapids: Baker Book House),2: 88.

[4]See H. Densinger, trans., *The Church Teaches: Documents of the Church in English Translation* (London: B. Herder Book Company, 1955), 165. This passage is also quoted by John Hick, *God and the Universe of Faith* (London: Collings Faunt, 1977), 120.

[5]Hick, *God and the Universe of Faiths,* 121.

[6]Ibid.

[7]There are, however, rather famous examples of sixteenth century Jesuit missionaries in both China and Japan who did "pass over" to the dominant religious perspectives of these cultures and "return" to their original perspectives creatively transformed. The most famous of these were Francis Xavier (1506-1552), who led the mission to Japan, and Matteo Ricci (1552-1610) who was in charge of the mission to China. Neither of these priests regarded the people, culture, or religious perspectives they encountered in Japan and China as simply forms of spiritual darkness where God was completely unknown. In fact, Francis Xavier found the meditative practices and insights of certain sixteenth century Zen monks a challenge to his own religious faith, and Matteo Ricci in China passed the most difficult civil service examinations, based on Confucianism, which were given by the Chinese bureaucracy, becoming one of the highest ranking administrative officials in China. He, as Xavier did in relation to Japanese Zen, appropriated much from the Chinese philosophical and religious tradition into his own Christian faith. But such examples are always the exception, never the rule in Christian history. See Louis J. Gallagher, S. J., trans., *China in the Sixteenth Century: The Journals of*

Matthew Ricci, 1583-1610 (New York: Random House, 1953) and Richard H. Drummond, *A History of Christianity in Japan* (Grand Rapids, Mich.: William B. Eerdmans Publishing Co., 1971), chap. 2.

[8]Quoted by Hick, *God and the Universe of Faiths*, 123.

[9]Walter M. Abbot, S. J., ed., *The Documents of Vatican II* (New York: Guild Press, 1966), 35.

[10]Ibid., 662.

[11]Karl Rähner, *Theological Investigations* (Baltimore: Helicon Press, 1966), 5: 131. Also see related essays in other volumes of *Theological Investigations*, especially volumes 6, 9, 12, and 14.

[12]See *On Being a Christian* (New York: Pocket Books, 1978), 89-116 for Küng's fullest treatment of the non-Christian religious Ways and how Christians ought to encounter them.

[13]Ernest Troeltsch, "The Place of Christianity Among the Religions of the World," in *Christianity and other Religions* ed. John Hick and Brian Hebblethwaite, (Philadelphia: Westminster Press, 1981), 20.

[14]Ibid., 21.

[15]Ibid., 11-31.

[16]Ibid., 26.

[17]See Van Harvey, *The Historian and the Believer* (Philadelphia: Westminster Press, 1964), 68-101, 226.

[18]Karl Barth, "The Revelation of God and the Absolutism of Religion," in *Church Dogmatics* (Edinburgh: T. and T. Clarke, 1956), vol. 1, part 2, section 17.

[19]Paul Tillich, *Systematic Theology*, (Chicago: University of Chicago Press, 1951), 3-68. Also see his *Christianity and the Encounter with the World Religions* (New York: Columbia University Press, 1963).

[20]See Richard J. De Martino ed., "Dialogue, East
and West: Paul Tillich and Hisamatsu Shin'ichi,   *The
Eastern Buddhist* 4 (October 1971):   39-107 and   5
(October 1972): 107-128.

[21]Jürgen Moltmann, *The Church and the Power of the
Spirit* (New York: Harper and Row, 1975), 151.

[22]Ibid., 159.

[23]John B. Cobb, Jr., *Christ in a Pluralistic Age*
(Philadelphia: Westminster Press, 1975), 44-61. Also
see Cobb and David Ray Griffin, *Process Theology, An
Introductory Exposition* (Philadelphia: Westminster
Press, 1976), 128-142.

[24]See Cobb and Griffin, *Process Theology*, 136-142
for more specific information. Also see my response to
this in my "To John Cobb: Questions to Gladden the Atman in an Age of Pluralism," *Journal of the American
Academy of Religion* 45 (1977): 753-88.

[25]Cobb and Griffin, *Process Theology*, 139-40.

[26]Cobb makes this point the center of his discussion of the Buddhist Way in *The Structure of Christian
Existence* (Philadelphia: Westminster Press, 1967), 60-
72.

[27]See my study, *The Dharma of Faith: An Introduction to Classical Pure Land Buddhism* (Washington, D.
C.: University Press of America, 1977).

[28]Alfred North Whitehead, *Process and Reality* (New
York: Macmillan Company, 1967), 31.

[29]Literally, "one whose essence is enlightenment."
In the Mahayana version of the Buddhist Way, the central meaning of this notion refers to a being who has
earned his own enlightenment through eons of self-discipline and rebirths, but who has also renounced all of
the fruits of his self-efforts, including his own full
participation in the experience of *nirvāṇa* until all
other unenlightened sentient beings achieve enlightenment.   Therefore, motivated by compassionate wisdom,
the Bodhisattva vows to work for the enlightenment of
all sentient beings or not accept his own enlighten-

ment.   Objects of faith and devotion for most Mahayana Buddhists, Bodhisattva veneration plays a more prominent role than the practice of meditation.

[30]John B. Cobb, Jr., "Buddhist Emptiness and the Christian God," *Journal of the American Academy of Religion*, 45, (1977): 11-25.

[31]Whitehead, *Process and Reality*, 53.

[32]Cobb and Griffin, *Process Theology*, 142.

[33]John B. Cobb, Jr., "Can a Christian Be a Buddhist, Too?" *Japanese Religions*, 10 (December 1978): 1-20.   Also see "Christianity and Eastern Wisdom," *Japanese Journal of Religious Studies* 5, (December 1975): 298.

[34]A notion eloquently stated by Wilfred Cantwell Smith, *The Meaning and End of Religion* (New York: New American Library, 1964), 19-49.

CHAPTER THREE
The Buddhist Encounter with Non-Buddhist Religious Ways

Now I know well that when I approached various large
assemblies, even before I had sat down there or had begun to talk, whatever might have been their sort I made
myself of like sort, whatever their language, so was my
language. And I rejoiced them with talk on Dhamma,
made it acceptable, set them on fire, gladdened them.

Dīgha-nikāya II, 109.

ON BEING BUDDHIST

Being a Christian has always meant confessing
that while God is the god of all existence, it is
through Jesus as the Christ that all persons are
finally brought into a saving relationship with God.
Likewise, being a Buddhist has always meant taking
refuge in the Three Jewels--the Buddha, the Dhamma, the
Samgha--as the only means of achieving self-transformation and liberation from continual rebirth in the realm
of suffering constituting life in the world of samsaric
existence. And just as the Christian Way includes
several different, yet authentically Christian, theological versions of the meaning of faith as trust in
Christ, so the Buddhist Way includes several different
Buddhist versions of the meaning of taking refuge in
the Three Jewels. Finally, just as the Christian
proclamation of Jesus as the central agent through whom
God effects the salvation of all human beings is simultaneously a claim for the universality of the Christian
Way itself, so the Buddhist proclamation that taking
refuge in the Three Jewels is the only means available
for obtaining spiritual release (*nirvāṇa*) from suffer-

ing existence is simultaneously a claim for the universality of the Buddhist Way.

However, "taking refuge in" the Three Jewels is something quite different from the Christian experience of faith as trust in Christ. The first jewel, taking refuge in the Buddha, has never meant trusting the historical Gautama the Buddha as the source of the salvation of the Buddhist seeker in quite the same manner, at least, of worshipping or trusting a God or a savior in the hope such beings will grant salvation as a gift. All of the earliest Buddhist traditions agree in emphasizing that Gautama was only a man, no more and certainly no less, who had achieved insight into the nature of universal suffering, the cause of suffering, and the means of achieving release from suffering. It was this discovery that transformed him from an ordinary human being to an extraordinary human being worthy of the honorific title "Buddha," or an "Enlightened One." But throughout this extraordinary man's life he remained fully human. And when he died, he literally ceased to be, for at this death his *nirvāṇa* attained the completion of *parinirvāṇa*, or final release from all further rebirths. Gautama the Buddha literally ceased existing and therefore could not become an object of devotion.

This earliest conception of the religious role of Gautama the Buddha is classically expressed in the last words he is said to have uttered to his disciples just before his death:

The the Blessed One addressed the brethren, and said, "Behold now, brethren, I exhort

you, saying, decay is inherent in all compo-
nent things! Work out your own salvation
with diligence."[1]

But when the disciples began grieving over
the Buddha's death, the venerable Anuruddha exhorted
his brothers:

Enough my brethren. Weep not, neither
lament! Has not the Blessed One formerly declared this to us, that it is the very nature
of all things near and dear to us, that we
must divide ourselves from them, leave them,
sever ourselves from them? How then, can
this be possible--that whereas anything whatever born, brought into being, and originated
contains within itself the inherent necessity
of dissolution--how then can this be possible
that such a being should not be dissolved?
No such condition can exist! Even the spir-
its, brethren, will reproach us.[2]

So the Buddha is a man like any other man.
But he was also extraordinary in a way unlike any other
human being. For according to the earliest texts,
Buddhists always regarded the historical Buddha as more
than merely the wisest of all *arhats*, or "saints" who
had achieved enlightenment. He was also the
sammasambuddha, the "fully enlightened one," for he had
discovered the way that all human beings must follow to
achieve enlightenment. Therefore, the Buddhist is a
"way follower" somewhat less in spiritual capacity and
attainment than the Buddha who discovered the Way.
Accordingly, taking refuge in the Buddha can only mean

imitating the Buddha's example by following his teachings, or Dhamma (Sanskrit, Dharma). This relationship
between the historical Buddha and his Way or teachings
(the Dhamma) is illustrated in the following dialogue
between the imminent monk, Nāgasena, and King Menander,
who was seeking to comprehend the Buddhist Way through
Nagasena's instructions at his court.

"Reverend Nāgasena," said the King, "does
the Buddha still exist?"

"Yes, your Majesty, he does."

"Then is it possible to point out the Buddha as being here or there?"

"The Lord has passed completely away in
Nirvana, so that nothing is left which could
lead to the formation of another being. And
so he cannot be pointed out as being here or
there."

"Give me an illustration."

"What would your Majesty say--if a fire
were blazing, would it be possible to point
to a flame which had gone out and say that it
was here or there?"

"No, your Reverence, the flame is extinguished, it can't be detected."

"In just the same way, your Majesty, the
Lord has passed away in Nirvana. . . .He can
only be pointed out in the body of his doctrine, for it was he who taught it."

"Very good, Reverend Nāgasena!"[3]

The Buddha is, in other words, incarnated in
the Dhamma. But the Dhamma can only be preserved,

since the Buddha no longer exists, by the Samgha, the community of persons actually following the Buddha's example through practicing the Dhamma. Taking refuge in the Samgha accordingly becomes an absolute necessity for the Buddhist seeker for two principle reasons: enlightenment is not likely to occur apart from a community accurately preserving the Buddha's memory and his teachings; and all persons, with the possible exception of the Buddha, require the support of a community to achieve the goal of his teachings, enlightenment. In short, while it is true all seekers must experience the reality of enlightenment for themselves through their own self-efforts, they require the support of a community accurately preserving the Dhamma and guiding its practice. The Samgha provides this guidance.

In summary, then, being a Buddhist means for all traditions of the Buddhist Way taking refuge in or trusting the Buddha as an example to imitate by practicing his Dhamma within the communal context of the Samgha, which not only preserves the Dhamma, but doctrinally defines it. Even so, the meaning of taking refuge in the Three Jewels has been and continues to be a subject of debate and interpretation within all the various traditions and schools of the Buddhist Way. The key to understanding the main characteristics of the Buddhist Way's encounter with non-Buddhist religious Ways is to be found here.

THE THERAVADA TRADITION

In the year 480 B.C.E. there occurred a great assembly of five hundred monks meeting in council

at Rajagrha. This council was the first of a long series, somewhat comparable to the ecumenical councils of
Christian history. The monks in attendance are said to
have recited the Pāli Canon of Buddhist scripture,
called the *Tipiṭaka* (Sanskrit, *Tripiṭaka*, meaning
"three baskets"), thus fixing the earliest official
oral version of the Dhamma. However, the *Tipiṭaka* was
transmitted orally until the Fourth Council, when it
was finally put into its first written form. The second Buddhist Council was held a century later, in 380
B.C.E., at Vesāli. This council witnessed the first
signs of the split within the Samgha that eventually
evolved into the Theravada and Mahayana divisions of
Buddhist teaching and practice. The Second Council was
also marked by disputes over monastic discipline, some
monks apparently seeking a relaxation of the rules for-
bidding the use of gold and silver, liquor, beds, and
meals after midday.

The Third Buddhist Council was convened about
240 B.C.E. at Pataliputra under the sponsorship of
King Aśoka. Led by this king, the Third Buddhist Council was a milestone in Buddhist history, for its decisions transformed the Buddhist Way from one sectarian
Indian religious movement among others into a universal
religious Way.

Aśoka was the grandson of the founder of the
Mauryan Dynasty, Chandragupta Maurya, and its third and
perhaps greatest king. Under his rule India came
closer to political unification than under any previous
ruler until the arrival of the British in the seventeenth century. After he had stabilized his conquests,

he converted to the Buddhist Way and established it as the state religion of his empire, although religious tolerance was also an important legal principle of the society he hoped to establish. One of his first actions after completing his conquests was calling the Third Buddhist Council to establish once and for all which of the numerous versions of the Dhamma was authentic, an important question for him because he had to define authentic Buddhist teaching and practice before he could give it official sponsorship.

Although a Buddhist adherent and patron, Aśoka had nevertheless a lay person's faith centering on moral discipline, devotion to the Buddha, and social service. He thought of the Buddhist Way as a universal religious Way rather than as one Indian sectarian movement among others. He also saw Buddhist faith and practice as a way of extending his political interests abroad. Thus he sent the first Buddhist missionaries beyond the borders of India, most notably to Sri Lanka. The form of Buddhist faith and practice these missionaries represented later came to be called Theravada, or "School of the Elders." Other forms of Buddhist faith and practice that came to be designated Mahayana ("Great Vehicle") also began spreading north from India during this time, specifically into Tibet, China, Korea, and finally, in the fourth and fifth centuries into Japan. The northern spread of the Buddhist Way beyond the borders of India was not, however, part of the official missionary activity sponsored by King Aśoka.[4] Even so, the fortunes of the Buddhist Way under Asoka's sponsorship are somewhat parallel to the fortunes of the Christian Way during the rule of Constantine the Great, emperor of Rome from 306-337.

The Theravada Dhamma is often characterized by its apparent denial that lay persons are capable of attaining enlightenment, along with the rather passive role it assigns to the religious life of the laity. Indeed, the core teachings of the Theravada interpretation of the Dhamma assume most persons lack the emotional and intellectual capacities required for undertaking the meditational and ethical disciplines of monastic life that are absolutely necessary for the achievement of enlightenment. Doctrinally and institutionally, the Theravada Saṃgha is limited only to ordained monks, because femininity is assumed to be a hindrance to the achievement of enlightenment. Presently, therefore, there is no order of nuns in the Theravada Samgha, although an order of nuns was established during the Buddha's lifetime somewhat against his will.[5] The usual reason given for this sharp separation between lay Buddhist practice and monastic practice is that the laity are of necessity too preoccupied with earning a living, with family life, and with other worthy, yet secular involvements and tasks to undertake the rigors of meditation. The search for enlightenment requires a twenty-four-hour-a-day effort, and lay persons simply do not have the time. Once more, being a lay person or a female is also the negative result of an individual's *kamma* (Sanskrit, *karma*), meaning the cumulative effects of an individual's deeds in his or her past lives. Lay status implies diminished mental and spiritual capacities precluding the successful performance of meditational disclosure.

But what at first glance seems like a very rigid separation between religious professionals and lay followers is greatly softened by the recognition that both monks and laity are liable to the same suffering and anxiety and that lay persons also possess spiritual potential. In short, even though the earliest Buddhist teachings and discipline are directed primarily to a cloistered male monastic community, all of the Theravada *suttas* indicate the Buddha's profound concern for the spiritual welfare of the ordinary lay follower. This concern continues to be expressed by monks of the Theravada Saṃgha.

Consequently, while laypersons possess little hope in achieving enlightenment until after passing through many rebirths, they can raise themselves up the spiritual ladder leading to enlightenment through service to the monastic order, trusting the Buddha's Dhamma as preserved by the monastic Samgha, and living according to the ethical precepts as uncompromisingly as possible in the secular world. Doing so acquires for the lay follower positive kammic merit, which in future lives assumes the form or capacities and endowments required for the rigors of monastic practice. The point is, the attribution of soteriological value to faith in the Three Jewels remains an absolute requirement for both lay persons and fully ordained monks:

All who have faith in me and love me have heaven as their destiny.[6]

Faith is the seed...faith in this world is
the best property of man.[7]

Incapable of meditative wisdom, the lay follower must especially rely on faith as his or her frame
of reference for practicing the Dhamma, although there
are currently movements in Theravada Buddhist countries
aimed at teaching meditation to interested female and
male lay disciples.[8]

To better understand how the separation between lay and monastic practice of the Dhamma relates
to Theravada interpretation of non-Buddhist religious
Ways, it is necessary to contrast the religious role of
the Buddhist laity with the specific goal for which
cloistered Theravada monks are ideally supposed to
strive twenty-four hours a day every day--the *arhat*
ideal. An *arhat* is a person who has achieved through
meditative insight what the Buddha achieved, so that an
arhat is also technically a Buddha since anyone experiencing enlightenment is an "enlightened one." But an
arhat is not "the" Buddha, of course, for he remains a
follower of the Buddha's Dhamma, not its discoverer.

The earliest Pali texts describe the *arhat* as
an enlightened being possessing numerous characteristics. He has, for example, achieved the insight of enlightenment because he has meditatively comprehended
the twelve *nidanas* (spokes) or interdependent causes of
the Wheel of *pratītya-samutpāda* (interdependent origination). Thereby, he eradicates the three *asravas*
(intoxicants), the three errors of sensual desire, love
of existence, and speculative opinion. He perfects the
Seven Factors of Enlightenment (Pāli, *samba jjhanha*):

mindfulness, investigation, energy, joy, serenity, concentration, and equanimity. He lets go of the five
nirvaranas (hindrances): sensuality, malice, sloth,
worry, and excitement. He perfects the discipline of
self-restraint and meditation, thereby acquiring various wonder-working powers. He fulfills the Triple Discipline of virtuous thought, concentration, and wisdom.
He destroys the Ten Fetters of belief in substantial
reality, individuality, perverted notions about good
works and ceremonies, doubt, sensual desire, hatred,
love of life, pride, excitement, and ignorance. He
knows by experience the Three Sublime States of compassion, sympathetic joy, and equanimity. In short, the
arhat is he who has attained total and complete self-
realization. No longer bound to the world of samsaric
existence, he attains release from all further involvement in the chain of endless rebirth into the world at
the moment of death, just as the historical Buddha did.
He achieves his goal through his own disciplined self-
efforts, not relying on any other sentient being, be
this a deity, the Buddha, a great teacher, or another
arhat. Utterly alone, he is the zealous, earnest master
of his destiny.[9]

Clearly, therefore, the Theravada interpretation of the meaning of taking refuge in the Three Jewels has two interdependent meanings. For the lay Buddhist, it means serving the monastic Samgha and disciplining his life in the secular world by observing the
ethical precepts of the Buddhist Way in the hope of
achieving *nibbāna* during another life time. For the
ordained monk, taking refuge in the Three Jewels means

total and committed participation in the monastic community, where time is spent solely in the practice of meditation, ethical discipline, teaching, and study.

It was this double-structured Dhamma, one for the laity and one for the monk, which was officially sent abroad with the missionaries sponsored by King Asoka. But in the process, this Dhamma also encountered non-Buddhist religious Ways, not only in India but throughout Southeast Asia. And because Theravada teaching claims the only way to "salvation," *nibbāna*, was through *its* system of meditative discipline guided by doctrine, the Theravada Buddhist Way was forced to develop an articulate understanding of its relationship with non-Buddhist Ways. The central notion under which this understanding evolved was the doctrine of *upaya* or "skillful means."

Essentially, *upāya* refers to any method skillfully applied for the purpose of leading human beings to the experience of enlightenment. Therefore, any method of meditation, religious ritual, ethical discipline, or doctrinal formulation can be used to help persons spiritually advance beyond where they are as unenlightened beings toward the final truth of enlightenment. In short, *all* religious teachings and practices, including the specific teachings and practices originating in the Buddhist Way, that help advance the seeker towards enlightenment are forms of *upaya*.

One of the earliest literary expressions of this notion is found in the *Tevijja Sutta*. The dialogue of this *sutta* (discourse) is set in Kośala where the Buddha stayed at a village where he was asked by two young Brahmins to resolve their argument about which of their teacher's methods was best suited to lead them to union with Brahmā, the Creator God. Each of these teachers was equally well-versed in the Three Vedas, as well as equally wise and virtuous. The Buddha responds that the superior method is one that:

lets his mind pervade one quarter of the world with thoughts of love [mettā], and so the second, and so the third, and so forth. And thus the whole wide world, above, below, around and everywhere does he continue to pervade with a heart of love, far reaching, grown great, and beyond measure.

Just . . . . as a mighty trumpeter makes himself heard--and that without difficulty-- in all four directions; even so of all things that have shape or life, there is not one that he passes by or leaves aside, but regards them all with mind set free, and deep felt love.

Verily this . . . .is the way to a state of union with Brahma.[10]

Now the fact the *Tevijja Sutta's* only topic is the achievement of union with Brahma at first seems quite confusing, for the text has, at least on the surface, nothing to do with the specifically Buddhist goal of achieving enlightenment. But, as Alicia Matsunaga notes, this confusion is easily dispelled when the topic of this text, union with Brahma, is compared with a similar theme in the *Mahā-govinda Suttana*. In this discourse the Buddha recollects how once in a former life he was a Brahmin high steward (mahā-govinda) who led all of his followers to union with Brahma, while at the same time teaching this state was inferior to Buddhist enlightenment:

> I do remember . . . . I was the High Steward
> of those days. I taught my disciples the way
> to communion with the Brahma-world. But . .
> . . that religious life did not conduce to
> detachment, to passionlessness, to cessation
> of craving, to peace, to understanding, to
> insight of the higher stages of the Path, to
> Nirvana, but only to rebirth in the Brahma-
> world. On the other hand, my religious sys-
> tem . . . . conduces solely to detachment, to
> passionlessness, to cessation of craving, to
> peace, to understanding, to insight of the
> higher stages of the Path, to wit, right
> views, right intention, right speech, right
> action, right livelihood, right effort, right
> mindfulness, right rapture.[11]

Only the practice of the Noble Eightfold Path leads to true enlightenment. The practices leading to union with Brahmā may create very intense states of religious experience, but they are declared inferior to the Buddhist goal of enlightenment. This is clearly the central thrust of the Tevijja Sutta, where the Buddha teaches non-Buddhists, i.e., Brahmins, an idealized form of Brahma veneration opposed to usual Hindu understandings of this deity. Once more, he teaches them a method of achieving union with Brahma by means of Bud-

dhist interpretations of ethical principles. In other words, the Buddha is pictured as teaching non-Buddhists by instructing them in an idealized practice related to his hearers' own level of understanding. By this process, non-Buddhists are gently led to specifically Buddhist teachings and forms of meditation. This method is known as *upāya*.

Buddhist tradition has, accordingly, interacted with non-Buddhist religious Ways with much more sympathy and less overt hostility than has historically characterized Christian interaction with non-Christian religious Ways. Non-Buddhist ideas and practices were not categorically rejected as forms of error and spiritual darkness. Rather, they were assimilated into the Buddhist Way as methods of teaching non-Buddhists specifically Buddhist standards of morality in order to prepare them for the practice of meditation.

The major assumption motivating this doctrine--"truth" must be apprehended and communicated in relation to the abilities and capacities of the individuals being taught--made it possible to approach non-Buddhist religious Ways as partial truths which could be skillfully appropriated for the purpose of raising non-Buddhists beyond their original doctrine and practices to the full truth of the experience of enlightenment. But even specifically Buddhist doctrines and practices are forms of *upāya*, for the truth of enlightenment and the methods of achieving awareness of this truth are not identical. Therefore, any method can be employed as a vehicle for achieving enlightenment if it is "skillfully" applied to the specific endowments and capacities of the individual seeker.

The doctrine of upāya became the foundation of what Alicia Matsunaga has suggestively called the "Buddhist philosophy [12] of assimilation." The notion of "skillful teaching" was even applied by the doctrinally conservative Theravada tradition of the Buddhist Way as it assimilated originally non-Buddhist teachings and practices into its version of the Dhamma. However, the Buddhist philosophy of assimilation is most fully developed in the Mahayana Buddhist tradition.

THE MAHAYANA TRADITION

Certainly, the outstanding feature of Theravada forms of the Buddhist Way is its emphasis upon self-reliance, for according to its version of the Dhamma, enlightenment can only be achieved through intense meditational practice apart from reliance upon anyone else: a teacher, a deity, or even the Buddha. Even so, until the individual seeker can stand alone, any and all methods of instruction should be utilized, including the worship of deities and the practice of non-Buddhist disciplines, to help that person advance beyond the need to cling to these "devices." As a result, wherever Theravada tradition was transmitted, originally non-Buddhist teachings and practices were incorporated into its Dhamma.

But the Mahayana Dharma, while maintaining the original Theravada teaching of self-reliance, went far beyond this tradition in its assimilation of non-Buddhist teachings and practices through its application of the doctrine of upāya. The distinctive notion separating Mahayana from Theravada tradition, the Bodhisattva ideal, represents the clearest example of the extent of Mahayana appropriation of originally non-Buddhist teachings and practices.

The Mahayana tradition is the culmination of forms of Buddhist faith and practice originating in the second and first centuries B.C.E., which were deeply influenced by popular bhakti (devotional) movements occurring within the Hindu Way. These devotional movements, centering upon veneration of both vedic and non-vedic Hindu deities, swept across India as more or less a reformation of, as well as a protest against, the ritualism and legalism of Brahmanic Hindu tradition. The Buddhist Way too came under the influence of these movements and incorporated much from them into its teachings and practices. The resulting transformation of the Buddhist Way involved the emergence of the distinctively Mahayana practice of Bodhisattva veneration.[13] As a consequence, the Mahayana Dharma assumed a lay character absent from Theravada tradition, although monasticism and meditational discipline are still emphasized in its teachings. However, the meaning of "Saṃgha" was widened to include the lay community, whose religious role and importance was regarded as of equal value to that of cloistered monks and nuns.

Specifically, the devotional-sectarian movements of the Hindu Way created the religious environment for the evolution of two distinctively Mahayana doctrines that together created the philosophical and religious foundations of its separation from Theravada tradition: the doctrine of the transfer of merit, called *parivarta* (turning over merit to the advantage of others), and the conception of a large number of Bodhisattvas who are active in assisting human beings in the attainment of enlightenment.[14]

"Merit" (*karma*), as normally conceived by Buddhist thought, is a quality within each person that assures some future positive benefit.[15] The Mahayana schools drew the conclusion that hoarding, storing, or accumulating personal merit, which according to their understanding is what the Theravada *arhat* does, implies egoistic self-seeking. Instead, the seeker should renounce his store of merit accumulated because of his religious practices and "transfer" or offer it freely to unenlightened beings for their own use. In other words, the Mahayana schools expected their followers to endow others with the merit they had acquired through the practice of the Buddhist Way, for this is what the Buddha himself is said to have done. It is the Bodhisattva who specializes in the transfer of merit.

A Bodhisattva is one whose "being" or "essence" (*sattva*) is "enlightenment" (*bodhi*). Accordingly, a Bodhisattva is a "Buddha in the making" who understands that final enlightenment cannot occur if there exists even one unenlightened being. Motivated by the compassionate awareness of his interdependency with others, the Bodhisattva actively strives for the enlightenment of all sentient beings before accepting the fruit of his own enlightenment. The method by which Bodhisattvas aid unenlightened beings is through turning over or "transferring" a portion of their infinite supply of merit to any sentient being desiring to draw upon it for their own religious advancement.

The pivot of the doctrine of the transfer of merit and the Bodhisattva ideal is the vow that all Bodhisattvas take to renounce their own final enlightenment unless they can assist all unenlightened beings in their quest for nirvāṇa. For this reason, all Mahayana Bodhisattva figures represent symbolic personifications of compassion (karuṇā) skillfully (upāya) guided by wisdom (prajñā) directed toward the release of all sentient beings from suffering. A classical example of the Bodhisattva's vow is the following passage from a Mahayana text called the Bodhicaryavatāra (Entering the Path of Enlightenment), written by the poet Śāntideva (early eighth century):

Let by all the good I have thus attained through these righteous performances all sorrows of all beings be completely pacified . . . . All my existence--all my goods in the three worlds unconditionally do I renounce for the fulfillment of the desire of all beings. My mind is bent on nirvāṇa, and everything has to be renounced for the sake of nirvāṇa, but if I am to sacrifice everything, let all be given to all beings. . . .Let them sport with my body--let them laugh and amuse; when the body is dedicated to them why should I take any more thought of it? Let them do any work they please to do with this body of mine; my only prayer is--let not any evil come to them with reference to me.[16]

The Bodhisattva is obviously different from the Theravada *arhat*. There are also numerous Bodhisattva figures and Buddhas functioning like Bodhisattvas involved in the Mahayana interpretation of this notion. But the following morphology seems doctrinally characteristic of them all: (1) Bodhisattvas are beings who may have been human, as was the historical Buddha, who, possessing infinite compassion, have taken vows to become fully enlightened on the condition that once attaining enlightenment, they will be able to work for the enlightenment of all unenlightened sentient beings; (2) the disciplines that Bodhisattvas practice during many rebirths acquire for them an infinite supply of merit; (3) from this store of merit Bodhisattvas create "Buddha Lands" in which they dwell, over which they reside, and to which any being placing faith in them and compassionately serving other sentient beings are reborn at death; (4) rebirth into a Buddha Land is accomplished when the residing Bodhisattva transfers a portion of merit to the devotee, which in turn cancels out any negative karma the devotee might possess; (5) the transfer of merit results in the rebirth of the devotee into a particular Bodhisattva's Buddha Land, so that when he or she hears the residing Bodhisattva teach the correct Dharma, they perfectly comprehend it, practice it, and thereby attain enlightenment. In other words, what the Theravada *arhat* must accomplish in this life, the Mahayana devotee may choose to accomplish after death and rebirth into a Buddha Land. In this regard, however, it is important to note that Bodhisattvas do not *give* enlightenment to devotees as a

gift of grace. They merely create the conditions making the achievement of enlightenment "easy" for those
beings choosing Bodhisattva veneration as a devotional
upāya.

Relative to the character of the Buddhist
Way's encounter with non-Buddhist religious Ways, three
observations concerning the Mahayana development of
Bodhisattva and Buddha veneration require clarification. First, all forms of Buddhist teaching stress the
role of meditation as the only means for achieving enlightenment. In fact, if any practice comes close to
possessing the character of what Christians mean by the
word "sacrament" in Buddhist teaching it is the practice of meditation. But any discipline, especially
meditation, must be tailored to the specific physical,
psychological, and developmental character of the meditator. All meditative disciplines are forms of upaya,
so that while the truth of enlightenment possesses absolute validity, the methods of meditation used to attain enlightenment must be skillfully related to the
specific abilities of each seeker, no two of whom are
alike. But the wisdom that transforms an ordinary
seeker into a Buddha is impossible apart from some form
of meditative Practice skillfully tailored to each
seeker's specific needs and abilities.

Second, Bodhisattva and Buddha veneration are
the logical continuation of trends having their beginnings in the earliest traditions of Theravada doctrine
and practice. Even Theravada tradition teaches that
not every seeker is capable of meditational self-discipline for any prolonged time, as each Buddhist hears

and comprehends truth differently according to the specific experiences and endowments of each individual.
Therefore, the truth of enlightenment must be communicated to each human being in a version uniquely appropriate to the needs and capacities of each. For just
as skillful parents do not communicate to a child about
love, sexuality, justice, or a particular religious
teaching in the same way these realities can be communicated to a mature adult, so the truths of Buddhist
religious experience will not be communicated to a
child, lay Buddhist, or non-Buddhist in identical ways.
Understood in this way, the doctrine of upāya makes
room for lay-oriented religious practices based on veneration of the Buddha and the worship of non-Buddhist
deities, even in Theravada tradition. The Mahayana emphasis upon Bodhisattva and Buddha veneration represents, therefore, essentially the logical continuation
of trends already existing in Theravada teaching and
practice.

Third, not only were savior figures and
deities originally part of Hindu religious tradition
assimilated into Mahayana Dharma as Bodhisattvas; other
deities and savior figures outside of Indian culture
were also assimilated into the Buddhist Way as upaya-
forms of Bodhisattvas and Buddhas. This process has a
long and complex history involving every Asian culture
into which Mahayana teachings and practices were
transmitted. But perhaps the following example of this
process will suffice as an illustration. In all
probability, the most well known Chinese Bodhisattva in
the West is Kuan-yin, the "goddess of mercy."

Originally Kuan-yin was a feminine "community deity" (*shen*) almost universally worshipped by the Chinese as a protector against disasters and bad fortune. She symbolized to pre-Buddhist Chinese pure nonjudgmental compassion always active in relieving all forms of human suffering. But when Mahayana tradition was transplanted into China, beginning around the end of the last century B.C.E., this divinity was "assimilated" into the Buddhist Way and identified with the Indian Bodhisattva Avalokiteśvara, the "Lord Who Looks Down in Compassion." In the process, "he" became a "she," for compassion is a peculiarly feminine virtue according to Chinese cultural traditions.[17] The resulting assimilation of originally two very distinct savior figures is but by one example among many that helped translate forms of Indian Buddhist teaching and practice, foreign to Chinese cultural and religious experience, into forms the Chinese could understand and appropriate. The cumulative effect of this process was the creative transformation of the Indian Mahayana Buddhist Way.

Perhaps the most interesting expression of the use of the doctrine of *upāya* involving the Buddhist philosophy of assimilation, because historically it was the most systematically developed, is the way in which elements of the indigenous religious Way of Japan, usually called Shintō ("the Way of the deities"), were assimilated into the Japanese Buddhist Way. The Japanese technical term for this process is *honji-suijaku* ("true nature-manifestation"). According to this theory, the indigenous Japanese deities, collectively called *kami*, are in reality incomplete "trace manifestations" (*suijaku*) of various Buddhas and Bodhisattvas. The first literary account of *honji-suijaku* thought appeared in Japanese Buddhist history during the early part of the tenth century, but its philosophical origins are much earlier in Chinese Buddhist thought.

The term *honjaku* (Chinese, *pen-chi*) was first used in China by Seng-chao (374-414) in his refutation of Neo Taoist ideas, which had in his time been assimilated into early Chinese Buddhist thought. In the eighth century, Chih-I of the Chinese T'ien-t'ai (Japanese, Tendai School applied this terminology in his commentary on the *Lotus Sutra*. He called the first section of the *Lotus Sutra* chi-men (Japanese, *jakumon* or *shakumon*), since it deals with the "manifested," and therefore limited, historical Buddha and his teachings. He entitled the second half of this sutra *pen-men* (Japanese, *hommon*), since he believed this section of the *Lotus Sutra* taught the Absolute or Original Buddha was the ultimate reality of which Gautama the Buddha was, like all Buddhas, only a finite incarnated manifestation.

The practical application of the *honjaku* theory to the relation between Bodhisattvas and the indigenous Japanese *kami* is unique in Buddhist history. The essential method of application involved identifying specific *kami* as partial "trace manifestations" (*suijaku*) of realities most completely revealed in their "true nature" forms (*honji*) as Bodhisattvas and Buddhas. The implication was that because worship of the *kami* is in reality merely veneration of inferior

forms of Bodhisattvas and Buddhas, devotees were un-
knowingly worshipping the *kami* as preparation for the
specific disciplines of the Buddhist Way. Accordingly,
the *kami* of the indigenous Japanese religious tradition
were assimilated into the Buddhist Way as a method of
teaching Buddhist ethics and meditation to non-Buddhist
Japanese.

The oldest Buddhist lists of *kami*, identified
with their specific *honji* Bodhisattvas and Buddhas,
date from the early twelfth century, although systematic application of this theory actually began during
the time of Prince Shōtoku (574-622), who is commonly
regarded by Japanese Buddhists as comparable to King
Asoka because of his activities in establishing the
Buddhist Way in Japan. One interesting fact about
these lists is their inconsistency. Even the lists of
single Shinto shrines and Buddhist temples over different periods of time usually alternate or change *honji*
because of the increase or decrease in the popularity
of various Bodhisattvas or Buddhas. However, the *honji*
list of the Kasuga Shrine deities, dating from the year
1175, should suffice as an illustration of the process
of assimilation in Japan.[18]

Suijaku (The Kami)	*Honji* (Bodhisattva)
Ichinomiya-Kashima	Fukukenjaku Kannon (Amo-ghapasa Avalokiteśvara)
Ninomiya-Katori	Yakushi Nyorai (Bhaisaj-yaguru)
Sannomiya-Hiraoka	Jizō Bosatsu (Ksitigar-bha)
Shinomiya-Aidonnohime	Juichimen Kannon
Wakamiya	Monjushiri (Mañjuśrī)

It is interesting that Jizo Bosatsu (Jizo Bodhisattva), whose speciality is delivering all sentient beings, especially children who have died before reaching old age, from suffering in the various Buddhist hells, was at one time or another listed as the *honji* of twenty-two different *kami*.[19]

The popularization and application of the *honji-suijaku* theory in the Buddhist Way's encounter with Japanese Shintō was as quickly accepted by the Japanese people as it was propagated by the Buddhist clergy. Of course, the Buddhist philosophy of assimilation, especially as it functioned in Japan, was much more complicated than I have outlined. However, the essential structure of *honji-suijaku* in Japan should be clear enough to prepare the way for some general conclusions about the essential character of the Buddhist Way's encounter with non-Buddhist religious Ways.

CONCLUDING OBSERVATIONS

Neither Theravada nor Mahayana versions of the Dharma categorically evaluated non-Buddhist religious Ways as realms of spiritual darkness and error, nor did a Buddhist doctrine comparable with the Christian doctrine of no-salvation-outside-the-Christian-Way explicitly develop in the Buddhist Way. Rather, Buddhist understanding and assessment of non-Buddhist religious teachings and practices were guided by the doctrine of upāya. What could, therefore, be assimilated into the Buddhist Way as a "skillful means" of preparing non-Buddhists for the practice of specifically Buddhist ethical and meditational disciplines was readily, even eagerly, appropriated. In the process, the Buddhist Way creatively transformed itself far beyond the original teachings of Gautama the Buddha. The clearest and most consistent expression of the philosophy of assimilation is the honji-suijaku theory in Japanese Buddhist teaching. But even this example of the doctrine of upāya was established on precedents going back to the earliest Indian traditions of the Buddhist Way. In light of this, three observations are pertinent.

First, Buddhist interaction with non-Buddhist religious Ways has been thoroughly dialogical, especially in comparison with traditional Christian interaction with non-Christian religious Ways. Accordingly, the Buddhist Way has historically been more open to the process of creative transformation than has the Christian Way. There has been very little religious imperialism in Buddhist teaching and practice. Its philosophy of assimilation allowed Buddhists to assume very positive attitudes toward non-Buddhist religious teachings and practices, even allowing Buddhist faith to appropriate ideas, disciplines, and deities having little or no historical connection with or philosophical support from Gautama's own strong emphasis upon self-reliance and meditation. Since Buddhist doctrine has never strictly identified "truth" with "method," "doctrine," or "meditation," any form of method, doctrine, or meditation can be a means for achieving enlightenment if skillfully applied to the individual seeker's own special abilities and endowments.

Conversely, however, traditional tolerance and assimilation of non-Buddhist religious ideas and practices was also highly selective. Only that which could be transformed into a means of preparing non-Buddhists for the practice of specifically Buddhist forms of ethical training and meditational discipline was assimilated. And, even though Mahayana teaching and practice make room for devotional practices directed toward the worship of Bodhisattvas and Buddhas, no form of the Dharma has ever assimilated notions of God as exemplified by Jewish, Christian, or Islamic theology as a skillful means of teaching non-Buddhists specifically Buddhist forms of doctrine and practice. In spite of its philosophy of assimilation, the Buddhist teaching remains as categorical in its rejection of anything compromising faith in the Three Jewels as Christian theology is in its rejection of anything compromising faith in Jesus as the Christ.

But can Christians through dialogue with Buddhists transform themselves in an authentically Christian way through appropriating Buddhist insights, experiences, and practices? Stated more poetically, can a Christian be a Buddhist while remaining Christian? Likewise, can Buddhists, through contemporary applica-

tion of their philosophy of assimilation in dialogue
with Christians, appropriate Christian insights and experiences while remaining authentically Buddhist? My
answer to both questions is "yes," and the remainder of
this study will be devoted to what I take to be the
meanings and possibilities of this conclusion.

NOTES

[1]T. W. Rhys-Davids, trans., *The Mahaparinibbana Suttana* in *Sacred Books of the East*, ed. Max Muller (Oxford: Clarendon Press, 1894) II:118.

[2]Ibid., II:119.

[3]*Milindapañha,* quoted in William Theodore de Bary, ed., *The Buddhist Tradition* (New York: Vintage Books, 1972), 30.

[4]For an excellent and readable account of King Aśoka's role in the early Buddhist missionary enterprise as well as an account of the historical context of the formation of the Theravada and Mahayana traditions, see Richard H. Robinson and William L. Johnson, *The Buddhist Tradition, An Historical Introduction,* 2d. ed. (Encino, Calif.: Dickenson Publishing Co., 1977), 64-95.

[5]See Diana Y. Paul, "Buddhist Attitudes Towards Women's Bodies," *Buddhist-Christian Studies,* 1 (1981): 63-71.

[6]V. Trenkner and Lord Chalmers, eds., *Majjhima Nikaya I: Pali Text Translation Series* (Oxford: Oxford University Press, 1888), 100.

[7]Dines Anderson and Helmer Smith, eds., *Suttanipata I: Pali Text Translation Series* (Oxford: Oxford University Press, 1913), 12.

[8]See Winston L. King, *In Search of Nibbana, An Essay on Theravada Buddhist Ethics* (La Salle, Ill.: Open Court Publishing Co., 1964), chapts. 1-3, for the best available account in English of this aspect of the Theravada Dhamma as applied to the life of the laity.

[9]*Svbbhava-Sutta,* in *Sacred Books of the East,* 2: 296-307.

[10]T. W. Rhys-Davids, trans., *Dialogues of the Buddha,* part I, *Sacred Books of the East,* 2: 310. Also quoted in Alicia Matsunaga, *The Buddhist Philosophy of Assimilation,* (Tokyo: Charles E. Tuttle Publishing Co, 1969), 12.

[11]Quoted in Matsunaga, *The Buddhist Philosophy*, 13.

[12]Ibid. I have heavily relied on Matsunaga's research in my preparation of this chapter.

[13]See Robinson and Johnson, *The Buddhist Religion*, 86-95, for a good summary of this process of Buddhist-devotional Hindu interaction.

[14]Ibid., 96-115.

[15]See, for example, the statement on merit in H. Kern, trans., *The Saddharma-pundarika-sutra* in *Sacred Books of the East*, 21: 63.

[16]Quoted in S. B. Dasgupta, trams., *An Introduction to Tantric Buddhism* (Calcutta: University of Calcutta Press, 1958), 4. For a more recent translation and interpretation of this text, see Marion L. Mantics, *Entering the Path of Enlightenment* (New York: Macmillan Co., 1976).

[17]Laurence G. Thompson, *Chinese Religion, An Introduction*, 2d. ed., (Encino, Calif.: Dickenson Publishing Co., 1975), 59-93 and Robinson and Johnson, *The Buddhist Religion*, 106.

[18]Daigan and Alicia Matsunaga, *Foundations of Japanese Buddhism*, (Tokyo: Buddhist Books International, 1974), I: 240-241.

[19]Ibid., 241.

CHAPTER FOUR
Buddhist and Christian Experience of Faith

And of what sort, monks, is the faculty of faith?
Herein an aryan disciple has faith: he has faith in
the enlightenment of the Tathagata, thus: "He is indeed the Lord, Arahant, perfect Buddha, endowed with
knowledge of right conduct, wellfarer, knower of
worlds, incomparable charioteer of men to be tamed,
teacher of devas and mankind, a Buddha, a Lord."

Saṃyutta-nikāya V, 199-200

What room then is left for human pride? It is excluded. And on what principle? The keeping of the law
would not exclude it. but faith does. For our argument
is that a man is justified by faith quite apart from
success in keeping the law.

Romans 3:27-28, *New English Bible*

INTRODUCTION

The center around which everything revolves
in the Christian Way is faith in Jesus as the Christ.
The center of everything bearing the name "Buddhist" is
faith in the Three Jewels as the absolute prerequisite
for attaining release from further rebirths in this impermanent and painful world of samsaric existence. Accordingly, comparing the ways in which Buddhists and
Christians have experienced faith should be useful in
specifying what the Buddhist and Christian Ways have in
common and how they differ. In turn, this procedure
should help clear away some of the misunderstandings
between Buddhists and Christians hindering their dialogical interaction.

Specifically, in this chapter I shall concentrate on: (1) establishing a generic conceptualization

of the meaning of the word "faith," which will reveal
its function in both Buddhist and Christian experience;
(2) summarizing the essential doctrinal formulations of
Theravada and Mahayana understandings of the nature of
faith; (3) summarizing the essentials of the Christian
conception of the nature of faith; and (4) concluding
with some comparative observations.

FAITH AND BELIEF

From a global perspective, as Wilfred
Cantwell Smith has observed, there is less diversity in
the ways in which human beings have experienced something called "faith" than in the ways in which human
beings have propositionally articulated the meaning of
faith through systems of "beliefs."[1] In Smith's words:

> Beliefs have changed, and will go on chang-
> ing; but that, it emerges, is not and has
> hardly ever been the point at issue. Various
> beliefs may have conduced to faith, but they
> have not constituted it. Also *vice versa*:
> beliefs have at times remained relatively
> constant, while faith has varied. Two per-
> sons may have believed much the same thing,
> but the faith of one has been strong and
> good, been beautiful, warm, humble, loving,
> joyous, while the faith of the other may have
> been minor, inept, awry. Beliefs may have
> conduced to faith, but they have not guaran-
> teed it.[2]

Smith's analysis of the comparative history
of faith's interaction with belief is probably as close

to the truth about how human beings have experienced
this reality as is possible, given the status of contemporary investigation into this subject. And as far
as I am aware, Smith is the only historian of religions
of any importance who has applied the methodological
principles of comparative religions to the interaction
of faith and belief in the religious traditions of the
world. Therefore, while I do not intend to summarize
the conclusions of his research, I do acknowledge that
my own reflections on the generic nature of religious
faith, as well as my discussion of the role of faith in
both the Buddhist and Christian Ways, are profoundly
informed by his work. I also, of course, assume full
responsibility for my use of his work, including my application of it in the following discussion.

Western scholarship, and indeed popular Western public opinion, most often defines faith in terms
of its "object." Thus "faith" is "faith in God" or in
"the Three Jewels." The problem with this approach has
always been its failure to indicate *what* faith *is*,
since it only points to *where* faith is *directed*. Not
that the object of faith is unimportant, for the object
to which faith is given greatly qualifies and conditions how a person experiences this object and how
faith expresses itself in a person's life. But since
the historical evidence seems to indicate that something called "faith" is universally present in all religious Ways, conceptualizing about faith in terms of
its "object" merely obscures the generic nature of
faith as universally experienced by all faithful human
beings. For example, when Christians define faith as

"faith in Christ," the religious actions and beliefs of persons whose "object of faith" is not Christ may be too quickly labeled as "unfaith." Not that Christians are wrong in defining their faith in this way. But if we are looking for a means of conceiving the generic nature of faith in order to understand what makes Christian faith or Buddhist faith "faith," then focusing too quickly on specific objects of faith will not prove particularly useful. Nor will it be conducive to interreligious dialogue. Concluding that faith is only authentic when its object is Christ or the Three Jewels constitutes a theological abstraction divorced from the facts of religious history that historians of religions have been bringing to light for the past hundred years.

By the same token, defining faith as "belief" is not particularly useful either, for they are not identical. Faith may indeed be engendered and sustained by doctrines and belief systems. This is especially true in Christian tradition: no other religious Way places such great emphasis upon propositional understanding. But faith is best understood as a quality of a person, not as a quality of belief, or for that matter of rituals, disciplines, or myths. These might express faith, but in themselves they are not faith.

However, particularly in modern Western intellectual tradition, governed as it is by the dualism of Cartesian epistemology underlying contemporary secularism as well as the popular religious imagination, the word "belief" as descriptive of "faith" greatly obscures the meaning of faith even within the teachings and practices of particular religious Ways. My point, one I have learned from Wilfred Cantwell Smith, is that today in modern secularized English-speaking countries "belief" now denotes the assertion of propositional conclusions, the truth of which remain uncertain. "Belief" normally denotes "improbable." And once more, most contemporary English dictionaries define "belief" as an "opinion" or "conviction," which the Random House Dictionary illustrates with the example, "the belief that the world is flat."[3] "Belief" in contemporary scholarly and popular usage means "the propositional assertion of ideas which are at best opinion, but at worst falsehood."

Accordingly, "belief" now connotes something like "the opposite of knowledge." "To believe" anything involves uncertainty, lack of knowledge, while in normal contemporary usage "to know" means "not to believe." Anything contradicting what we "know" to be true is a "belief" or an "opinion." The meaning of the statement "I *know* that my redeemer lives," for example, is not identical with the statement "I *believe* that my redeemer lives." Contemporary modern persons do not "know" God exists, while only a few "believe" in the existence of God. And even believers in God usually understand their belief as unprovable "opinion." In modern secularized, pluralistic cultures, believing in the existence of a transcendent reality named God bears the same relation to knowledge that believing in a flat world bears to knowledge—no relation at all.

This has not always been the case. Etymologically, the original meaning of the word "belief" meant "to hold dear," "to love," "to be loved," "to cherish."

The object of these verbal forms was for many centuries primarily a person to whom esteem, affection, trust, and self-giving was directed on that person's behalf. This was the original meaning whether the object of the verb was a human being or God. The noun form, "belief," denoted "endearment," "holding as beloved," "trust," "commitment," or "confidence in" another person immediately known and experienced in one's life. Originally, therefore, "belief" did not denote "opinion" but "knowledge."

The history of the change in meaning of the word "belief" from "trust in a human being because of knowledge of that person" to "an opinion based upon lack of knowledge" is not the topic of this chapter,[4] but the implications for understanding the relationship between faith and belief in the modern world implied by this history are of utmost importance.

First of all, the human sense of reality is primarily linguistic. That is, language is the primary mode through which we are rooted in history and culture and through which we interpret and structure our experience into a human vision of "the way thing really are." Whatever language we speak not only creates for us a sense of meaning and reality, it also enables us to discover new realities. The reverse is equally true, however, because the uncritical use of language also falsifies our sense of reality.[5] Relative to modern English usage of the term "belief," the realities of religious faith have been profoundly falsified for most modern religious and nonreligious persons. In point of historical fact, no religious Way has ever

simply equated "faith" with "the assertion of propositions" in which to believe. Not even mainline Christian tradition, which emphasizes doctrinal and propositional understanding of the implications of faith more
than any other religious Way, has identified "faith"
with "belief" in propositional assertions.

What then is "faith," generically understood?
Perhaps Paul Tillich's definition of faith as "ultimate
concern" is as close to a generic understanding as any
in contemporary theology:

> Faith is the state of being ultimately con-
> cerned. *The content matters infinitely for*
> *the life of the believer, but it does not*
> *matter for the formal definition of faith.* .
> . .it happens in the center of the personal
> life and includes all its elements. Faith is
> the most centered act of the human mind.[6]

As "the most centered act of the human mind,"
faith functions as a kind of paradigm in ways not un-
similar to the ways paradigms function for research
scientists.   In the natural sciences, for example, a
paradigm is a set of primary, perceptual assumptions
underlying all of a scientist's thinking, feeling, and
doing that by their very nature are most often unexamined, and perhaps even unknown.   They are also
"unprovable" in the sense in which scientific "beliefs"
or theories are "provable." But scientific paradigms
open the way to the "discovery" of new knowledge and
the application of old knowledge to developing new
technologies.[7] Now because religious faith possesses a
sort of paradigmatic quality, it also opens up reli-

gious persons to the "discovery" of realities not simply "given" in mundane experience. Religious faith engages a person's total being emotionally, intellectually, morally--with whatever the "object" of faith
might be, just as a paradigm totally engages a working
scientist with his "object," be this a subatomic parti-
cle, a new chemical process, or a possible connection
between a virus and the cause of a particular form of
cancer. Faith requires total personal involvement and
commitment to its "object," just as a scientist's trust
in the paradigms requires total involvement and commitment to the objective of gaining knowledge of the natural world.

In stressing the personal character of the
paradigmatic function of religious faith, care must be
taken that "personal" not be confused with
"individual." The opposite of "individual" is "social,"
while the opposite of "personal" is "impersonal." All
societies, in varying degrees, intermix personal and
impersonal methods of social interaction and control.
But as every religious Way teaches, individuals only
become persons within a community of faith. Being personal, which is synonymous with being human, demands
social involvement in the quest for community. Faith
does not exist apart from some form of social context.
It touches both the corporate and the private dimensions of our lives because "it has much to do with the
gregarious and lonely aspects of human life."[8]

The paradigmatic nature of faith is constituted by trust of the human sense of transcendence,
meaning the experience of hope that the "givens" of

phenomenal existence are not all there are, as many be-
havioral scientists would have us "believe." Accordingly, faith is universally experienced as a specific
mode of orientation of an individual's personality to
self, neighbors, the universe, or the Sacred, however
it is named, best characterized in English by the word
"trust." Faith is trust and commitment to whatever we
apprehend as ultimate, and which thereby evokes in us
the capacity for living at a more than mundane level of
existence. This is why the opposite of faith is not
"unbelief," but nihilism, meaning the inability to experience either the world around us or our lives as
significant. Without faith, in other words, we are incapable of responding to the universe or our immediate
neighbors in the hope of being responded to in return.

But faith as trust is always symbolically expressed through myth, ritual, moral action, social organization, corporate institutions, and intellectual
abstractions such as creeds, doctrines, or theological
and philosophical systems of belief. Of course, different Ways place great emphasis upon myth and ritual,
while others like the Buddhist and Christian Ways place
a greater emphasis upon intellectual abstractions. But
religious persons do not "believe" symbols in the same
way persons formulating opinions believe propositions
to be true. We either respond to symbols or we do not;
we more or less adequately apprehend the realities and
meanings to which symbols point; we are more or less
grasped by what a symbol has meant, now means, or may
mean if it opens us up to trusting the transcendent reality to which it points. Consequently, symbols, in-

cluding beliefs, may be expressions of faith, but they should not be equated with faith. Human beings may live by the most profound faith, and yet their beliefs about the reality to which their faith points be in error. Likewise, a human being's beliefs may be propositionally "true" and "orthodox" while yet expressing no faith at all in the transcendent reality to which their beliefs point. We can be doctrinally in error and yet possess deeply profound and moving faith, and *vice versa*.

But even though the comparative study of religion has clearly demonstrated that generically faith is central in all religious Ways, this does not imply faith is everywhere the same. Nor is religious faith always necessarily admirable. Trust can be misplaced, ignorant, and delusive. Even when faith is placed in an object that is "really ultimate," to paraphrase Tillich, this does not guarantee faith will engender human creativity or establish human community. Faith often expresses quite pathological behavior and has led to the wholesale slaughter of millions of human beings. Faith has everywhere been defined, conditioned, and realized within the constraints imposed by the social, political, historical, and biological limitations and finitude of persons of faith.

Finally, and in spite of the finitude of human existence, generically faith is a way of saying "Yes!" to the truth we apprehend and to which we are thereby wholly committed as an ultimate concern. It is, therefore, neither historically accurate nor even theologically appropriate to minimize the "truth" to which Buddhists or Christians or Muslims or Jews or Native Americans or others have apprehended and trusted, and in terms of which they have created and sustained cultured, human existence. Faith is not belief in a set of doctrines or opinions stated in propositional form. It is not even belief in trust. Faith is "assent" to truth in the dynamic sense of linking up to it, betting our lives on it, delighting in it, yoking ourselves to it, while remaining in awe of it.

But how is the generic nature of faith specifically structured by Buddhist and Christian existence? What are the distinctive characteristics of Buddhist and Christian faith?

THERAVADA BUDDHIST FAITH

A common Western, and especially Christian, misconception of the Buddhist Way maintains that faith plays a minor role in its teachings and practices. This seems particularly true of Theravada teaching and practice. Thus the fundamental differences between the Buddhist and Christian Ways appear, at least at first glance, to originate at this point. After all, Gautama and the earliest tradition thereafter rejected the quest for a transcendent God, along with the notion of an individual soul entity's (ātman) remaining self-identical through time. And even though all Buddhists venerate the historical Buddha, as well as numerous other Buddhas and Bodhisattvas as upāya forms, Buddhist teachings and practice have always aimed at preparing the seeker for going beyond the need for "faith" in any sort of permanent entity. Faith, according to the Bud-

dhist world view, too often resembles clinging to entities having no existence, other than in the believer's
mind, in an impermanent universe. Understood from this
perspective, faith becomes a source of suffering
(duḥkha), and thus Buddhists normally regard Christian
teachings about faith as expressions of ignorant clinging.

Buddhist tradition, with the possible exception of the Japanese Pure Land teachings of Shinran
Shonin, to which I shall again refer in another section
of this chapter, denies the necessity and even the possibility of clinging to any sort of permanent entity
thought to exist objectively to the individual seeking
enlightenment. Eventually, we must rely on our own
self-discipline and our own gradually accumulated wisdom, for ultimately we must "save" ourselves without
relying on anything or anyone else. Accordingly, what
Christians label "faith" seems to Buddhists to be nothing more than one more attachment keeping us karmicly
bound to the processes of rebirth in samsaric suffering.

Faith, then, in the earliest teachings of the
Buddhist Way appears as one of a number of "mental
states" blocking the achievement of enlightenment:

By getting rid of three mental states: passion, aversion, and confusion, one is able to
get rid of birth, aging, and dying. By getting rid of three mental states: false view
as to "own body," doubt, and dependence on
rite and custom, one is able to get rid of
passion, aversion, and confusion. By getting

rid of three mental states: unwise reflection, treading the wrong way, and mental
laziness, one is able to to get rid of false
views as to "own body," doubt, and dependence
on rite and custom.[9]

Because there is no "object" of faith transcending the
self, nor indeed is there any "self" to transcend,
there exists nothing in which to have faith. Furthermore, this is why most Western interpretations of the
role of faith in Buddhist teachings and practices agree
with John Cobb's judgment that Gautama rejected the
"quest for a transcendent self, and he purified the reflective consciousness from the last traces of mystical
influences."[10] If Cobb's judgment is valid, then what
Christians have meant by faith cannot be an important
experiential element of the Buddhist Way because all
sense of a transcendent reality infusing meaning into
mundane existence seems to be utterly rejected by the
Buddhist world view.

However, not only is this interpretation of
the Buddhist Way stereotypical, it is also inaccurate
because it fails to take into account how Buddhists understand their own experiences as Buddhists. There is
little doubt the earliest Buddhist movement was
"atheistic," although not in the sense of denying the
existence of divine realities or in the sense of dis-
pensing with ideas of divinity altogether. Theravada
and Mahayana teachings are atheistic in the sense of
denying soteriological functions to any deity, especially as this involves the attainment of enlightenment. But even this judgment requires qualification

because of certain forms of Mahayana Pure Land teachings and practices. Even so, the Buddha himself displaced the older Hindu deities of his time in his teachings while not replacing them with new deities. Nor did he teach concepts of deity. For him, the goal of human life was the attainment of enlightenment, not union with nor dependency upon any transcendent divine entity. All Theravada and most Mahayana forms of the Buddhist Way strictly adhere to this aspect of the Dharma.

Another reason a sense of transcendence, and hence faith, appears lacking in the lives of Buddhists relates to the utterly negative language of the doctrinal descriptions of the goal of Buddhist self-discipline, *nibbāna*. Most of this language was deduced from the root meaning of the term, "extinction" or "going out." As with all true religious ultimates, *nibbāna* symbolizes an essentially indescribable state, and no religious Way so consistently maintains the ineffability of its ultimate experiential goal as the Buddhist Way. And yet, Buddhists have also said much about *nibbāna*, for the question implied in its quest is always "the extinction of what?"

Most often, Buddhist doctrine describes *nibbāna* as the extinction of greed, hatred, and delusion. Other descriptions stress *nibbāna* as a state of freedom from desire resulting from the final destruction of the cause of "suffering" (*duḥkha*), "thirst" (*trsita*), or "desire" (*taṇha*). Still again, *nibbāna* is described as the absence of the ignorant delusion that we are separate individual substantial selves. In other words, "*nibbāna* is the consummation of the *anatta* doctrine."[11]

All doctrinal descriptions of *nibbāna* also portray it as a progressive realization of the emptiness of independent selfhood obtained by means of meditational discipline. The meditator, usually a monk, gradually but directly realizes that the changing states constituting his body and mental functioning, along with the momentary rise and disappearance of his emotional states, reveal no permanent soul or self-entity (*attā*, Sanskrit, *ātman*) remaining self-identical through time. The final state of this realization is the full "going out" or "extinction" of *nibbāna*".

No wonder, then, non-Buddhist Western interpreters of the Buddhist Way, particularly Christian interpreters, have not perceived "transcendence" in Buddhist teaching, and, therefore, nothing resembling Western or Christian conceptualizations of faith. A perceived negativism, erroneously labeled "nihilism," obscures other more positive considerations that Buddhists themselves emphasize--considerations that point to the transcendence of *nibbāna* itself. For example, one point often unnoticed in the West is that while *nibbāna* may be indescribable, it *is* knowable. It is also very pleasant, moving, and indeed blissful and joyous to the individual attaining it. The experience not only transforms an unenlightened seeker into a Buddha, an "enlightened one," *nibbāna* remains knowable after the death of the *arhat* as *khandha-parinabbāna*, or "the full extinction of the elements of existence," although this state is not often discussed in Buddhist literature.[12] This form of enlightenment is consequent to another form described as *kilesa-parinibbāna*, or "the full extinction of defilements." This latter form of enlightenment involves the extinction of greed, hatred, desire, and all other delusions binding the seeker to the realm of suffering existence, while the former *nibbāna* represents the final culmination and perfection of the release from suffering occurring after the death of the *arhat*.

Consequently, what is "extinguished" in *nibbana* is anything hindering the attainment of whatever is supremely valuable, good, and real. For the person attaining it, *nibbāna* thus turns out to be an absolutely positive experience of a transcendent reality, the seeking for which gives purpose and meaning to the mundane world of ordinary existence. It is, in the fullest English meaning of the word, "salvation." As the Buddha himself is reported to have described *nibbāna*:

> Verily, there is an Unborn, Unoriginated. Uncreated, Unformed. If there were not this Unborn, Unoriginated, Uncreated, Unformed, escape from the world of the born, the originated, the created, the formed, would not be possible.[13]

But while Buddhists experience *nibbāna* as a fully dynamic, positive, transforming, and transcendent reality, enlightenment does not correlate with what Christians and other Westerners usually understand by the word "God." *Nibbāna* does not denote a cosmically creative reality sustaining the natural order of the universe. This is the function of Dhamma in Buddhist philosophy. However, *nibbāna* does represent an immutable reality for Theravada Buddhists, which in turn means it is also a transcendent reality by any ordinary definition of transcendence. Accordingly, *nibbāna* plays a religious role in the Buddhist Way significantly comparable to that played by God in Christian faith.

But on this side of the "further shore" of *nibbāna*, however, the universe of on-going flux, processive change, and impermanence involves one permanent pattern. Within the ebb and flow of existence, the Buddha taught, only one force is absolutely effective for human salvation—the Dhamma (Sanskrit, Dharma). "Dhamma," generally translated as "law" or "teaching" in English, actually means the ideal "standard" by which the "correctness" or the "reality" or the "truthfulness" of an entity, event, or principle is measured. Thus it can mean something like "natural law" or "the way things really are" in the universe as opposed to what unenlightened human beings normally wish things to be. Dhamma can also refer to the rules and norms of ethical and social behavior, as well as the ideal principles of a craft or a discipline, such as, for example, the principles of medical science that a physician applies to individual persons in the treatment of illnesses. Finally, Dhamma refers to the specific teachings of a philosopher, guru, or religious movement. All of these meanings and more are involved in Buddhist understandings of the Dhamma.

From a specifically Buddhist point of view, however, Siddhartha Gautama did not "invent" his version of the Dhamma. The Dhamma is not a human contrivance, nor can it be simply reduced to Gautama's ideas, for he first discovered it as something ontologically prior. Only afterward did he begin teaching what his discovery implied for the attainment of release from the round of suffering and death. In other words, the teachings of the Buddha began in the sixth century B. C. E., but the Dhamma did not originate then. It has always existed. Therefore, the Dhamma, in the sense of the Buddha's teachings about it during the last forty years of his life, does not owe its authority to Gautama's wisdom and virtue. On the contrary, Gautama became the "Enlightened One," thereby attaining wisdom and virtue, only through his discovery of the eternally operating and preexistent Dhamma. It was this "discovery" that he taught his followers in doctrinal form as the Four Noble Truths, the Noble Eightfold Path, and the dependent coorigination of all things and events constituting the universe at any single moment of space-time.

That human beings can transform themselves from ordinary, suffering human beings into fully enlightened *arhats* by meditatively discovering this eternal Dhamma, just as Gautama did, sounds "Pelagian" to Christian ears because of the heavy emphasis the Theravada Buddhist Way places on self-salvation. But in at least one sense, this is an inaccurate caricature of both the Buddha's and the Theravada teaching. For if the "way things really are" in the universe is constituted only by the flux of samsara, only by the coming and going of phenomena apart from an eternal Dhamma around which existence "this side of nibbana" revolves, then no person can "save himself." The Buddha taught, and the Buddhist Way consistently follows his teaching, that any decision about how to live is always the individual's, but the fact that living according to the Dhamma brings salvation in the form of enlightenment remains ontologically prior to and independent of human decision, effort, and achievement.

Confidence in, trusting, "taking refuge in" this Dhamma constitutes "faith" in Theravada tradition, the technical term for which is sraddha. "Being a Buddhist" through "taking refuge in the Three Jewels" is an "act of faith" in the eternal Dhamma in all traditions of the Buddhist Way. And although there are differences among Buddhist schools regarding doctrinal conceptualizations of the meanings of śraddhā, authentic Buddhist faith declares that the theology, doctrine, philosophical world view or secular ideology a person espouses carries no ultimate importance. Nor do ritual action, mystical training, ethical self-discipline, or meditative practice ultimately matter. These practices are forms of upaya, but if and only if skillfully applied to the task of apprehending the Dhamma in the search for enlightenment. The only "ultimate concern" that is really ultimate, and which demarcates the Buddhist Way from all other religious Ways, is the eternal Dhamma, the discovery of which is enlightenment.[14]

MAHAYANA BUDDHIST FAITH

As the "faith paradigm" from which a Buddhist initiates the quest for enlightenment, through which the universe is meaningfully apprehended, by which the meaning of enlightenment is intellectually conceived, and according to which teachings about enlightenment become experientially verified through the discipline of meditation, śraddhā also forms the heart of the Mahayana understanding of Buddhist faith. However, the elements that Mahayana tradition brings to its own unique understanding of śraddhā, while not identical with the essential operational meanings of Theravada conceptions of faith, profoundly transform the ways in which faith energizes and expresses itself through specifically Mahayana doctrines and practices.

The Mahayana transformation of śraddhā centers on the concept of the Bodhisattva, a concept stretching the older meanings of Theravada conceptions of sraddha to their furthest logical limit. In this regard, two important doctrinal points require brief discussion.

First, the goal of Mahayana teaching and practice is identical with the goal of Theravada teaching and practice, namely, the attainment of enlightenment. Of course, Theravada doctrine absolutely rejects Mahayana practices of Bodhisattva veneration as forms of clinging. Not only do Bodhisattva and Buddha veneration possess no substantial doctrinal standing in Theravada tradition, devotionalism plays no soteriological role at all in its version of the Dhamma. These are not even recognized as forms of upāya. Still, the faith guiding the Mahayana Buddhist's devotionalism is structurally and experientially no different from the *sraddhā* around which the Theravada Dhamma revolves. Both are instances of Buddhist faith.

Second, even though Bodhisattvas and Buddhas, but usually excluding Siddhartha Gautama, are "saviors," these beings are not normally conceived as giving *nirvāna* to a devotee as a gift of grace. Mahayana teachings are just as rigorous in insisting the seeker must achieve enlightenment through personal disciplined effort and skillful practice of meditation. All, which turns out to be a very great deal, Bodhisattvas do for their devotees is to make it "easier" to practice the required meditational disciplines *after* attaining rebirth into a Buddha Land. Consequently, the majority of Mahayana Buddhists do not meditate "this side of *nirvāna.*" Instead, most utilize various *upāya* forms of devotional practices directed towards particular Bodhisattvas and Buddhas, coupled with ethical self-discipline, in the hope of achieving rebirth into a Buddha Land. Afterwards, the devotee must practice meditation to finally attain enlightenment. Thus even though the vast majority of Mahayana Buddhists follow some form of Bodhisattva or Buddha veneration, devotionalism remains an *upāya* option. The individual possessing sufficient mental, physical, and emotional endowments may also achieve enlightenment "this side of *nirvana*" apart from seeking rebirth into an Buddha Land through devotional practices. For such a person, devotionalism plays little, if indeed any, significant role. Some Mahayana schools, for example the Zen

(Chinese, Ch'an) or "Meditation School," emphasize meditational self-discipline in this life here-and-now as
the best means for achieving enlightenment, while down-
playing the importance of devotionalism.

There exists, however, one Mahayana form of
sraddha that does not completely fit the pattern I have
described: it carries the Buddhist faith paradigm to
its most extreme "non-Pelagian" form. I am referring
to the Pure Land tradition, especially as expressed
through the teachings of the Japanese Pure Land master,
Shinran Shōnin (1173-1212) and his fifteenth century
disciple, Rennyo Shōnin (1414-1499). Originating in
India as an optional upaya practice, Pure Land faith
quickly evolved into the most systematic form of Mahayana Buddha-bhakti.[15] The object of Pure Land faith
is not the historical Gautama the Buddha, but Amitabha
Buddha, the "Buddha of Infinite Light," also sometimes
called Amitayus Buddha, the "Buddha of Infinite Life."
Soon after the transmission of Mahayana tradition into
China, toward the end of the last century B. C. E.,
Pure Land teachings and devotional practices became so
popular that no school of the Chinese Buddhist Way
could ignore it. Therefore, it was incorporated into
the teachings of all schools of the Chinese Mahayana
Dharma.

Pure Land teachings also arrived in Japan in
the fifth century as an aspect of the teachings and
practices of each of the schools that were introduced,
at various times, from China via Korea. Thus the Pure
Land School became an independent Buddhist movement for
the first time in the twelfth century, mostly because

of the life and work of Hōnen Shōnin (1133-1212), the founder of Jōdo Shū or "Pure Land School." Hōnen's most important disciple, as well as his favorite one, Shinran Shōnin, created a second independent Pure Land movement known as Jodo Shinshu or "True Pure Land School" after Hōnen's death. The institutionalization of Jōdo Shinshū was in turn accomplished by Rennyo Shonin in the fifteenth century, although Jodo Shinshu received no legal recognition as an independent Buddhist School until the seventeenth century. Today, Jodo Shinshu is the largest school of the Buddhist Way and is divided into several branches.

The Pure Land schools, as do most Mahayana sectarian movements, base their special interpretation of the Dharma upon a collection of *sūtras* (Pāli: *sutta,* or literature purporting to be a "discourse" of the Buddha), regarded as the most fully developed expression of the Buddha's teachings, all other sutras being *upāya*-discourses expressing doctrines in less fully developed forms leading up to the teachings of the Pure Land sutras.[16] This does not mean the Mahayana "schools" were originally institutionally separate. Usually several schools existed side by side in the same temple or monastery. This was, in fact, the general situation in Japan and China until the twelfth century, when Buddhist movements such as Jōdo Shū, Jōdo Shinshū, the Rinzai and Sōtō traditions of Zen, and Nichiren Shū, named after its founder Nichiren, began assuming doctrinal and institutional independence from one another and the older schools of Japanese Buddhist tradition.

The textual foundations of Pure Land teachings lie in three Mahayana sutras.[17] The first and most important sutra, the *Larger Sukhāvatī-vyūha* (The Larger Discourse on the Happy Land), translated in Japanese as *Muryōjukyō*, contains the mythological account of the origins of the object of Pure Land devotionalism, Amitābha Buddha, more widely known by his Japanese name, Amida Buddha. Pure Land teaching is primarily a philosophical interpretation of this text.

Gautama the Buddha, according to the oldest Buddhist traditions, has always been an object of devotion. But the Pure Land movement reduced his role to that of announcer of the merits of Amida Buddha, who now resides in a Buddha land known as "the Happy Land" or "Land of Bliss" (Sanskrit, *sukhāvatī*; Japanese, *gokuraku*). As the most blissful and perfect of all Buddha Lands, located "far to the West," the Pure Land was created as the karmic result of the completion of Amida's forty-eight Bodhisattva vows, which he made many *kalpas* ("eons") ago during his incarnation as the monk and seeker of enlightenment, Dharmakara. Through contemplation, devotion, and trust in Amida and his forty-eight Bodhisattva vows to rescue all sentient beings from the sufferings of life in samsaric existence, a seeker may gain rebirth into this wonderful place at the moment of death.

The Japanese Pure Land movements initiated by Honen and Shinran particularly emphasized the eighteenth of Amida's forty-eight vows, called the "Original Vow" in Pure Land doctrinal terminology:

If, when I become a Buddha, all sentient beings in the ten quarters [of the universe]
should not desire in sincerity and trustful-
ness to be reborn into my Land by thinking on
me only ten times, excluding only those who
have committed the five irreversible actions
and have slandered the Dharma, may I not receive perfect enlightenment. [18]

The key term of the Eighteenth Vow is
"thinking on me," which is my translation of the
Japanese *nen*, literally "reflection." In its original
meaning, *nen* denoted several styles of meditation involving fixing concentrated attention upon either an
actual image of a Buddha or a Bodhisattva or a mental
image of these beings. It also carried the sense of
"invocation," as when a meditator repeats the name of a
Buddha or Bodhisattva over and over in a *mantra* formula
as an aid in developing the power of concentrated attention. In Japanese, each of these meditative techniques is referred to as *nembutsu* or "Buddha reflection." The point is, Hōnen and Shinran read the Eighteenth Vow as a promise of rebirth to any individual
"thinking on" Amida Buddha in perfect trust (*nembutsu*)
in his vow to lead all sentient beings to rebirth into
his Pure Land, excepting those committing the "five irreversible actions" (Japanese, *gogya*): patricide, mat-
ricide, killing an *arhat*, killing a Buddha or a Bodhisattva, and causing disunity within the Samgha.
Those slandering the Dharma by spreading false teachings and practices also exclude themselves from rebirth
into Amida's Pure Land.

The second Pure Land text, the *Smaller Sukha-vatī-vyūha* (Japanese, *Amidakyō*), is a condensed version of the *Larger Sutra* known for its detailed description of the basic features and attributes of the Pure Land. But unlike the *Larger Sutra*, this text teaches that even those committing the "irreversible actions" and "slandering the Dharma" may gain entry into the Pure Land if they possess but one moment of authentic and undoubting trust in Amida's vows to save all sentient beings.

The final Pure Land text, the *Amitāyur-dhyāna-sūtra* [Discourse on the Buddha of Infinite Light], in Japanese, *Kammuryōjukyō*, was probably written as a manual to encourage steadfastness in Pure Land devotional practices. Its main features are its vivid description of the beauties of the Pure Land coupled with its rather detailed analysis of sixteen forms of meditational practice meant to aid seekers obtain rebirth there.

The general patterns of Pure Land teaching and practice were originally no different from any other form of Mahayana Bodhisattva or Buddha veneration. Through placing faith in Amida Buddha, contemplating him and his Bodhisattva vows, and disciplining the moral life according to the ethical precepts of the Buddhist Way, the devotee can hope for rebirth into the Pure Land. After this event, Amida confronts the reborn seeker with the correct version of the Dharma, after which the seeker meditatively comprehends its meaning and thereby achieves enlightenment. Hōnen's interpretation of Pure Land tradition, however, initiated a process of change in Pure Land faith and practice for which there exists no precedent in any previous form of Mahayana teaching. Understanding how different Honen's Pure Land teachings were from any form of Buddhist teachings and practice prior to his time will require a brief summary of the historical conditions of twelfth century Japan--the context of his and Shinran's respective Pure Land movements.[19] The twelfth century was the beginning of an age of tumultuous social, moral, political, economic, and religious chaos lasting for the next four centuries. The main features of this period were its almost continuous civil warfare and political intrigue. The first six decades of the twelfth century were especially violent because the existing social and political institutions according to which Japanese persons structured their lives into meaningful relationships simply collapsed with nothing taking their place. Even Buddhist institutions were in a state of decay, and in fact were themselves largely responsible for the social unrest and violence of the times. And if the records of this period are to be believed, human life was held rather cheaply. But out of this general disorder the Buddhist Way also began reviving itself, the result of work among the masses by dedicated and caring monks like Hōnen and Shinran, who had left their monastic seclusion to take up the life of itinerant teachers. Because of the work of these monks, the Buddhist Way began evolving forms of faith and practice suited to the religious needs of common ordinary human beings struggling to survive and find meaning during these difficult times. The result was the creation of uniquely Japanese sectarian forms of the Buddhist Way that, while rooted in older Chinese forms, for the first time ceased being mere imitations of these forms.[20]

Much of the revival of the Japanese Buddhist Way occurring during these years was based on a fairly ancient understanding of history that is found in several variations in some of the Mahayana sutras and *sastras* ("commentary"), but which had little doctrinal importance in non-Japanese Buddhist traditions. To twelfth century Japanese, however, this theory of history, which assumed a cyclic understanding of historical processes in which each world-cycle was divided into three ages,[21] seemed empirically verified by their own experiences.

The first age is called, in Japanese, the age of *shōbō* (Sanskrit, *saddharma*) or "true Dharma." The stated length of time for this age differs from Buddhist text to Buddhist text, but Honen and Shinran believed it to have lasted for five hundred years after the death of Gautama.[22] Since this is an age in which a Buddha is incarnated into historical existence, it is a golden age. Consequently, persons born during the age of *shōbō* are naturally virtuous and spontaneously wise, endowed with all of the capacities required for the easy achievement of enlightenment. There exists neither natural nor moral evil, for truth and goodness are the sole realities of this period. But as a world cycle "runs down," history enters a period of decline called *zōbō* (Sanskrit, *pratirūpadharma*) or "counterfeit

Dharma," lasting for the next one thousand years. Beings born during this age are not as fortunate as those
born during the age of shōbō, for with the disappearance of the spiritual influence of an incarnated Buddha, evil in the form of egoism begins dominating the
lives of persons. As a result, very few individuals
attain enlightenment through personal discovery of the
eternal Dharma because humanity's natural endowments,
along with existing forms of the Buddhist Way, have begun to decay. Finally, a cycle of history reaches its
lowest point, the terrible age of mappō (Sanskrit,
paschimadharma), the "end of the Dharma" or "the latter
days of the Dharma," an age of total moral and natural
evil, infecting not only human nature but even the Buddhist Way itself. No human being born during this age
can attain enlightenment through the practice of any
form of the Buddhist Way, since nothing is effective in
rescuing human beings from the bondage of continuing
death, suffering, and decay--the karmic results of human egoism. The length of time the age of mappō is
said to last is ten thousand years, after which another
age of shōbō begins with the appearance of a new Buddha
in history. The next expected historical Buddha is
Maitreya (Japanese, Miroku), whose appearance will end
the present age of mappō.

The experiences of persons living in Japan
during the twelfth century seemed to most Japanese to
be empirical evidence for the arrival of the age of
mappō. In fact, following the traditional way of dating the Buddha's life and death assumed by most
Japanese, it was even calculated the present age of

mappō had begun in the year 1010, almost precisely the time when the tragic events initiating the wars of the twelfth century occurred.

Accordingly, Hōnen advised his followers to place faith (*śraddhā*, Japanese, *shin*) in Amida Buddha's other-powered efforts to bring all sentient beings into the Pure Land. He characterized faith as possessing three interdependent mental attitudes or "minds" (*sanshin*, literally "three minds"): (1) *shijōshin* or "sincere mind," meaning steadfast devotion to Amida Buddha to the degree no event in a devotee's life, either good or evil, hinders his devotion; (2) *jinshin* or the "mind of devotion" to Amida Buddha and no other Buddha, Bodhisattva, or deity; and (3) *ekōhotsuganshin,* the "mind" or "desire of transforming the merit" accumulated through faith in Amida Buddha into rebirth into the Pure Land.

According to Hōnen, a person "achieves" the three minds of faith through *nembutsu*, which he taught not as a form of meditation but as an invocation of Amida's saving power. *Nembutsu,* for Honen was simply the practice of repeating over and over the phrase or *mantra,* "*namu amida butsu*," meaning "I take refuge in the Buddha of Infinite Light." Only one chanting of this invocation with undoubting faith, he said, is all that is required for the achievement of rebirth into the Pure Land. But because undoubting faith is not only difficult to achieve, but also an absolute requirement for rebirth, Hōnen advised his followers to practice *nembutsu* many times a day throughout their lives, he himself claiming to have chanted it seventy thousand times daily.

Clearly, Hōnen's *nembutsu* teaching represents a very simplified form of traditional Buddhist Practice indeed. But quite apart from his emphasis on simplifying practice and doctrine, Honen's teachings added nothing essentially new to the tradition of Mahayana Bodhisattva veneration. An inconsistency in his teachings, however, proved troublesome for some of his younger disciples, especially Shinran. For if, as he taught, no one can be saved by any sort of self effort, then how can anyone develop the three minds of undoubting faith in Amida Buddha's vow to save all sentient beings? But Honen also taught that no one can achieve rebirth into the Pure Land by any sort of self-effort during this degenerate age. The problem, of course, centers on his definition of faith as a self-powered act of the human will to believe the promises of Amida Buddha's Bodhisattva vows. But how can anyone will to believe anything with an undoubting mind in the age of *mappo*?

Of all Hōnen's disciples, Shinran most clearly perceived this difficulty in his teacher's understanding of faith. Shinran believed the problem was not merely an obvious lapse of logical consistency in Honen's doctrinal formulation of Pure Land teachings and practice; he believed something much more important was at stake. Because of his own difficulties and frustrating lack of success in achieving enlightenment through his participation in most of the monastic disciplines of the Buddhist Way then available to him,

Shinran took Hōnen literally at his word: no religious practice of any sort depending upon human self-effort (Japanese, *jiriki*, literally "self-power") is effective in helping human beings achieve salvation during the age of *mappo*. The only thing anyone can do during this terrible degenerate age is totally trust Amida's "grace" (Japanese, *tariki,* literally "other-power") to effect human rebirth into the Pure Land.

Faith, meaning trust in Amida Buddha's vows to save all human beings and non-trust in any form of human self-effort to achieve enlightenment, is the key for Shinran. In his view, faith is not an act of the will to believe, but a gift Amida Buddha gives to an individual through the operation of his "other-power." Restating it in Shinran's own terminology, the "three minds" of faith in Hōnen's teachings are mental atti- tudes or modes of trust that Amida, through his "other- power," creates in an individual's mind. No one "decides" to "have faith," but rather one "discovers" one is already possessed by it. Thus in a way similar to Martin Luther, Shinran taught a doctrine of salva- tion by faith through absolute "other power" (*tariki*) alone as humanity's only option for salvation in the age of *mappō*.

The word "faith" in this slogan-like summary denotes, as already stated, the three mental attitudes of Honen's definition of faith, except Shinran believed these same interdependent qualities are created in an individual's mind by Amida's "other-power" through the "transfer of merit" from Amida to the individual. Con- ceived from this perspective, all religious actions

cease being "self-powered" (*jiriki*) methods of achieving any religious benefit such as rebirth into the Pure
Land or enlightenment. On the contrary, religious action or "practice" is transformed into an expression of
gratitude for the gift of faith. No human being, according to this understanding of faith, can do anything
to attain enlightenment either in this life or after
rebirth into the Pure Land. Not even *nembutsu* as
taught by his teacher, Hōnen, has any bearing on the
salvation of humanity in Shinran's understanding of
Buddhist faith. For even trusting Amida's other-power
and rejecting all forms of human self-effort in the
practice of religious disciplines is given to the devotee by Amida. Ultimately, Shinran even understood this
act of "other-power" to be, appropriating Christian
language, "irresistible." The devotee cannot even say
"no" to it. So necessary is Amida's gift of faith for
the achievement of *nirvāṇa*, that even after rebirth
into the Pure Land, no one is unable to attain enlightenment through any form of self-powered practice. Thus
beings are reborn into the Pure Land as enlightened
Buddhas.

　　Many scholars, including me, have noted Shinran's conception of Buddhist faith exactly parallels
the understanding of faith explicit in the teachings of
Saint Paul, Saint Augustine, Martin Luther, and the
main theological tradition distinguishing classical
Protestant theology from medieval Roman Catholicism.
Even though Amida Buddha, the object of Pure Land faith
and practice, is not at all similar to traditional
Christian understandings of God as revealed through

Christ, the structural relation between "faith" and "other-power" in Shinran's interpretation of Pure Land tradition exactly parallels the relation between "faith" and "grace" in classical Pauline-Augustinian-Lutheran theology. In neither does any form of human self-effort play a positive role in the creation of faith and "salvation."

Obviously, Shinran's understanding of faith is the most "non-Pelagian" understanding ever occurring in the history of the Buddhist Way. In fact, his doctrine of faith is so different from anything previously taught about faith in Buddhist doctrine that the strong emphasis he placed upon Amida Buddha's "other-power" was rapidly deemphasized in Jōdo Shinshū teachings and practices after the death of Rennyo Shōnin in 1499. The reason that energized Shinran to teach a doctrine of *śraddhā* so utterly foreign to traditional Buddhist concepts is a controversial subject among Buddhist scholars. Most likely, his own admitted frustrations with his inability to achieve the experience of enlightenment during twenty years of monastic self-discipline had much to do with it. And, of course, his sense of personal failure only deepened his belief he was living during the age of *mappō*. But even here Shinran was unique. He was the first Buddhist ever to question the need for self-effort in the quest for enlightenment. This fact alone is evidence against the notion that "faith" is not a constitutive part of the Buddhist Way, or that nothing in Buddhist experience parallels what Christians doctrinally define as "faith through grace."

THE CHRISTIAN WAY OF FAITH

The Christian Way is pre-eminently a Way of faith, at least according to the New Testament and the major theologians who have articulated the meaning of biblical faith in both Protestant and Roman Catholic tradition. While there has always existed much diversity of interpretation of the experience of faith, all authentically Christian theological reflection is united by one central thread: in Jesus as the Christ, God decisively acted in history to establish the salvation of all of creation. Thus while there have always been important theological differences of opinion regarding *how* God has acted through Christ in effecting humanity's salvation, and indeed even about what salvation means, *that* God has so acted always remains the starting point, the point of faith as trust, for all Christian theological reflection. According to the Christian Way in all of its regional, historical, and institutional forms, "faith" (Greek, *pistis;* Latin, *fides*) always denotes "trust" in God's action through Christ, never trust in theological assertions and opinions about what this action means. Doctrinal belief is one expression of faith's seeking understanding, along with other expressions of faith such as devotional practices and ethical self-discipline, but it does not in itself constitute faith.

The meaning of this contention can be easily illustrated by the historically important controversy between Saint Augustine (354-430) and Pelagius (who died sometime before 420) about the role of human will in the origin of distinctively Christian faith.[24] The importance of the debate between Augustine and Pelagius lies not only in the way in which it clarified specific theological issues concerning the nature of faith, but also because of their representing opposed doctrinal extremes of Christian understanding. Even today, Christian doctrines of faith may be labeled either "Augustinian" or "Pelagian."

Both Pelagius and Augustine assumed, trusted, "took refuge in," had faith in the life, death, and resurrection of Jesus as the Christ as the final source of God's saving action on humanity's behalf. Neither took this to mean God had not acted in other ways in the past, nor indeed would cease acting in the future. But they never doubted God had encountered humanity ultimately and finally under the conditions and limitations of sinful historical existence through the incarnation of God in Jesus the Christ. They may have disagreed concerning the implications of God's act in Christ, but *that* God had so acted was their common faith. Thus neither accused the other of "unfaith" or of being "unchristian." Pelagius believed his theological conceptualization of Christian faith more accurately expressed what God had done through Christ than Augustine's did, and Augustine believed Pelagius's interpretation of faith was in error. Both thought theological conceptualization of the meaning of Christian faith was important, because how human beings express and live faith in part reflects how faith is conceptually understood. The point of their controversy was not whose faith was "true" or "false" or "Christian" or "unchristian." The point was whose propositional-theological interpretation, whose "beliefs" most fully correlated with what for both of them was the experientially prior or "given" reality of faith in Christ.

Pelagius understood faith moralistically, and in so doing sharply distinguished his thought from Augustine's. Since he assumed God created human beings with a free will, he believed all individuals must be held accountable for their choices, even the choice of placing or not placing faith in God's saving action on humanity's behalf through Christ. Pelagius never doubted human beings are free to act, are able to act in conformity with God's will, and are able to achieve whatever is willed because God created human nature in this way. In other words, human free will is a gift of God's grace because grace is built into the structure of God's creation. As part of the structure of human reality, grace, and so therefore free will, is not supernatural. Human beings are free and able to respond to God through Christ or to reject Christ. A positive response to God through Christ is what Pelagius called "faith."

Not placing faith in Christ is "sin" in Pelagius's theology. Sin is rebellion against what God wills for human beings, and, according to Pelagius, God wills that all human beings should relate to him through Christ. However, he did not teach sin is a reality built into human nature as the result of humanity's primal act of disobedience at the Fall. "Sin" carries sociological meaning in his thought, for no human being is born into this world "originally sinful," an idea that he believed compromised the justice and love of God for his creation as taught by the Hebrew Scriptures and New Testament. Rather, persons learn to sin from the environment in which their lives must be lived. According to this view, sin is rebellion against God, the primary form of sin being lack of faith in Christ. Sin is not an ontological reality structured into the human soul, since unless individuals *can will* what is not best for them, unless individuals *can choose* to do good or evil, unless individuals *can decide* to have or not have faith in God through Christ, unless individuals *are free* to sin or not sin, no one is responsible for one's own actions, including one's own sin. Instead, God becomes responsible for everything, and human beings cease being responsible for anything, including their sinful disobedience of God. God becomes unjust and unloving if he punishes human beings when they disobey him, a notion clearly contrary to the Scripture's teachings about a just and loving God revealed through Christ. Therefore, according to Pelagius, God neither wills faith nor anything else in his world in an ontological sense. That is, Pelagius rejected any suggestion that God predestines faith or anything else by his will in the world before he created the world. For him, "predestination" meant "foreknowledge," meaning God did not ontologically determine events, including who would have faith in God through Christ and who would not, before they happened, but rather "foreknew" before the creation of the world who would freely make the decision of faith in Christ and who would not.

Augustine opposed Pelagius on all of these points.[25] His conception of faith was grounded in the writings of Saint Paul, especially Paul's bifurcation of "law" and "gospel," most systematically expressed in his Epistle to the Romans. By "law" Augustine meant all the commandments of the Hebrew scriptures, the "theological function" of which is not helping human beings free themselves from sin through obedience of God's commandments. In his view, doing "works of the law" cannot establish a saving relationship between God and an individual. Rather, the function of the law is simply to make God's demands known. And by so doing, sin, meaning rebellion against the will of God, becomes more powerful because the law teaches human beings they have, in fact, disobeyed God. But the law possesses no power to free human beings from sin. It only convicts and declares a person, *all* persons according to Augustine, guilty and deserving of divine punishment. Freedom from sin and its consequent penalty, death, requires God's grace. This, too, is revealed by the law, for the more one tries fulfilling God's commandments through obeying the law, the more one becomes aware of not possessing the ability to do so apart from God's grace. No human being can establish a saving relationship with God through self-efforts, doing "works of the law." The more one tries, the more one rebels against God, and the more one becomes entrapped by the power of sin. The law can only be fulfilled by the aid of divine grace.

The basic problem preventing human fulfillment of God's law is "original sin." Because of Adam's primal disobedience of God in the Garden of Eden (Genesis 2:4-3:24), which Augustine also believed was an actual historical event, human nature thereafter became corrupted. No one after Adam can do anything other than rebel against God, for humanity has inherited Adam's sin and Adam's punishment. Some persons may will to do what is pleasing to God, but no human being now has the power to act accordingly. In other words, after the Fall no human being is free not to disobey God, and thus all human beings deserve only God's punishment for sin, death.

Therefore the law reveals a person's guilt because there is no "sin" unless there is a law convicting a person of sin, just as there is no murder unless there exists a law making murder a crime. Augustine's image for this idea is taken from the legal procedures of Roman civil law. Law defines the nature of a crime, the specific penalties for engaging in a crime, and the means by which the penalties are to be carried out. Law can only determine the guilt and the penalty for a crime: it cannot free a criminal from guilt or the penalty. But a judge can declare a guilty human being under the law free from having to pay the legal penalty for breaking the law. When such an event occurs, a criminal remains guilty while remaining free from having to pay any legal penalties. The authority by which a judge in a court of Roman law could free a convicted criminal from having to pay the penalty for breaking a law was called "justification." "To be justified" meant being declared formally free from the penalty of the law while remaining guilty of breaking the law.

Augustine appropriated this image in his theology. Because all human beings stand guilty of sin under the law of God, humanity's only option is to rely upon the work of Christ accomplished in his death and resurrection. This and only this pays the penalty for sin and satisfies the justice of God. Now God as a merciful judge is able to justify persons of faith. In other words, humanity remains guilty of sin, but those who trust Christ are "justified" by God, meaning they are granted freedom from death, the penalty for sin, while yet remaining guilty of sin.

Faith, then, means trust in God's work of justification through Christ and non-trust in our own self-efforts in establishing a saving relationship with God. Augustine believed this to be humanity's only hope of salvation. But even faith as trust in Christ's saving work is not a free act of the human will to believe. This, too, is a gift that God gives to some and not to others. No one simply "decides" to trust God's work through Christ apart from God's grace.

Consequently, a person receives grace, forgiveness, and salvation, meaning eternal life with God after death, the moment when one begins trusting God's revelation through Christ. However, no one is capable of trusting God's work through Christ without the reception of God's prior grace to do so. For Augustine, following Saint Paul, salvation occurs totally and absolutely by "faith through grace alone." Once more, God's grace is so absolutely decisive that God "decides" or "predestines" by divine will who will be given grace and who will not. Augustine did not believe this implied injustice on God's part, as Pelagius did, because humanity itself brought about the state of universal sinfulness, the origins of which he located in Adam's primal act of disobedience at the Fall. Accordingly, God's gift of "faith through grace" to any human being shows God to be a merciful judge. But also God's requirement that the penalty for sin must be paid through Christ's death shows God to be absolutely just. For as Adam's act of disobedience brought sin and death into the world, so Christ's act of obedience brought grace and eternal life for whomever God decides to grant it. And the standards by which God makes his decision to offer grace to some but not others remains a mystery to human understanding, since God's nature is ultimately beyond finite comprehension.

Even though the major conceptualizations of the nature of faith in Christian history have fallen between these two extremes, neither Pelagius's nor Augustine's propositions *about* faith *were* faith. They represent two opposite versions of the trust both had in God's prior work of salvation through Christ.

The theological definitions of faith, whether labeled "Pelagian," "Augustinian," or "semi-Pelagian," which have played important roles in the history of the Christian Way and which have come to be regarded as definitive understandings by most Christians, should never be confused with faith. Faith is never "belief" or "opinion," but always something prior to belief and opinion. Faith engenders belief and opinion, but can never be reduced to them. Both Pelagius and Augustine assumed the difference between faith and belief in their theological debate.

Distinctively Christian faith is, therefore, "trust," "setting the heart on" ("For where your heart is there will your treasure be also."), "taking refuge in" (to borrow Buddhist phrasing), centering one's "ultimate concern" upon the events of the life, death, and resurrection of Jesus of Nazareth as the "Christ," the final means by which God has entered human history itself to effect the salvation of all human beings. All else is interpretation, opinion, "belief." What "saves" an individual is not what one believes, but what one trusts. The Christian Way is always the way of trust in God through Christ, not the way of trust in propositional statements and theological systems. For the mystery of God revealed through the Christ event for Christians is beyond the limitations imposed by doctrinal or propositional abstractions. Theological conceptions may symbolically point to the mystery of God, but cannot completely contain it. Theological conceptualizations of faith that have most fully pre-served this distinction have also been the most lasting and influential in Christian history.

CONCLUDING OBSERVATIONS

In so sharply separating "faith" from "belief" in both Buddhist and Christian conceptualiza-tions, I am not implying belief is unimportant for ei-ther Buddhists or Christians. How we understand the implications and the meaning of whatever we "set our hearts on" conditions how faith is lived. But faith always remains prior to belief in both Buddhist and Christian experiences. Saint Anselm of Canterbury perhaps most accurately summarized the relation between faith and belief in his statement, "I believe in order that I may know." Here, of course, "belief" does not carry its modern connotations, but the original meaning, "I set my heart on." Anselm's point was that we do not have knowledge about anything apart from prior trust in realities transcendent to the mere givens of mundane experience. The Christian "knows" because of possessing faith, not "belief," in Christ. Likewise, the Buddhist "knows" only because of faith in the Buddha, the Dharma, and the Samgha.

Clearly, however, the object of Buddhist faith is not identical with the object of Christian faith. The object of faith, what a person trusts, makes all the difference. Faith in Christ is not the same as faith in the Three Jewels. But, generically understood, faith as trust is universal, and plays a role of fundamental importance in all religious Ways. Once more, both Buddhists and Christians experience faith as a gift, even though grace is, no doubt, doctrinally more strongly emphasized in the Christian Way. However, the sense of grace is more highly developed in the Buddhist Way than is commonly recognized by Christian interpretations, especially in the Pure Land teachings of Shinran. Therefore, Christian theological reflection about the Buddhist Way might have a rather unexplored dialogical entry point into the Buddhist experience of faith through Jōdo Shinshū teachings and practices.

One negative observation cries out for consideration. Conceiving faith as essentially "trust" or the experience of "taking refuge in" a reality or realities transcendent to the ordinary givens of mundane existence, whether this reality is named "God" or "the Dharma," does not mean Buddhists or Christians have never confused faith with belief. Historically, most Buddhists and Christians have tended to take refuge in doctrines, practices, and institutions, thereby confusing these with the transcendent realities to which they point. For it is always easier to trust our symbols than to trust transcendent realities. But the scriptures and the teachers of the mainline traditions of both religious Ways consistently separated faith from belief. Faith represents an ideal all Buddhists and Christians are taught to seek for themselves, but which apparently few succeed in realizing.

Finally, while the truth to which faith points transcends conceptualization and institutionalizations, the trust of faith is always experientially grasped by faith. So far as our own systems of beliefs about what we trust are concerned, where the immanence of this transcendent reality is most evident, it is extremely important that we hold fast to the truth we find while recognizing that truth transcends all belief systems. So far as another person's beliefs are concerned, it is equally important for us to strive to apprehend the truth perceived there as well, especially those truths we undoubtedly miss because our own belief systems may very well hide these other truths from us. In short, Christian faith need not cut Christians off from the truths to which Buddhist faith point, and *vice versa*. We are apt to be cut off from one another to the degree we confuse truth with ideology, faith with belief, thereby giving our beliefs an absolute author- ity that may be idolatrous. Doing so represents a mis- understanding of both the Buddhist and the Christian Ways of faith.

NOTES

[1]I wish to acknowledge my debt to Professor Smith's studies. I have, for the most part, followed his lead in formulating the understanding of faith and its relationship to belief informing my analysis and conclusions in this chapter. See especially *Belief and History* (Charlottesville: University Press of Virginia, 1977) and *Faith and Belief* (Princeton: Princeton University Press, 1979).

[2]Smith, *Faith and Belief*, viii.

[3]Ibid., 120.

[4]See Smith, *Belief and History*, 36-9 for a fuller analysis of the history of this change in the meaning of the world "belief."

[5]Benjamin Lee Whorf, *Language, Thought, and Reality* (New York: John Wiley and Sons, 1956).

[6]Paul Tillich, *Dynamics of Faith* (New York: Harper and Brothers, 1957), 4, emphasis supplied.

[7]See Thomas S. Kuhn, *The Structure of Scientific Revolutions* (Chicago: The University of Chicago Press, 1962), 43-51.

[8]Smith, *Faith and History*, 2.

[9]*Anguttara-nikaya* V, 147.

[10]John B. Cobb, Jr., *The Structure of Christian Existence* (Philadelphia: Westminster Press, 1967), 107.

[11]Winston L. King, *In the Hope of Nibbana* (La Salle, Illinois: Open Court Publishing Co., 1964), 82. Also see his *Theravāda Meditation: The Buddhist Transformation of Yoga* (University Park: Pennsylvania State University Press, 1980), 1-40.

[12] King, *In the Hope of Nibbana*, 83. Also see Rune E. A. Johansson, *The Psychology of Nirvana* (Garden City, N. J.: Anchor Books, 1970), 52-59. The main thrust of these pages is *nibbāna* "does not imply anni-

hilation, but rather a different type of existence; perhaps a diluted, undifferentiated, 'resting' existence, more or less impersonal but still recognizable." Ibid., 59.

[13] *Udāna* VIII, 3. Also quoted by King, *In the Hope of Nibbana*, 85.

[14]Buddhists are usually silent, or at least not prone to discussing what the state of existence in *nibbana* after death is like, and in this they follow the example of the Buddha himself, who also refused to discuss such questions. But the following passage does affirm what Buddhists *hope* is the case after death: "For those who in mid-stream stay, in great peril in the flood--for those adventuring on aging and dying--do I proclaim the Isle. Where is nothing, where nought is grasped, this is the Isle of No-beyond. Nibbana do I call it--the utter extinction of aging and dying." *Suttanipata,* 1093-94. Therefore, the "monk of wisdom *here*, devoid of desire and passion, attains to *deathlessness, peace, the unchanging state of Nibbana*" *Suttanipata,* 204, emphasis supplied.

[15]There are numerous studies of Pure Land faith and practice. For example, see my study *The Dharma of Faith: An Introduction to Classical Pure Land Buddhism* (Washington, D. C.: University Press of America, 1977); Allan A. Andrews, *The Teachings Essential for Rebirth* (Tokyo: Sophia University Press, 1973); Alfred Bloom, *Shinran's Gospel of Pure Grace* (Tucson: University of Arizona Press, 1965): and Akamatsu Shunshu, *Kamakura Bukkyō no Kenkyū* [Studies in Kamakura Buddhism] (Kyoto: Byorakuji Shoten, 1957).

[16]For a brief but good summary of the nature of Buddhist sectarian movements (Chinese, *tsung*; Japanese, *shu,* which I have translated as "school"), see Ocho Enichi, "The Beginnings of Buddhist Tenet Classification in China," *The Eastern Buddhist*, 14, (Autumn 1981): 71-94.

[17]Since the Japanese Pure Land masters worked from Chinese translations of these texts, all further references will be taken from the following critical edition of these works: *Shinshū Shōgyō Zenshō* [Complete Works of Shinshu Teaching], (Kyōto: Kōkyo Shōnin, 1958), 5

vols., hereafter abbreviated as *SSZ*. All Pure Land materials cited in this chapter are my own, unless otherwise indicated.

[18]*SSZ* 1:9-10.

[19]See Edwin O.Reischauer and John K. Fairbank, *East Asia: The Great Tradition* (Boston: Houghton and Mifflin, 1960), 544 ff., for an informative summary of the conditions of life in Japan during the twelfth century.

[20]For a fuller description of this process, see Daigan and Alacia Matsunaga, *Foundations of Japanese Buddhism*, (Los Angeles: Buddhist Books International, 1974), I and II:11-36.

[21]See Watanabe Shoko, *Nippon no Bukkyō* [Buddhism in Japan] (Tokyo: Iwanami Shinsho, 1964), 54 56.

[22]The specific periodization Hōnen and Shinran followed is that of the *Candagarbhāvaipula-sūtra* and the *Mahāmaya-sūtra*.

[23]The remainder of this section's analysis of Hōnen's and Shinran's specific Pure Land teachings are based on my previous work, *The Dharma of Faith*.

[24]See Etienne Gilson, *The Christian Philosophy of Saint Augustine* (New York: Random House, 1960), 27-55, 113-184; Otto W. Heick, *A History of Christian Thought,* (Philadelphia: Fortress Press, 1965), I:196-206; and Williston Walker, *A History of the christian Church* (New York: Charles Schribner's Sons, 1959), 168-172, for historical background on the issues of the Pelagian controversy.

[25]See Augustine, "The Spirit and the Letter," *Library of Christian Classics*, ed., John Burnaby, (Philadelphia: The Westminster Press, 1955), 8:182-250.

CHAPTER FIVE
Faith as Practice: The Buddhist Way

A man buries a treasure in a deep pit, thinking: "It will be useful in time of need, or if the king is displeased with me, or if I am robbed or fall into debt, or if food is scarce, or bad luck befalls me."

But all this treasure may not profit the owner at all, for he may forget where he has hidden it, or goblins may steal it, or his enemies or even kinsmen may take it when he is careless.

But by charity, goodness, restraint, and self-control men and women alike can store up a well-hidden treasure--a treasure which robbers cannot steal. A wise man should do good--that is the treasure which will not leave him.

Khuddaka Paṭha 8

Students of the Way must not worry about clothing or food. They must merely follow the Buddhist rules and not concern themselves with worldly things. The Buddha said: "For clothing, use tattered cast-aside garments; for food, use what can be begged." In any kind of world these two things will not be exhausted. Don't forget the swiftness of change, not let yourself be needlessly troubled by worldly affairs. While in this brief dewlike existence, think only of Buddhism, and don't concern yourself with any other problem.

Dōgen Zenji, Shōbōgenzō Zuimonki 16

ON THE MEANING OF "PRACTICE"

As the most centered act of which human beings are capable, faith becomes a force for integrating a person's emotions, intellect, physical needs, social involvements, and aesthetic sensibilities. The life of faith is, in other words, a life of practice. The interrelationship between faith and practice in Buddhist experience is the topic of this chapter.

Since much of the ongoing discussion between
Buddhists and Christians focuses on the necessity of
following a clearly defined religious practice, the interrelationship between faith and practice involves
matters of great importance.[1] There is no lack of examples of religious practice: prayer, meditation, contemplative study of sacred texts, obedient submission
to ethical and social norms, monastic self-discipline,
social reform. But much confusion also exists about
what practice means and how practice and faith are interrelated, especially among religious people living in
modern, secularized cultures. Is it possible, or even
desirable, to live a life of faith without practice?
Is is possible to practice a religious Way without
faith? What should the goal of practice be?

The concerns underlying such questions are
greatly increased in the case of seemingly private religious practices such as meditation or contemplative
prayer. Persons who practice meditation, for example,
are often asked by those who do not what "good" it does
for society. The assumptions motivating this question
view religious practice as an instrumental activity for
achieving ends or objects not part of the practice itself. That is, meditation is "practiced" to achieve
enlightenment, or prayer is "practiced" to surrender
completely to the will of God.

Consequently, when modern persons use the
word "practice" in conjunction with religious faith,
the meaning most often assumed expresses dualistic connotations opposing practice with theoretical knowledge.
We tend, in other words, to habitually separate theo-

retical knowledge conceived as an end in itself from practice as an instrumental means applied to achieving theoretically conceived ends.[2] Relative to Buddhist and Christian religious life, practice then assumes the character of a method for achieving enlightenment or salvation as each Way doctrinally theorizes about the ultimate goal of human existence. Thus meditation, prayer, ritual, and ethical self-discipline are transformed into methods for achieving what theory determines as the goal of religious faith.

Historically, however, this conception of religious practice is quite misleading, especially in Buddhist and Christian teaching. Neither religious Way dualistically separates faith as an end from practice as a means for achieving an end. In both Ways, in fact, practice and theory are so inseparable in their difference that they are like two sides of the same coin. One cannot exist apart from the other, just as there cannot be "heads" apart from "tails" in an American coin. Living faith requires practice, and practice is the way in which religious human beings express their faith.

If instrumental understandings of practice inadequately characterize the life of faith in Buddhist and Christian teachings, then delineating the specific meanings of practice in both religious Ways should clarify many of the crucial issues now coming to light in current Buddhist-Christian dialogical encounter. The conception of practice I wish to consider, because it most closely approximates the meaning of this notion in traditional Buddhist and Christian teaching, involves the disciplined performance of some skill. As John C. Maraldo[3] has described this notion, practice in the sense of skilled action is, generally speaking, akin to the Greek notion of *askesis,* from which the English word "asceticism" is derived. But the original meaning of *askesis* had nothing to do with bodily or mental self-mortification as a means of achieving enlightenment or salvation. On the contrary, the ancient Greeks understood *askesis* within the context of athletic training, and therefore for them it expressed positive valuation of bodily existence, coupled with the exertion of athletic prowess as a means of perfecting the body and the mind. Accordingly, any activity that "takes practice" to be proficiently performed will provide an excellent metaphor for understanding what is involved in the religious practice of an individual's faith.

The first fact that becomes evident for anyone engaged in learning a particular skill, for example, playing the piano, performing a dance, learning a foreign language, doing floral arrangement or the tea ceremony, competing in a particular athletic event, or studying medicine is the absolute necessity for repeated, concentrated effort and performance. At least for anyone beyond the novice stage in the skill being learned, all of these examples are daily disciplines exercised for no other reason than their performance.[4] Furthermore, anyone performing any skilled discipline for any length of time knows perfection in a disciplined skill can never be achieved and retained without continuing practice because the performer's skill *is* the practice and the practice *is* the skill. Practice in this sense does not make perfect, as the master of any skilled discipline knows. For example, when a musician performs a concert he or she performs the identical activity during the concert as was performed during the "practice" sessions. Thus, to the degree an activity becomes "practiced," meaning proficiently and artistically performed, there exists no gap between what an artist *wills* to do and *what* the artist does. Even during practice, there is no room for desires and intentions separating performance from an imagined theoretical idea, that is, separating *what* he or she is doing from *how* he or she wishes it were being done.

This concept of practice directly opposes much contemporary Western understanding, which dualistically separates theoretical knowledge from practice. The model underlying this concept is, as I have indicated, athletic training. But this model can be stretched to include any disciplined activity requiring training, repeated exertion, and concentration of body and mind. It can even include an individual's most routine daily activities. Accordingly, "practice" as disciplined performance is the topic of not only this chapter, but the remainder of this study. I hope to demonstrate that neither the Buddhist Way nor the Christian Way dualistically opposes faith (*theoria*) and practice (*praxis*), because in the concrete religious experiences of Buddhists and Christians, faith and practice name polar opposites of a single religious reality.

THERAVADA BUDDHIST PRACTICE

The earliest forms of Buddhist practice originated in Theravada tradition. The specific forms of
Theravada practice were also continued in Mahayana discipline conjoined with its own unique forms. Consequently, most of the foregoing discussion will focus on
Theravada traditions of practice. But as the Mahayana
version of the Dharma made significant modifications to
Theravada disciplines of practice in light of its own
distinctive doctrines. I shall address only these modifications in my discussion of Mahayana practice.

All traditions of the Buddhist Way doctrinally conceptualize the practice of Buddhist faith as
the Noble Eightfold Path (āryāṣṭāṅgika-mārga):

1. Right Views   (samyak dṛṣṭi)
2. Right Aspiration   (samyak saṃkalpa)
3. Right Speech   (samyak vāca)
4. Right Action   (samyak karmānta)
5. Right Livelihood   (samyak ājīva)
6. Right Effort   (samyak vyāyma)
7. Right Mindfulness   (samyak smṛti)
8. Right Concentration   (samyak samādhi)

The Theravada Dhamma, however, has always maintained
the most doctrinally uniform interpretation of the Noble Eightfold Path, primarily because there exists much
less theoretical and practical deviation among Theravada Buddhist schools than among the numerous schools
and sectarian divisions of the Mahayana movement. So
even while there are wide-ranging discussions and differences of opinion concerning the specific details of
Buddhist practice, the fundamental elements of the No-

ble Eightfold Path were settled very early in the history of the Theravada version of the Buddhist Way. As a result, the structure of Theravada practice has remained remarkably stable.

Right Understanding involves rational comprehension coupled with emotional appreciation of the "truth" of the Buddhist world view to which the doctrine of the Four Noble Truths points and which the *arhat* experientially comprehends through the practice of meditation. Right Understanding describes the novice stage of the Path, for before the seeker can experience enlightenment, he must first accept the Buddhist conception of existence as an accurately realistic description of his own existential situation. At this stage of practice, propositional understanding of the Buddhist world view functions as an *upāya* ("skillful means") guiding the seeker toward realistically comprehending the conditions of human existence, along with the possibilities for release from these conditions.

Of course, the complete realization of the truth of enlightenment cannot be experientially known until the seeker attains skilled proficiency in the final three meditative stages of the Noble Eightfold Path called Right Effort, Right Mindfulness, and Right Concentration. But Right Understanding provides the intellectual context guiding the actual practice of all facets of Buddhist faith. Doctrinal understanding of the Buddhist world view is thus an absolute prerequisite guiding the practice of meditative and ethical self-discipline. For if the seeker practices specifi-

cally Buddhist forms of meditation apart from intellectual understanding of and commitment to the Buddhist
world view, then the experience of enlightenment as
Buddhists understand it is impossible, even though profoundly moving insights might indeed be achieved.

This last point may be illustrated by a simple example. When a Christian practices a specific
Buddhist meditative technique such as, for example, Zen
Buddhist *kōan* meditation guided by commitment to some
doctrinal expression of Christian faith, experiences
and insights will not be the same as those of a Rinzai
Zen Buddhist practicing the same meditative techniques
guided by the presuppositions of the Buddhist world
view. The experiential results, in other words, will
likely be quite different. Even if they are not, the
Christian meditator will interpret the meaning of the
experience differently from a Buddhist colleague.[5] As
William James noted some eighty years ago in his *Varieties of Religious Experience*, we experience whatever
our religious conceptualities prepare us to experience
as we practice our religious faith.[6] Therefore, Christian "enlightenment" attained through specifically Buddhist techniques of meditation will, in all probability, not be recognized by Theravada Buddhists (and perhaps Mahayana Buddhists) as authentically *Buddhist* enlightenment experiences, although the power, goodness,
beauty, and truth of a Christian's meditative experience would certainly be positively affirmed.

James's point becomes even clearer as we remember, along with intellectual assent to the doctrinal
formulation of the Buddhist world view, that the Bud-

dhist Way simultaneously involves the seeker's intention of devoting total disciplined self-effort toward
putting doctrine into practice in the anticipation of
achieving enlightenment. Putting total effort into
practice, guided by doctrine, is called "Right Aspiration." The goal of Right Aspiration is "shaping together" or "shaping up" (*samkalpa*) the seeker's mental
framework in order to attain freedom from anything hindering his devotion to distinctively Buddhist teachings
and practices. Thus one must not only possess Right
Understanding of the Buddhist world view, one must be
exclusively committed to this world view, while simultaneously rejecting non-Buddhist teachings and practices.

The doctrines summarizing the Buddhist world
view and guiding Buddhist practice, and which are also
represented as the "original teachings" of the Buddha,
are the Four Noble Truths (*ārya satyas*), the Three
Marks (*lakṣaṇa*) of Existence, the Five Aggregates
(*skandhas*), and Dependent Co-origination (*pratītya
samutpāda*). Indeed, a volume could be written, and
many have been, about each of these doctrines. But for
purposes that I hope are now clear, a brief descriptive
summation of each of these doctrines should illumine
the specific ways in which faith and practice are interconnected within the Theravada Buddhist Way. In
turn, this should also prove useful in establishing a
point of departure for analyzing similar interconnec-
tions between faith and practice in the Mahayana
Dharma.

According to the most ancient literary sources, the Buddha preached a sermon at Benares, actually his second "discourse" (*sutta*), to a small group of ascetics who, upon hearing the Buddha's words, became his earliest disciples. Known as the *Anattā-lakkhana-sutta* (Sanskrit, *Anatmālakṣaṇa-sūtra*) or "Discourse on the Marks of Nonself," this text's central teachings concern not only the doctrine of nonself, but also the doctrines of "impermanence" (*anicca*) and "suffering" (*duḥkha*), which together constitute the "three marks" or characteristics of existence.[7]

The first mark of existence is *anattā* (Sanskrit, *anātman*) or "nonself." The primary axiom of the Brahmanic religious tradition contemporary with the Buddha posited every sentient being's possession of an unchanging "Self" (*attā*) or "Soul" comprising the ontological center of its existence. This Self, whose nature is pure, subtle, substantial, and eternal is the carrier of a being's karmic residues from one existence to the next during its process of transmigration. But the Buddha, as is well known, rejected all concepts of a permanent self-entity remaining identical through the processes of time. Accordingly, he attacked all concepts of permanent selfhood in two ways. First, he emphasized the necessity of nonattachment to any entity or state understood to be permanent as the absolute prerequisite for the achievement of enlightenment. In an impermanent universe, there are no permanent entities to which to cling, including an eternal non-changing self-entity. Second, the Buddha stressed the illogic of the concept of permanent selfhood. How could anything pure, subtle, and unchanging be associated with something as impure, gross, and impermanent as a body transmigrating through samsaric existence? On the other hand, of course, if the self is *not* in some sense permanently self-identical through time, what transmigrates? This latter question has never been satisfactorily answered by subsequent Buddhist philosophical speculation, although the earliest attempts to do so involved the doctrine of the five *skandhas* Nevertheless, all Buddhists follow Gautama's utter rejection of a permanent, substantial self-entity underlying the core of personal existence, and the philosophical puzzles that this doctrine creates are, Buddhist teaching stresses, dissolved away at the moment of enlightenment.

The second mark of existence, impermanence, is an interpretation of the nature of the "elements" (*dharmas*) comprising existence by means of two categories: the "condition" and the "unconditioned." According to the Theravada version of the Buddhist Way, only *nibbāna* is an unconditioned *dharma,* meaning that its existence does not depend upon anything other than its own being. But all other elements comprising existence at any moment of time, because they are subject to change and processive becoming, are impermanent. That is, becoming is the defining characteristic of samsaric existence; nonchange is ontologically impossible. Therefore, as the only permanent, unchanging *dharma,* only *nibbāna* is a worthy object of human striving.

Now if all things and events "this side of
nibbāna" are without selfhood because they are impermanent, to what do the terms "being" or "individual" or
"person" refer?   The standard Theravada response to
this question declares that all individual entities are
constituted by five interdependent "aggregates" or
skandha.   Literally, *skandha* means "heap" or "bundle,"
and all individual entities during any single moment of
existence are interconnected aggregates of these physical and mental "bundles of energy."[8]

The first *skandha,* called "form" (*rupa*), denotes the four "great elements" (*mahābhūtas*), which in
their relationship with one another comprise the physical nature of all entities: earth, water, fire, and
air.   Because the *rūpa skandha* includes all material
objects of the past, present, and future, along with
whatever is internal and external or gross or subtle,
this aggregate is the physical ground for those aspects
of existence involving emotion and mentality.

The second *skandha,* "feeling" (*vedāna*), originates from the contact of our physical and mental organs (in Buddhist physiology the mind is an organ of
sense identified with the brain) with objects in the
external world.   At this level of development awareness
is not conscious, but rather more like stimulus-re-
sponse reactions to sense data.

"Cognition" *(saṃjñā)*, the third *skandha,* determines the characteristics of a thing or event.   Like
"feeling," "cognition" originates from "contact" with
the external world through sense perception.   But unlike "feeling," "cognition" involves differing degrees

of conscious judgment about *what* is perceived through "feeling." For example, "there is perception of a patch of sense data" would represent a "feeling." But, "I perceive a blue sky" represents a cognitive judgment about what is perceived as mere sense data at the level of "feeling." Because of the factor of judgment about what is perceived through feeling, consciousness in varying degrees and intensity originates with this *skandha*.

The fourth *skandha*, "mental constituents" (*saṃskāra*), points to the volitional aspects of experience, for with this *skandha* value judgments are placed on what is perceived through cognition. Thus, because of "feeling," sense data originating from the external world are unconsciously experienced, cognitively judged to be a patch of blue sky, to which an emotional reaction is given. For example, I might react to a blue sky as pleasant and feel a warm sense of enjoyment. The same blue sky in the middle of a midwestern American winter might be experienced as bitterly cold, and then my emotional reaction might be quite negative. This *skandha*, as the source of emotional and volitional reaction to the external world, is also the source of the karmic results of action. In other words, *how* an individual attaches himself to events and entities judged to be positive, negative, or emotionally neutral determines an individual's character, or *karma*.

The final *skandha* is "consciousness" (*vijñāna*). Consciousness arises as our physical and mental organs come into contact with objects in the external world. Now since the Buddhist Way places such great stress upon meditative self-discipline, the operations of the five *skandha* have been an object of prime concern in the "scholastic" literature of early Buddhist tradition.   This literature, collectively called the *Abidhamma-piṭaka* [Basket of Scholasticism], is the concluding section of the Pali Canon.[9]

Originally, the doctrine of the Five Aggregates was formulated as a descriptive account of human nature along with the mental states occurring during the process of meditation. The doctrine's major intention is thus "psychological" in the widest possible meaning of this term. However, the Five Aggregates were quickly appropriated to provide metaphysical descriptions of all the constituting elements (*dharmas*) of the Buddhist world view. Even so, the doctrine of Dependent Co-origination remains the central Buddhist conception of the "way things really are," and the entire meditative system of the Theravada tradition was structured as a means of internalizing this world view.[10] The doctrine of Dependent Co-origination also distinguishes Buddhist teaching and practice from traditional Christian teaching and practice: unless this is clearly perceived and fully understood by those participating in Buddhist-Christian dialogical encounter, very little mutual creative transformation is apt to occur.[11]

Dependent Co-origination asserts all of the elements comprising existence during any single moment of space-time are what they are because of how they causally interact with every other element of existence at that moment. Furthermore, the becoming of every el-

ement of existence occurs in interdependent relationship with the becoming of every other element of existence. As a means of illustrating the dynamic, processive, and interdependent causal relationship among all
existent things and events, Buddhist doctrine symbolizes this aspect of its world view as a wheel possessing twelve links or "spokes" (nidāna) arranged in a
circle, variously referred to as the "wheel of existence," "the wheel of birth and death," or the "wheel
of Samsara." The twelve nidāna are related to one another in the following pattern: "Because of this, that
becomes; because of that, something else becomes."[11]
The twelve "spokes" are as follows: because of ignorance (avidyā), mental constituents (saṃskāras) arise;
because of mental constituents, consciousness (vijñāna)
arises; because of consciousness, name and form (nāma-
rūpa), the physical and the non-physical dimensions of
existence, arise; because of name and form, the six
senses (ṣaḍāyatana), sight, sound, touch, taste, smell,
and mind arise; because of the six senses, contact
(sparśa) with the external world arises; because of
contact, feeling (vedanā) arises: because of feeling,
craving (tṛṣṇa) arises; because of craving, clinging
(upādāna) arises; because of clinging, becoming (bhava)
arises; because of becoming, birth (jāti) arises; because of birth, old age and death (jarāmaraṇa) arise.
Because of old age and death, ignorance arises--the
wheel of existence continuing its cyclic process of becoming with no beginning or ending, except for the individual's transcending of this cyclic treadmill with
the attainment of enlightenment.

Specifically, the attainment of enlightenment depends upon breaking three *nidāna* that Theravada teaching concludes are the interdependent sources of humanity's involvement in the processes of becoming: ignorance, craving, and clinging. For the moment, however, one point requiring clarification is how the doctrine of Dependent Co-origination dispells all notions concerning the creation of the universe by a god or gods, along with the idea of a changeless, substantial "self-entity" or soul or Self underlying the processes of phenomenal existence. For if there really is nothing permanent in the universe, thinking or hoping otherwise along with the resulting clinging to such nonexistent entities forces us to structure our lives contrary to the way reality really is. The karmic result of this is *duḥkha* ("suffering"), which is also the third "mark of existence."

When the Buddha preached his first sermon, the *Dharmacakrapravartana-sūtra* [Discourse on the Turning of the Wheel of the Law], to the ascetics who became his earliest disciples, he declared the Four Noble Truths to be the central teachings of his Dharma. The first noble truth is the truth of suffering, although "existential anxiety, while not a literal translation of the technical term denoting this truth (*duḥkha*), more completely captures its meaning.[12] In the Buddha's words, "Birth is suffering, old age is suffering, disease is suffering, death is suffering, association is suffering, separation is suffering"[13] The usual Western interpretation, that the first noble truth summarily dismisses all pleasure and happiness, is stereotypical. Rather, the Buddha intended to point out the transiency of all mental and physical pleasures. Furthermore, he apparently thought *duḥkha* was encountered through three interrelated modes of human existence: *duḥkha-duhkhatā*, or ordinary mental and physical suffering; *vipariṇāma-duḥkahatā*, or suffering resulting from change, such as pleasure transformed into pain; and *saṃskara-duḥkhatā*, or suffering because of conditioned or finite being. The three forms of suffering also correlate with the "three marks of existence."

The second noble truth is the cause of suffering, *tanha,* or "desire," but sometimes also called *tṛṣṇa,* or "thirst." Again in the Buddha's words, *tanha* is "that which is craving tending to rebirth, connected with pleasure and lust, finding delight here and there, namely: craving for sensual desire, craving for becoming, and craving for non-existence."[14] Thus the second noble truth must be understood in conjunction with the doctrine of Dependent Co-origination, for to desire anything is to desire that entity permanently--otherwise why would anyone desire it? But in a universe of continual becoming, desire is metaphysically impossible of fulfillment. Consequently, while ignoring the real nature of things, unenlightened persons identify themselves with what possesses no existence--numerous forms of permanency. The karmic effect of such clinging desire is "suffering," "anxiety," "unsatisfactoriness."

The third noble truth is a simple declaration: release from suffering is possible provided we extinguish the cause of suffering, desire. The fourth noble truth is the Noble Eightfold Path, the means by which desire and attachment are eradicated. I have already described the first two steps of the Eightfold Path, Right Understanding and Right Aspiration as minimally involving intellectual ascent to the Buddhist world view summarized by the doctrines of the Three Marks of Existence, the Five Skandha, Dependent Co-origination, and the Four Noble Truths. The next three steps of the Noble Eightfold Path--Right Speech, Right Action, and Right Livelihood--summarize ethical disciplines meant to prepare the seeker for the practice of meditation, for as the earliest Buddhist doctrines teach, enlightenment is never an unethical event.[15]

Right Speech alludes to the disciplined use of language, the central vehicle through which human beings structure individual and collective experience into distinctively human understandings of reality. Since language is also the chief means by which individuals also either consciously or unconsciously falsify their conceptions of the external world, Right Speech means refraining from improper forms of speech such as lying, malicious talk, harsh or frivolous language, or ignorant speech.

Right Action involves avoiding three primary actions: killing, stealing, and any misconduct that might injure others. Thus all Buddhists must live according to the Five Precepts: not to kill, steal, lie, be sexually aggressive, or drink intoxicants. But more positively understood, Right Action intends a compassionate, noninjury attitude towards all sentient beings.

Right Livelihood means expressing noninjury towards all sentient beings, at least as much as possible in a world in which all forms of life must feed off other forms for any to survive. Specific vocations and occupations that Buddhists should avoid mentioned in the earliest texts include using and practicing of astrology and magic, interpreting dreams and omens, acting as a go-between, trading slaves, and doing military service.

The final three steps of the Noble Eightfold Path--Right Effort, Right Mindfulness, and Right Concentration--epitomize Buddhist understanding of meditative practice. The lines separating these meditative stages from one another are not, however, sharply drawn by Buddhist meditators, because very often a meditator slips back and forth between the experiences defined by each of these stages. Furthermore, while practicing meditation the seeker, simultaneously practices all of the disciplines involved in the previous five steps of the Eightfold Path. In other words, Buddhist practice is not a hierarchy of eight successive stages through which the seeker must progress before proceeding to the next. Several Indian meditative traditions do take this approach to the practice of meditation, for example, the system of Patañjali known as Rāja Yoga. But since Buddhist practice reflects the Buddhist world view, each particular step achieves its intended purposes in interdependent conjunction with the other seven steps.

Right Effort defines the novice stage of meditative practice, and is characterized by the initial efforts of cleansing the mind of all existing "evil thoughts," meaning any thought of or emotional attachment to all conceptions of permanency. More positively, Right Effort points to the meditator's beginning efforts to develop powers of focused concentration on "good thoughts" as these are demarcated by Buddhist doctrinal teaching. The most crucial technical goal of this stage, however, is deepening the seeker's power of concentration so that during later stages of meditation the highly developed ability to direct fully concentrated attention can be employed at will to the topics reserved for advanced meditators.

Right Mindfulness continues developing the technical skills of concentrated attention that the meditator learned as a novice during the stage of Right Effort.[16] During this stage, the meditator's power of concentration becomes so highly developed that when attention is focused on an object, no external stimuli are allowed to interfere with concentration. Technically, the main difference between this stage and Right Effort is that the seeker at this stage directs attention inwardly, focusing on the self's subjective mental, physiological, and psychological processes as "objects" of concentration. The goal of the procedures of Right Mindfulness is experientially discovering there is nothing permanent about any of these internal processes that the meditator can identify as a permanent self. That is, the seeker begins to apprehend the truth of the Buddhist doctrine of universal becoming and impermanency as the experiential truth of his or her own existence. Gradually, awareness of impermanency deepens and broadens to include all beings, which in turn helps the meditator begin eradicating the mechanism underlying the self's peculiar forms of attachment. Gradually becoming aware of the nonexistence of permanent entities to which to cling, the seeker stops clinging.

As this realization gradually deepens to full maturity--a moment that differs for each individual meditator--the seeker experiences entrance to the final stage of practice called Right Concentration. Right Concentration denotes meditative practice at its most completely developed and experiential depth, because during this stage "practice" becomes "enlightened," just as the "practice" of a musician gradually becomes the Practice of a master artist. Now the meditator becomes a fully enlightened *arhat*, finally free from *duḥkha*; freedom from all attachment and clinging is achieved, even attachment and clinging to enlightenment.[17] Even though the Noble Eightfold Path constitutes a "Buddhist transformation of yoga," according to Winston L. King, Buddhist practice involves "the total, supersaturated, existentializing of the Theravada world view that all existence in personal and individual modes of being, intrinsically embodies impermanence, pain, and impersonality."[18] In other words, the disciplines of distinctively Buddhist practice are guided by the doctrine of Dependent Co-origination. But for purposes of discussion and teaching, the eight steps of the Path are traditionally broken down into three interdependent groupings. Steps three to five are called *sīla*, meaning "moral casualty and responsibility."

Steps six to eight are referred to as *samādhi* or
"concentration" involving the techniques of meditation,
while steps one and two are called *paññā* (Sanskrit,
prajñā) or "wisdom" or the "understanding" that brings
enlightenment. This organizational structure is Buddhaghosa's, a fifth century translator of Buddhist
texts from Singhalese into Pali and a writer of numerous commentaries. Buddhaghosa understood *sila* and
samādhi as the two legs of Buddhist practice, with
paññā as its body--an image beautifully capturing the
interdependency of each step of the Eightfold Path.
This image continues guiding Theravada practice.
"Wisdom" refers to the beginning doctrinal understanding of the Buddhist world view, the truth of which the
seeker must existentially confirm through the practice
of moral self-discipline and meditation.[19]

Moral causality is a central element of enlightenment; therefore, Buddhist practice always entails ethical self-discipline. Before an individual
can achieve spiritual perfection, that is, he or she
must achieve moral perfection because both the status
of the enlightened and the unenlightened are directly
correlated to the moral condition of the individual.
The Buddhist Way, accordingly, bases its ethical
teachings on a theory of universal causality popularly
known as the Law of Karma (Pali, *kamma*).

Karma means not only "cause" but the
"effects" of cause operating universally at all levels
of existence during any moment of time. But Buddhist
teaching and practice, unlike many forms of Hindu
teaching, rejects all deterministic understandings of

the operations of karma, for the Buddhist Way radically asserts human free will and responsibility. Human beings can freely determine and change the quality of their lives in the present through intelligent, morally good thought and action because an individual's past karmic residues eventually run themselves out. There is, consequently, justification for religious hope. We may be born in states of existence created by our own previous actions. Yet by our own well-directed efforts we can create new favorable environments even here and now. But are we bound to reap all that we sow in exact proportion to our deeds? This question, once asked of the Buddha, elicited this reply:

If anyone says that a man *must* reap according to his deeds, in that case there is no religious life, nor is an opportunity afforded for the entire extinction of sorrow. But if anyone says that what a man reaps *accords* with his deeds, in that case there is a religious life, and an opportunity for the entire extinction of sorrow.[20]

According to Buddhist interpretation of the Law of Karma, then, sīla is both the beginning stage of moral practice and the interiorized ethical perfection of the *arhat* that occurs spontaneously with the achievement of enlightenment. But in the beginning states of practice, especially the ethical practice of Buddhist lay persons, sīla defines those minimal ethical rules of behavior recognized as valid by all societies and cultures. These same rules are greatly expanded for ordained monks (and nuns in Mahayana Buddhist teaching). Guided by the *Vinaya-piṭaka* [Basket of Discipline], monks are required to govern their behavior by 227 major and 163 minor rules, while nuns were expected to govern their lives by 279 major and 390 minor rules.[21] The heart of lay Buddhist *sīla*, however, remains the Five Precepts.

As the guiding rule governing the moral conduct of Buddhist individuals living in secular society, the Five Precepts are, as I have indicated, primarily concerned with the prohibition of antisocial actions involving injury to living beings. When adopted as positive principles of living, the Five Precepts transform an individual into a sober and responsible member of society. If, however, they are "interiorized" through the practice of meditation, which they must be before enlightenment can be attained, the Five Precepts cease being merely external rules of "law" and become inner motivations naturally and spontaneously directing the *arhat's* interactions with others through what are called the Four Illumitibles: compassion (*karuṇā*), loving kindness (*mettā*), sympathetic joy (*muditā*), and equanimity (*upekkhā*).

Karuṇā is a heightened sense of fellow-feeling for the suffering of all sentient beings as if it were our own. But compassion does not merely mean emotional identification with the condition of others, which in Buddhist understanding is nothing more than sentimentality. The ideally compassionate person, exemplified by the Buddha, functions as a skillful physician who completely appreciates the suffering of every sentient being, works according to skillful means" for their release from suffering, but without letting their suffering "get to him."[22] *Mettā* means extending loving kindness towards others in such a manner that the individual experiences no distinctions between the self's and another's welfare.[23] *Mudita* is the capacity for sympathetic joy in another's joy or success, coupled with forgetfulness of our own successes or failures.[24] *Upekkhā* is the controlled balance of mind of an enlightened individual characterized by emotional nonattachment and disinterest.[25] Remaining completely unshaken by the world's mental and emotional turmoil enables an enlightened individual to extend nonjudgmental compassion and sympathetic joy equally to all sentient beings without regard to or interest in issues labeled "good" or "evil." Similar to the love of God expressed in the parables of Jesus in the New Testament, the enlightened *arhat's* compassion and sympathetic joy "falls on the just and the unjust."

The polar structure of Theravada ethical practice is clearly evident. *Sila* entails both the novice and final stages of the process of self-development toward enlightenment. Of itself, ethical practice will never bring a person to enlightenment. But at the initial stages of Buddhist practice, accordingly, ethical cultivation functions primarily as a preparation for meditation. On the other hand, the highest attainments must also be established on good ethical conduct because the religious perfection the seeker achieves through the practice of meditation *simultaneously* and *spontaneously* issues in ethical perfection. So during the novice stages of practice, *samadhi* stands above *sīla.* But with the achievement of enlightenment *sīla* itself becomes "enlightened."

However, even the techniques of meditation, like ethical training, are only forms of *upāya.* Still, if any particular Buddhist practice approaches what Christian theology defines as a "sacrament," it is meditation, because it is the only means of "salvation" in the Buddhist Way; "practice" *means* "meditation." The most ancient Theravada literary sources concerning Buddhist meditation are found in the Pāli Canon and Buddhaghoṣa's massive meditational manual, *The Path of Purification [Visuddhimagga].* Based on at least a thousand years of pre-Buddhist meditational tradition, both sources allegedly express Gautama the Buddha's actual practice--a claim that must not be taken too literally.

I previously noted how Theravada techniques of meditation apply the Buddhist world view in molding the seeker's consciousness of the self and the world. The major differences between Hindu yoga and Buddhist meditation occur here. The Buddhist concept of enlightenment as "going out" of space-time samsaric existence into *nibbāna* totally differs from Hindu yoga's quest for a pure and unchanging self, called *purusa* or "Person" in Rāja Yoga and *ātman* of "Self" in Advaita Vedanta, remaining self-identical through time. And while it is impossible to learn either Hindu yoga or Buddhist meditation apart from personal practice under the guidance of a teacher, just as it is equally impossible to learn how to dance by merely reading books about dance, an outline of the essential procedures of

Theravada meditation will clarify the central role of meditative practice in the Buddhist Way.

The seeker begins by finding an isolated place in which to assume the classical seated meditation position called the "Lotus"--sitting with legs folded so that each foot rests in the bend of the opposite knee. Sitting thus with spine and neck in a straight line, hands folded together on lap, eyes half-closed in a non-focused gaze, and the lower portion of the anatomy made immovable and unfeeling, the seeker can clearly attend to the specific subjects of concentration assigned by the teacher.

Traditionally, forty subjects are available as directed by the meditation master in accordance with the personal characteristics and progress of the student. Not all subjects are required by any single meditator, but only the ones most helpful to the individual seeker. Some of these subjects are preparations for later stages of more intense practice. Examples of this category include meditating on the Buddha and his virtues, on peace, sympathetic joy, compassion, or equanimity, all of which are meant to internalize Buddhist ethical virtues as well as to provide a model (the Buddha) to imitate in the student's own practice. Other subjects function as techniques intended to increase the skill and depth of the student's concentration. Examples of these subjects include various physical objects of differing shapes, sizes, and colors such as circles, squares, and other sorts of geometrical shapes. Finally, there are whole classes of subjects devoted to helping the meditator comprehend his or her own participation in the universal realities of impermanence. Subjects in this category include the decay of one's physical features, the processes of decay and aging of one's body, corpses in various stages of decay, the repulsiveness of one's digestive processes, and the waste products of one's body.

After a period of time, differing with each individual student, and occurring when the teacher judges the student's powers of concentrated attention have been sufficiently strengthened, two types of meditation are open: the *jhānic* states and insight awareness. The *jhānic* (Sanskrit, *dhyāna* or "meditation") form of meditation, variously translated in English as "musings," "absorptions," or "trances," involves eight stages of successively higher levels of internal abstraction. Buddhaghoṣa's term for these stages was "peaceful abidings," and this accurately portrays their experiential quality. The *jhānas* involve a trance-like calm in which consciousness of the external world is totally blocked off while the meditator focuses attention on a particular subject, such as a color or a decaying bodily state. At the deepest developmental level, the *jhānas* scarcely involve sensory awareness of their external objects, or indeed, even awareness of the student's own conscious attention. Historically, the sources of this type of Theravada meditation stem from Indian traditions of yoga. But by themselves, proficiency in the *jhānic* state does not lead to final enlightenment. Rather, the *jhānic* meditation functions as a method of developing the student's powers of concentration in order to undertake "insight" or *vipassanā* meditation.[26]

Insight meditation may be practiced either in conjunction with *jhānic* meditation or independently, but only insight meditation can internalize the Buddhist world view and thereby lead the seeker to enlightenment. That is, this method alone leads to liberating insight into reality, the "way things really are" as conceived by the Buddhist world view, because insight meditation alone transforms the propositions of Buddhist teaching into internally experienced truths. For example, the rise and fall of the abdomen in breathing, when given focused conscious attention, witnesses to the perpetual flux of the life cycle from existence to non-existence to reborn existence *ad nauseam*. Centering concentrated attention on the repulsiveness of his own bodily functions and stages of decay establishes for the meditator an existential sense of his own impermanence, which in turn tempers his attachment to life. Gradually, he ceases clinging to permanency in any form in the confirmed impermanence of this universe. Finally, clear and detached observation of his own mental and emotional states as they occur creates an experiential awareness of himself as only a fluctuating, impermanent succession of physical-mental states or "events" (*dhammas*). And if insight meditation is used in conjunction with *jhānic* meditation, the former deepens the realization of the inescapability of the life and death processes that, even during the peaceful *jhānic* trances, continually manifest themselves as the structure of existence.

The results of Theravada meditational practice are two-fold. Negatively understood, there occurs
a thoroughgoing experiential awareness of the tran-
sience (*anicca*) and suffering (*duhkha*) or existence.
Positively understood, however, as well as emphasized
by Buddhist if not by Western interpretations, insight
meditation issues in a foretaste of final *nibbana* itself. This experience appears in flashes of momentary
insight during only the most fully developed states of
insight meditation. They also do not appear to last
very long, which should not be of great surprise since
in the Buddhist view of reality nothing is permanent.
But the bliss and equanimity of these experiences
greatly qualify and condition the life and behavior of
the meditator after they occur. Everything happening
to the now enlightened seeker subsequent to these momentary flashes of insight is interpreted in terms of
these experiences until death. Restated in the terminology of Theravada conceptions, as the meditator advances in *vipassana* meditation he progressively becomes
a "stream enterer" (*sotapanna*) who will never again be
reborn in less than a human state, a "once returner" to
human existence (*sakadagamin*), a "nonreturner" to human
existence (*anagamin*), and finally an *arhat*, who, like
the Buddha, will "go out" into final *nibbana* upon
death.

MAHAYANA BUDDHIST PRACTICE

Mahayana Buddhist practice carries on the basic Theravada three-fold division of practice into *pra-
jña, sila,* and *dhyana* (Pali: *pañña, sila,* and *jhana*).

However, Mahayana tradition, as it spread through north and east Asia, was more willing and able to incorporate elements from the cultures it encountered into its own doctrines and practices than was the Theravada tradition. One reason for this was the tendency of Theravada tradition to define itself in a more rigid doctrinal fashion than Mahayana tradition. Consequently, the Mahayana Buddhist Way created numerous variations and occasionally radical modifications of the basic Theravada system of practice very early in its historical development. Three distinctive Mahayana teachings played an especially important role in these modifications.

The first is the Mahayana conception of the Bodhisattva, who is not merely a being striving for enlightenment--the Theravada interpretation--but a being on the verge of attaining final enlightenment. Rather than selfishly entering into this state, a Bodhisattva deliberately chooses to reincarnate himself endlessly until he has brought every sentient being to enlightenment. Accordingly, the Bodhisattva, who also personifies for Mahayana devotees what Buddhists mean by "compassion" (*karuṇā*), evolved into the Mahayana paradigm of spirituality, at times even superseding the Buddha as an object of veneration. The final Mahayana addition to the Buddhist Way was Nāgārjuna's revolutionary declaration that "*nirvana* equals *saṃsāra*", meaning there exists not one ontological iota of difference between either state of existence.[28]

The implications of these doctrinal extensions of the Buddhist Way for the evolution of Mahayana

practice were as varied as they were immense. The ancient Theravada language of world alienation, detachment, enlightenment, and final *nirvāṇa* was maintained.
However, the Mahayana conception of the Bodhisattva
brought the life of inner meditational discipline out
of the monastery, resulting in a blurring of the older
separations between the monastic *saṃgha* and the laity.
Not that monasteries ceased existing in Mahayana Buddhist countries or that meditation was no longer emphasized in Mahayana teaching and practice. But monastic
life was joined to life in the secular world in a way
unheard of in Theravada conceptions of Buddhist practice, so that even involvement in the affairs of secular existence itself could be appropriated by both
monks and laity, as well as by male and female
followers of the Buddhist Way, as instruments of religious practice and progress. The scriptural culmination of this transformation of Buddhist practice is a
famous Mahayana sutra entitled the *Vimalakirti Sūtra*.
In this text, the layman Vimalakirti is pictured as superior in understanding and wisdom to even Mañjuśrī,
the Bodhisattva of wisdom who stands beside Amida Buddha in the latter's Pure Land. Symbolized by Vimalakirti, the Mahayana ideal of becoming a Bodhisattva
replaced emotional alienation from the world, the result and goal of the Theravada *arhat's* practice, with
disinterested involvement in the world.

One of the more profound effects the doctrine
of the innate Buddha Nature within all things and
events had upon Buddhist practice was the way in which
it encouraged an expanded sense of intimacy with the

process of life in the phenomenal world. For example, unlike Theravada practice, Mahayana systems of meditation generally instruct the seeker to single mindedly concentrate on the impermanence and suffering of the self's existence because doing so only deepens the mechanisms of egoistic attachment. Rather, the seeker must experience his own mind, cured of such egocentric care for personal enlightenment, as the universal Buddha Mind itself of which all existence, enlightened or ignorant, is a limited expression. This enlightened discovery of unity with all existence is the truth discovered with the attainment of *nirvāṇa*.

Finally, Nāgārjuna's teaching of the ontological unity of *nirvāṇa* and *saṃsāra* extended and deepened the "monistic" implications of Mahayana teachings and practice, mostly by undercutting the dualism of the Theravada distinctions between what most Western interpreters tend to label sacred and profane, religious and secular, and religious professionals and laity. Thereby, Theravada techniques of meditation were transformed into methods for experiencing the innate Buddha Nature in all things and events and the unity of samsaric existence and enlightened existence. As a byproduct, spontaneity and integration became the defining characteristics of true progress towards *nirvāṇa*. Harmoniously interacting with others in what Westerners sometimes call "community," the meditator experiences detachment from all transitory elements and forms of existence in a sort of "being in the world but not of the world" involvement.

In all probability, the Zen tradition (Chinese, *ch'an;* Sanskrit, *dhyāna*) most simply and coherently expresses these distinctively Mahayana variations in its practice. As a specifically meditative discipline--the word "Zen" means "meditation"--Zen conceives itself as a direct "wordless" continuation of the Buddha's own enlightenment shorn of the impediments of doctrine, ritualism, and scripture. How much truth there is to this self-evaluation is debatable, but Zen's two standard forms of practice, *kōan* ("public document") meditation and *zazen* ("seated meditation") are designed to break through all intellectual and emotional attachments so that the universal Buddha Nature that is simultaneously the seeker's own "true nature" may be brought into explicit focal awareness.

At the opposite extreme of Mahayana meditative practice, the Tibetan schools have created extremely complex forms of practice found nowhere else in the Buddhist world. Pre-Buddhist Tibetan Bon elements (primarily shamanistic in structure) were readily incorporated into the Buddhist Way, resulting in highly diversified patterns of ritual, devotional practices, and meditative styles. A "cover word" for Tibetan practice is "tantraism."[29] Buddhist *tantra* is the logical continuation of the doctrine of the unity of *nirvāṇa* and *saṃsāra*, a doctrine most completely articulated in Tibetan Buddhist philosophy. Consequently, Tibetan practice makes extensive use of sexual symbolism and other bodily functions to unite all elements of the seeker's mind-body organism with the creative energy (*kuṇḍalini*) of the whole universe. Tantric meditational practices are also noted for their extensive use of ritual chanting (*mantra*) and symbolic diagrams (*mandala*) employed as focal objects of concentrated attention in order to produce visualizations in the seeker's mind of various Buddhas, Bodhisattvas, and other beings along with their individual Buddha realms.

CONCLUDING OBSERVATIONS

The most ancient forms of Buddhist practice assumed that only the monastic environment was fully capable of sustaining successful practice, "successful" meaning practice leading the seeker to the achievement of enlightenment. In fact, the Buddhist Way originated as a monastic Way--perhaps the first in Indian religious history--growing and evolving around the person and practices of the Buddha himself. The earliest use of the word "*samgha*," in other words, denoted only the *male* monastic followers of the Buddha's Dharma, not the community of male and female lay supporters. In various guises, monastic self-discipline continues to provide the model governing Buddhist practice, primarily because meditation continues its role as, ultimately, the sole practice capable of leading the seeker to enlightenment.

But for lay Buddhists, practice mostly means the pious performance of good deeds in the hope of accumulating positive karmic merit so as to achieve more positive future rebirths, even rebirth in which the individual is endowed with sufficient mental, physical, and moral capacity necessary for undertaking the rigors of monastic practice. The dual structure of Buddhist practice--one form for the monastic community and one for the laity--is most consistently maintained by Theravada tradition. It also remains the usual approach of Mahayana practice as well, in spite of the more active religious role allocated to the lay Buddhist, the acknowledgement of the possibility that lay Buddhists are fully capable of achieving enlightenment as lay persons, and the more varied forms of practice available to the Mahayana Buddhist seeker.

However, during the past one hundred years, Theravada monks and Mahayana monks and nuns have become more actively involved in the life and concerns of the laity. Much of their practice is now devoted to community service in the fields of education, social work, medicine, and politics. In every region of the contemporary Buddhist world, practice for growing numbers of sensitive monks and nuns includes concerned social activism in such international and domestic issues as war and peace, ecology, human rights, and the economic redistribution of the world's wealth and natural resources. Clearly, the normal Western picture of an inert order of religious professionals physically and mentally isolated from the lives and concerns of lay persons, and indeed parasitically living off the labor of the laity, is at best superficial and at worst simply untrue.[30] Most Theravada and Mahayana Buddhists do not live in a monastic environment isolated from secular society; most do not even meditate, and "practice" normally means doing good works coupled with devotional reverence to past and present sages, Buddhas, and Bodhisattvas in the hope of accumulating positive karmic

merit leading to more positive future rebirths. Practice in the sense of intensive meditation remains, as
it has always been, the vocation of a select few monks
and, in the Mahayana tradition, nuns and lay persons.

On the other hand, contemporary meditation
trends indicate a general tendency toward adaptation
and simplification of method in order to widen the appeal of meditational practice to lay persons.[31] Part
of the motivation behind the current movement towards
lay meditation is the concern of many Buddhist teachers
to "renew" the Buddhist Way in order to provide more
resources for increasing the relevance of Buddhist
faith for personal life in a modernizing secular world.
In both Theravada and Mahayana regions of the Buddhist
world, lively lay interest and participation in meditation are presently an authentic part of "lay practice." And while it remains true that much of this impetus originated in lay demands placed upon the monastic Samgha, even the most conservative Theravada monks
are increasingly participating in this process of internal renewal.[32] The most noteworthy examples of this
trend include teaching Theravada lay men and women the
techniques of insight meditation, lay practice of several styles of Zen meditation, and Tibetan tantric meditation, which is becoming increasingly popular among
Western seekers of the Buddhist Way.

There continues to remain, however, one apparent exception to the generic pattern of Buddhist
practice I have described: the Jōdo Shinshū ("True
Pure Land School") tradition centering upon Shinran's
interpretation of the Buddhist Way of "salvation by

faith through other-power alone." For all forms of the Buddhist Way other than Jōdo Shinshū, "practice" means the discipline of meditation grounded in ethical perfection of the seeker according to the five precepts and guided by the doctrinal summations of the Buddhist world view. The goal of practice is the achievement of enlightenment, the assumption being that the seeker is *not* enlightened and must *do* something to achieve it. There are also many varieties of practice in the Buddhist Way, but they are all forms of upāya or "skillful means" of achieving enlightenment.

Shinran's understanding of Buddhist faith, however, was centered on his own experiences of frustrating failure as the practices he undertook as a Tendai (Chinese, T'ian-t'ai) monk did not achieve for him what he expected to achieve.[33] Because of these experiences, Shinran concluded none of the traditional forms of Buddhist practice can help an individual experience enlightenment during the present cycle of world history known as the Latter Days of the Dharma. The traditional practices of the Buddhist Way all demand the "self-powered" discipline of the seeker to be effective. But because the capacities and endowments of all persons born into this age are weakened and corrupted, no person can obtain enlightenment through any sort of self-powered practice. Accordingly, in Shinran's opinion, "practice" can only mean placing "faith" as trust in Amida Buddha's other-powered efforts to cause our rebirth into his Pure Land as enlightened Buddhas.

Surely, Shinran's Pure Land teachings have transformed the generic pattern of Buddhist practice in a direction unprecedented in any previous form of the Buddhist Way. According to him, meditation, chanting *mantra,* ritual action, devotional practices, ethical self-discipline, or scholarly study of the sutras achieve absolutely nothing for the seeker. On the other hand, the person to whom Amida Buddha grants trusting faith possesses everything necessary for "salvation"--Amida Buddha's totally nonjudgmental compassion. Consequently all religious action--all forms of "practice"--can only be expressions of gratitude for the unmerited gift of salvation, "salvation" conceived as rebirth into Amida Buddha's Pure Land as an enlightened Buddha. "To practice faith" meant for Shinran, in other words, doing works of compassion on behalf of other sentient beings, just as Amida Buddha has expressed compassion to the person of faith, as an act of gratitude for having received this unmerited gift. Because Shinran did not conceive practice as an instrumental means for achieving something an individual lacks, he renounced his monastic vows, entered secular life as a layman, married an ex-nun, brought up six children, and was generally active in the world in much the same way, and for many of the same reasons, Protestant minsters remain actively involved in the secular world.

Even though contemporary Jōdo Shinshū teaching continues to follow Shinran's conception of Buddhist practice, there are also currently moves among Pure Land teachers to reinterpret his emphasis upon the other-power of Amida Buddha in order to place them in closer conformity with the traditional Buddhist emphasis on disciplined self-effort.[34]   Thus much of Shinran's original emphasis upon Amida Buddha's prior efforts on humanity's behalf in effecting the salvation of all sentient beings through his other-power is now deemphasized in contemporary Pure Land doctrinal formulations and in the writings of non-Pure Land Buddhists.[35]   As a consequence, Pure Land Buddhists are now encouraged to undertake the self-powered practice of meditation and ethical self-discipline, although monasticism continues to be nonexistent in this form of the Buddhist Way.

But neither "practice" nor "faith" can be, in fact, so sharply distinguished in any form of the Buddhist Way.   The Pure Land and the Zen traditions most conveniently illustrate, at least for most Westerners, the classical interrelationship between faith and practice in the Buddhist Way, even though their doctrinal interpretations of the Dharma represent opposite extremes of Buddhist selfunderstanding.   To the unenlightened seeker, the devices of practice may indeed appear instrumentally distinguished from the goal of practice.   In this view, "practice" is an activity the seeker undertakes to achieve enlightenment.   This sort of dualism is, however, quite simplistic in view of the Buddhist doctrine of the dependent co-origination of all things and events constituting existence at any moment of existence.   For once enlightenment is achieved by whatever specific meditational techniques, the seeker concurrently discovers how deeply "practice" continues being part of the experience of enlightenment itself; one discovers nothing is achieved that one did not already possess at the beginning of one's practice of the Buddhist Way. Or as the Buddha supposedly described his own experience when asked what it was he achieved when he attained enlightenment: "I obtained not the least thing from unexcelled complete awakening. And for this reason it is called 'unexcelled complete awakening.'"[36] Faith and practice are unified by the practice of enlightenment. Master Dogen expressed it this way:

> The Dharma is amply present in every person, but unless one practices, it is not manifested; unless there is realization, it is not attained. . . .As it is already realization in practice, realization is endless: as it is practice in realization, practice is beginningless.[37]

NOTES

[1]This aspect of Buddhist Christian encounter is more heavily emphasized by Roman Catholic scholars than by Protestant participants in the dialogue, although Protestant concern for "practice" is not entirely absent. Protestant thinkers, however, have tended to be more concerned with Buddhist doctrinal understanding as a means of reformulating Christian theological reflection in the hope of more meaningfully articulating Christian faith in a religiously plural world. Roman Catholic discussions have tended to focus on Buddhist techniques of meditation as a means of renewing the contemplative traditions emphasized in the Church's monastic communities. Cf. Aelred Graham, *Zen Catholicism: A Suggestion* (London: Collins, 1964); Thomas Merton, *Mystics and Zen Masters* (New York: Dell, 1967); William Johnston, *The Still Point: Reflections on Zen and Christian Mysticism* (New York: Fordham University Press, 1970); and Joseph J. Spae, *Buddhist-Christian Empathy* (Tokyo: Oriens Institute for Religious Research, 1980). I shall return to this observation with a more completely developed discussion in the conclusion of Chapter 6.

[2]My understanding of the relation between practice and theory (Latin, *praxis* and *theoria*) is greatly indebted to John C. Maraldo's essay, "The Hermeneutics of Practice in Dogen and Francis of Assisi," *The Eastern Buddhist*, 19, 2 (Autumn 1981): 22-45. For a more detailed analysis of the theory-practice polarity from the time of Aristotle on, especially in Roman Catholic monastic theology, see Nicholas Lobkowicz, *Theory and Practice* (South Bend. Ind.: University of Notre Dame Press, 1967).

[3]Ibid., 25.

[4]See Michael Polanyi, *Personal Knowledge* (New York: Harper and Row, 1958), 49-65.

[5]See Agehananda Bharati, *The Light at the Center: Context and Pretext of Modern Mysticism* (Santa Barbara: Ross-Erickson, 1976), chap. 3.

[6]William James, *The Varieties of Religious Experience* (New York: New American Library, 1958), 292-328.

[7]Cf. Nalinaksha Dutt, *Early Monastic Buddhism* (Calcutta: Calcutta Oriental Book Agency, 1960), 133-147, and Walpola Rahula, *What the Buddha Taught* (New York: Grove Press, 1962). Also see *Digha Nikaya*, 2, 64 ff.

[8]See Bhikshu Sangharakshita, *A Survey of Buddhism* (Bangalore: Indian Institute of World Culture, 1966), 100-111. For the implications of the theory of the five *skandha* for the Buddhist understanding of human nature, see the chariot metaphor in *Milindapañha*, pp. 25 ff.

[9]This literature is mainly concerned with ordering and elaborating the meaning of the Buddhist world view, especially as related to the mental states encountered during the practice of meditation. The *Abidhamma-pitaka* therefore instructs the seeker in specific meditational techniques as well as provides guidance in the search for certain types of experiences regarded as positive signs of progress toward enlightenment. See Richard H. Robinson and Willard L. Johnson, *The Buddhist Religion, A Historical Introduction* (Encino, Ca.: Dickenson Publishing Co., 1977), 65-66.

[10]I am aware that Buddhist teachers are not particularly comfortable with the Western notion of metaphysics since this word connotes "speculation" *about* reality apart from personal experience of reality. The Buddhist view is that speculative systems of thought are too often objects of clinging that more often than not mislead the seeker from the reality being sought. In other words, philosophical systems and definitions of the nature of reality are more stable and easier to comprehend than the realities of change and becoming. But according to the Buddhist understanding, attachment to *anything* is a hindrance to enlightenment, including attachment to systems of philosophy and religious doctrines. Consequently, when I use the word "metaphysics" in reference to Buddhist thought I merely mean to indicate the vision of reality, "the way things really are," in the Buddhist world view as distinct from what enlightened persons *want* or speculatively believe things to be.

[11]The following exposition is indebted to Junjiro Takakusu, *Essentials of Buddhist Philosophy* (Honolulu: University of Hawaii Press, 1956), chap. 3. Also see Floyd H. Ross, *The Meaning of Life in Hinduism and Buddhism* (London: Routledge and Kegan Paul, 1952), 98-106. For references in the Buddhist *suttas*, see *Milindapanha* 71, 16; *Anguttara-nikāya* 3, 33; and *Samyutta-nikāya*, 2, 95.

[12]I have in mind Paul Tillich's analysis of "existential anxiety" in his *The Courage to Be* (New Haven: Yale University Press, 1952), 32-63. Tillich seems to have written of a universal human experience that is, in my opinion, a striking parallel to what Buddhist teaching means by *duhkha*.

[13]*Samyutta-nikāya* 5, 421 ff.

[14]Ibid.

[15]*Dhammapada* 1,5 and *Sutta Nipata* 1, 8.

[16]See *Majjhima-nikāya* 1. 40 ff.

[17]*Majjhima-nikāya* 1. 349-352, and *Vinaya-piṭaka* 3, 3-6.

[18]Winston L. King, *Theravada Meditation, The Buddhist Transformation of Yoga* (University Park: Pennsylvania State University Press, 1980), 16.

[19]Buddhaghosa, *Visuddhimagga* [Path of Purification], ed. Henry Clark Warren (Cambridge: Harvard University Press, 1950), chap. 14, sections 3-9, pp. 369-370.

[20]Narada Thera, "The Buddhist Doctrine of Kamma and Rebirth," *Life of the Dhamma,* 3 (June 1953): 45. Quoted by Winston L. King, *In the Hope of Nibbana* (La Salle, Ill.: Open Court, 1964), 17.

[21]There are currently no orders of nuns, with the possible exception of Burma, in Theravada Buddhist countries. However, at one time there were numerous communities of nuns. The higher number of major and minor rules governing their lives reflects the patriarchal attitude that feminine nature is a hindrance to

achieving enlightenment and requires more disciplining than masculine nature. For an excellent study of Buddhist attitudes towards women, see Diana Y. Paul, *Women in Buddhism: Portraits of the Feminine in Mahayana Buddhist Tradition.* (Berkeley: Asian Humanities Press, 1978).

[22]See Buddhaghoṣa, *Visuddhimagga,* chap. 9, 78.

[23]Ibid., 89-90.

[24]Ibid., 85.

[25]Ibid., 88.

[26]This point has been strongly emphasized by Winston L. King, *Theravada Meditation,* especially chapts. 4-6. From the Pāli Canon, see *Mahasatipatthanasutta* [Discourse on Great Mindfulness] in *nikaya,* 9, 2, 217-36.

[27]From *Shōbōgenzō* [Eye and Treasure of the True Dharma], quoted by Hee-jin Kim, *Dōgen Kigen--Mystical Realist* (Tucson: The Association for Asian Studies, 1965), 254. I shall treat the doctrine of the Buddha Nature in all things and the doctrine that *nirvana* equals *saṃsāra* more fully throughout subsequent chapters.

[28]The best treatment of Nāgārjuna's interpretation of the Buddhist way is still Frederic J.Streng's *Emptiness, A Study in Religious Meaning* (Nashville: Abingdon Press, 1967).

[29]Etymologically, the word *tantra* means any kind of "elaboration" (if derived from the root *tan,* "to spread"), or it may mean "knowledge" (if derived from the root *tantri*). *Tantra* is essentially any kind of expanded literature or knowledge; thus Buddhist *tantra* is "expanded knowledge" of methods to achieve enlightenment usually associated with the use of the body in ways no other Buddhist schools find suitable because they usually entail compromise with the standard Buddhist moral precepts. *Tantra* also carries the connotation of "esoteric" or secret teaching. See S. B. Dasgupta, *An Introduction to Tantric Buddhism* (Calcutta: University of Calcutta Press, 1958), 2-3.

[30]Although he is a journalist and not a Buddhist scholar, this point has been clearly made by Jerrold Schecter, *The New Face of Buddha* (Tokyo: John Weatherhill, 1967).

[31]See King, *Theravada Meditation*, 116-152 and Joseph J. Spae, *Buddhist-Christian Empathy*, 130-176.

[32]See Donald K.Swearer, "Reformist Buddhism in Thailand: The Case of Bhikkhu Buddhadasa," *Dialogue*, 8 (January-December): 27-42.

[33]For an excellent biographical study of Shinran's life and his sense of failure as he practiced monastic discipline for over twenty years, see Alfred Bloom, "The Life of Shinran Shōnin: The Journey to Self-Acceptance," *Numan*, 12 (1968): 1-62.

[34]D. T. Suzuki was perhaps best known for this. He, like most Zen Buddhists, tended to read Zen principles and teachings *into* Shinran's understanding of faith precisely because Shinran's doctrine of faith was so unusual within the context of traditional Buddhist doctrine. See Suzuki's *Shin Buddhism* (New York: Harper and Row, 1970). Also see my essay. "The Zen Critique of Pure Land Buddhism." *Journal of the American Academy of Religion*, 41, (June 1973): 184-200.

[35]For example, see Shinji Takuwa (trans.), *Perfect Freedom in Buddhism* (New York: Grove Press, 1960), p. 48.
[36]*Vajracchedikā* [Diamond Cutter] *Sūtra,* quoted by D. T. Suzuki, *Manual of Zen Buddhism* (New York: Grove Press, 1960), 48

[37]*Bendowa*, quoted by Maraldo, "The Hermeneutics of Practice in Dogen and Francis of Assisi," 29.

CHAPTER SIX
Faith as Practice: The Christian Way

Do not store up for yourselves treasure on earth, where it grows rusty and moth-eaten, and thieves break in and steal it. Store up treasure in heaven, where is no moth and no rust to spoil it, no thieves to break in and steal it. For where your treasure is, there will be your heart also.

Matthew 6:19-21, *New English Bible*

My brothers, what use is it for a man to say he has faith when he does nothing to show it? Can that faith save him? Suppose a brother or a sister is in rags with not enough food for a day, and one of you says, "Good luck to you, keep yourselves warm, and have plenty to eat," but does nothing to supply their bodily needs, what is the good of that? So with faith; if it does not lead to action, it is itself a lifeless thing.

James 2:14-17, *New English Bible*

THE HEART OF CHRISTIAN PRACTICE

As in the Buddhist Way, so also in the Christian Way: faith and practice are not two different things, but rather bipolar dimensions of one reality constituted by religious faith, as *yin* in polar opposition to *yang* constitutes the one reality the Chinese designated as the Tao ["the Way"]. Not that Christians have never dualistically separated faith, usually conceived as a set of propositional assertions in which we must "believe," from the practice of faith, conceived as a series of instrumental actions for achieving whatever we are supposed to "believe in." But dualistically separating faith from practice distorts the biblical images of their interdependence, as well as misrepresents the theological traditions that have been historically normative for the major body of Christian self-understanding.

The earliest scriptural passages alluding to the interrelation between Christian faith and practice in comparison to other religious Ways--in this case the Jewish Way of the first century of Christian history-- occur in the epistles of Saint Paul. Of these, his letter to the Romans is the primary source of the normative assumptions guiding Christian struggle to understand what it means to practice whatever is distinctively "Christian" about Christian faith. The following verses are especially pertinent:

> But now, quite independently of law, God's justice has been brought to light. The Law and prophets both bear witness to it: it is God's way of righting wrong, effective through faith in Christ for all who have faith--all without distinction. For all alike have sinned, and are deprived of the divine splendor, and all are justified by God's free grace alone, through his act of liberation in the person of Christ Jesus. . . What room then is there left for human pride? It is excluded. And on what principle? The keeping of the law would not exclude it, but faith does. For our argument is that a man is justified by faith quite apart from success in keeping the law. (Romans 3:21-28, *New English Bible*)

This passage[1] is historically the single most important scriptural source for the Pauline doctrine of "justification by faith through grace alone," a doctrine that is not only the axiomatic starting point of distinctively Protestant theology, but that is also an equally important tenet in contemporary Roman Catholic thought. Paul's teaching of justification by faith through grace transformed the primitive Christian community from a minor sectarian movement within the Jewish Way into a universal religious Way grounded within, yet independent of, the Jewish Way.[2] And since roughly one-third of the New Testament was written by Paul, while approximately another third of the New Testament, including much of the material in the synoptic gospels, was influenced by his theology, Paul's understanding of faith is the theological key unlocking the teachings around which the Christian Way has revolved. There are several elements in this key.

First, faith is not an act of the human will to believe whereby an individual decides to accept or reject God's plan for the salvation of humanity accomplished through the life, death, and resurrection of Jesus as the Christ. Salvation--meaning for Paul, release from death as sin's penalty coupled with eternal life with God--does not depend upon anything an individual does or accomplishes, including living according to particular ethical and ritual systems, participating in any sacred institution, or assenting to a set of doctrinal propositions regarded as "orthodox." Understood from this perspective, "faith" can only mean "trust" in God's prior action on humanity's behalf through the life, death, and resurrection of Jesus as the Christ, along with nontrust in any human contrivance meant to establish an individual's positive relationship with God. But even more, Paul believed the very ability to trust God's actions in the Christ event was itself totally dependent upon God's prior action, that is, God's "grace." Thus, anyone "having" faith does not simply "decide" to trust God because the stories about Jesus "make sense." Faith is a gift, never merely a human "work" or attitude created by human self-effort.

The mainline Christian traditions have remained loyal to the Pauline conception of faith. "Christian faith" names a trusting response to God's "work" of salvation through Jesus as the Christ, a "work" through which God lovingly relates to sinful human beings, none of whom deserves love. Or, in the language of Paul's writings, God "justifies" persons to whom he gives faith by regarding them as if they were really not sinful and deserving of death, as the penalty for sin, just as a judge in a Roman civil court of law during Paul's day could judge a criminal guilty of a crime and then declare that individual free from having to pay the legal penalty. In this way, a legally guilty criminal could be treated as if he or she were really not guilty. Trusting God's act of "justification" is "faith." But even the ability to trust God's justifying action is created in an individual by God's grace.

Second, because Christ's death has paid the penalty for sin--death for all humanity--anyone to whom faith has been graciously given is "free" in the most important meaning of this word. That is, faithful persons do not have to earn anything from God. Accordingly, Christians are free from the restraints of all religious and secular legalisms.

Finally, Christian freedom from all forms of legalistic behavior in order to please God did not mean that Paul believed human behavior possessed no intrinsic value. While it is true the heart of Paul's "gospel" is that salvation is a gift unrelated to anything anyone does to earn it, this does not mean human action has no religious or ethical consequences. Faith is never an unethical event. Accordingly, Paul devoted most of his letters to the question of *how* Christians *ought* to practice faith in human relationships. Simply because no human being establishes a saving relationship with God through any form of self-effort does not mean individuals are free to be immoral, unintelligent, uncaring, or socially irresponsible. Antinomian behavior is as much a sign of unfaith as its opposite--attempting to earn God's love through self-righteous behavior. Whatever faithful persons do, it is always an expression of gratitude for what God has first given to them through Christ. Thus, aiding the poor, praying, undergoing baptism, partaking of the Lord's Supper, studying the scriptures, practicing ethical self-discipline--all religious action--are included in the "practice" of Christian faith. But practice earns nothing for Christians that they do not already possess. In short, the practice of faith is completely without merit.

Viewed from this perspective, Christian practice is shorn of all instrumental meanings. "Practice"

and "faith" name two polar opposites unified by one re-
ality--trust in God as created by God's self-disclosure
through the life, death, and resurrection of Jesus as
the Christ. Christian faith *is* Christian practice, for
one cannot exist apart from the other.

To illustrate the generic relationship between Christian faith and practice I shall concentrate
on what I call "ethical practice," "theological practice," and "devotional practice." I shall also include
some brief observations relative to Christian monasticism for purposes of comparison with Buddhist monastic
practice. While the foregoing discussion does not pre-
tend to be an exhaustive analysis of all forms of
Christian practice, it does aim to illustrate the guiding assumption of the remainder of this chapter--one
provided by the author of the Epistle of James. His
understanding of Christian faith was not different from
Paul's. He wanted to combat antinomian misrepresenta-
tions of the Pauline teaching of the interrelation between faith and practice:[3] faith which "does not lead
to action" is "in itself a lifeless thing." (2:17)

ETHICAL PRACTICE

In common with the major theological traditions of the Jewish Way, as well as with those of Islam, the Christian Way has always stressed that the
life of faith is also a life of communal service to
others. Christian practice always necessitates personal and communal struggle against all the dehumaniz-
ing and debilitating forces operating in finite exis-

tence which hinder or destroy personal growth and creativity.

In short, "practice" in the Christian Way always means ethical involvement in the concrete affairs
of daily existence in the secular world. The picture of
Jesus of Nazareth preserved in the traditions in the
synoptic gospels remains the model for Christian ethical practice. This picture is aptly described by Edward Schillebeeck:

> In the care he shows for man and his record
> of suffering, for publicans and sinners, for
> the poor, the crippled and the blind, for the
> oppressed and for the people torn apart by
> "evil spirits," Jesus is a living parable of
> God: that is how God cares for man. In the
> story of Jesus is told the story of God. It
> is God himself who opens up to us in the
> story that is the life of Jesus a new world,
> a different experience of reality and way of
> living: thus the New Testament story *about*
> Jesus forms the response of the first Chris-
> tians to the story *of* Jesus himself.[4]

According to the biblical picture, the foundation of Jesus' ethical practice towards others was
love, the Greek word for which is *agapē*. The classical
Greek philosophical tradition distinguished *agapē* from
eros (love expressed as attachment and desire to control the object of love for one's own well being) and
philos (dispassionate "brotherly love" of the sort expressed between social equals who have nothing to lose
in their relationship because there would be no rela-

tionship if there were anything to lose). *Agapē* is "disinterested" love, not, be it noted, "uninterested" love, and might be best rendered into modern English as "love with no strings attached." *Agapē* is non-ego-involved love, expressed through concrete actions on behalf of another person's welfare, according to what that person really needs, which in the last analysis, may not be what that person necessarily desires or thinks he or she needs. Individuals loving in the sense of *agapē* care for the total welfare of others regardless of any rewards or benefits, or, indeed, lack of rewards or benefits. For example, giving aid to the poor *because* it makes the giver feel righteous is not an act of *agapē*. It is, however, an act of egoism because it only expresses concern about the giver's well-being and psychological comfort, even though a poor person might receive needed charity in the process.

Nor is legalistically obeying the objective demands and rules of a moral code or an ethical system an act of agapeic love. In fact, systems of law, more often than not, prevent the free exercise of acts of care for the needy, the poor, and those socially and religiously unacceptable persons always oppressed by any legal system. As Alfred North Whitehead once observed, love in the sense of *agapē* is "always a little oblivious to morals,"[5] as well as to social and ritual taboos, religious systems, and institutionalized conventions. Practicing faith through loving others with no strings attached may even require the breaking of specific laws, taboos, and social mores. Here again, Jesus of Nazareth is the biblical model for Christian practice, as illustrated by the following account from the Gospel of Matthew. When asked by a group of Pharisees which of the commandments of the Jewish Law ["Torah" or "instructions"] is the most important, Jesus reportedly summarized faithful religious practice as follows:

"Love the Lord your God with all your heart, with all your soul, with all your mind." That is the greatest commandment. It comes first. The second is like it: "Love your neighbor as yourself." Everything in the Law and the prophets hangs on these two commandments. (Matthew 22: 37-40)

Jesus' point was that God's love for all human beings, like rain, "falls on the just and the unjust." No human being has satisfied God's desire that we should live justly and exercise caring concern for one another's welfare. But Jesus believed God especially loves those persons who do not necessarily deserve love, at least as defined by traditional interpretations of Jewish Law during his day. Thus, as God's relation to the world is primarily expressed through the persuasive power of love, rather than through simple compulsion, so should an individual's faith issue in similar caring concern for others, "with no strings attached." Or as parents love their children, although no child needs to or can do anything to earn their loving care, so should faithful persons relate themselves to the world.

But *saying* that Christian practice is essentially and always the disinterested practice of love through concrete acts of caring concern of others, and determining *how* disinterested love ought to be practiced in the real world of complex social-ethical relationships, are two different matters. Accordingly, the discipline of ethics has been an ancient and honored topic of theological reflection in Christian history, beginning with the earliest writings of the New Testament, the epistles of Paul. No tradition of Christian theology and no major Christian theologian has ever denied that Christian practice must always be the practice of love. But how love should be transformed into distinctively Christian practice, the model for which has always remained the biblical pictures of the life of Jesus, has engendered a great amount of debate. Indeed, the actual practice of love has proven to be no simple matter.

"Ethics" is a rather abstract word possessing many nuanced meanings. It can, for example, refer to the study of the standards of moral conduct and the practical application of these standards to the concrete situations we face in the conduct of our daily lives. It can also refer to the ethical teachings of particular philosophers, religious thinkers, religious groups, or professions, as in "Aristotle's ethics," "Luther's ethics," "Buddhist ethics," or "medical ethics." Finally, ethics is closely related to, but not identical with, "morality." Thus "Aristotle's ethics," for instance, is not exactly synonymous with "Aristotle's morals," because the latter conveys something about his personal behavior and conduct that ideally ought to be, but might not be, an expression of his "ethics."

One common procedure of philosophical and theological ethical reflection employs a functional distinction between "first order" and "second order" types of judgments. I shall also follow this procedure. By "first order" I mean the rules of judgment, standards, principles, and conduct, both actual and ideal, of a particular group, whether this group be professional, national, or religious. First order ethical judgments are also similar to the term "morality," as well as the terms "ethical code" or "moral code." In much contemporary Western ethical reflection, morality is a subject of first order ethical principles, with the emphasis placed upon the standards, principles, and regulations of such matters as sexual conduct, basic honesty, justice, and general mores. First order ethical judgments are also concerned with "what ought to be," even when the meanings of first order judgments are not entirely fixed. For example, phrases such as "the manner and morals of. . ." simply denote general customs and habits.

"Second order" ethical judgments are conclusions about the meaning of first order ethical judgments. Second order ethical judgments have traditionally been regarded as synonymous with Christian moral philosophy and moral theology. When, for example, the ethics of the Christian Way or the Buddhist Way are subjected to critical analysis and comparison, we are engaged in second order ethical reflection. In other words, second order ethical judgments are concerned primarily with "what is," not with what "ought to be."

I am not qualified to discuss the history of first and second order ethical reflection in Christian tradition. Such an undertaking would serve no purpose anyway, given the special concern of this study. However, the central role of ethical practice in the Christian Way can be easily illustrated by the major types of contemporary first and second order Christian ethical teaching. Each type represents an answer to the question, *how* should Christians practice love within the give-and-take of social interrelationships. It should be born in mind, moreover, that while all of the types of ethical teaching I describe are contemporary, this does not mean they are "new" in the sense of never having been thought of before in Christian history. Some of the specific problems confronting contemporary Christians in the modern secular world are new, however, and this should add greater clarification to the special ethical character of Christian practice.

A central feature of first order ethical judgments is concern for establishing rationales justifying ethical decisions. One example of this procedure is often referred to as "ends oriented" or "teleological" theory because special emphasis is placed upon the ends or goals for which an action is undertaken. Joseph Fletcher is perhaps the leading exponent of this type of ethical theory.[6]

Fletcher's ethical philosophy is explicitly utilitarian: the greatest degree of happiness for the greatest number of persons should always guide Christian moral practice, even should this require breaking social and institutional standards and laws. But as a Christian thinker Fletcher interprets the utilitarian principle in light of the New Testament's norm of *agape*. Thus, in seeking the greatest degree of happiness for the greatest number of persons, Christians should imitate Jesus' practice of expressing radically loving their neighbors. Or employing Fletcher's words, the Christian should seek the "greatest amount of neighbor welfare for the largest number of neighbors possible." Fletcher regards this standard as the essential element of what he calls "agapeic calculus."

Fletcher's four most widely known examples of agapeic calculus are: (1) a physician forced to decide whether to save a mother of three children or a skid row drunk both ought to decide to save the mother because the welfare of more individuals will be served; (2) at the close of World War II a German woman, imprisoned by the Russians, was morally justified in committing adultery with a guard in order to become pregnant, secure her release from prison, and be restored to her husband and children; (3) President Truman's decision to drop the atomic bomb on the Japanese cities of Hiroshima and Nagasaki was morally justifiable on the grounds of agapeic calculus because the direct taking of innocent life is permissible if it prevents the death of a greater number of persons; (4) the Christian should favor the rights of women to seek and obtain abortions on demand, not only for the sake of the prospective mother's physical and mental health, but also for her self-respect and happiness since "no un-

wanted or unintended baby should ever be born."
Agapeic calculus, according to Fletcher's point of
view, points to the fact that the mother's welfare out-
weighs that of an unwanted fetus.

First order ethical decisions sometimes emphasize particular features of a situation that are determined to be the decisive indicators of the most
morally responsible action to undertake, regardless of
the consequences. This type of ethical principle is
sometimes called "duty-oriented" or "deontological
ethics." Among contemporary Christian theologians,
Paul Ramsey is the best known example of this approach.[7]

In numerous books and articles, Ramsey has
sharply criticized the ends-oriented conclusions of
Fletcher and others. The force of his criticism lies
in his assumption that there are, in principle, no
fixed restrictions on Christian ethical practice because the norm governing the life of Christian faith
must always be *agape*, as exemplified in the New Testament's stories of Jesus' interaction with his contempo-
raries. Among the most important of these restrictive
principles is what he calls "the practice of nonmaleficence," according to which no Christian may ever deliberately cause direct injury to an innocent person in
order to accomplish some presupposed "greater good."
Practicing Christian faith in any other way means
treating persons as dispensable means for achieving
other ends, which in Ramsey's judgment is absolutely
contrary to the Christian norm of New Testament love.
No person should ever be used as an instrumental means

for achieving a supposed greater good, which Ramsey believes is the primary danger of ends-oriented ethical
theories.

Ramsey cites Truman's decision to employ the
atomic bomb against the civilian populations of Hiroshima and Nagasaki as an illustration deontological
ethics. His conclusions, of course, are diametrically
opposed to Fletcher's. Truman's stated rationale for
dropping the atomic bomb--"shortening the war" and
"saving lives," particularly the lives of American military personal who would have been involved in invading
the Japanese islands had the atomic bomb not been
dropped--was to Ramsey's merely another way of needlessly injuring innocent persons. According to his
principle of nonmaleficence, Truman's decision was ethically repugnant.

It is not that Ramsey is a pacifist. He believes some armed conflicts are unavoidable and can be
justified on Christian principles, including his principle of nonmaleficence. But even in these circumstances only military personnel and targets ought to be
deliberately and directly attacked so that whatever
civilian casualties occur are inadvertent and indirect.

In a similar vein, Ramsey directs the principle of nonmaleficence to current problems and discussions in the field of nuclear policy. Here, consistent
with his evaluation of Truman's decision to employ the
atomic bomb against the Japanese, he argues that any
present policy targeting cities, and therefore civil-
ians, is in Principle contrary to the Christian norm of
agape. He consequently advocates targeting only mili-

tary installations, contending that civilian casualties caused by bombing these targets would not have been deliberately intended and therefore are ethically blameless.

Finally, and also in opposition to Fletcher, Ramsey thinks that in cases where life and death decisions must be made in situations with no clearly defined distinctions between what is good or evil, moral or immoral, or creative or destructive, Christians must act on a random basis and avoid computing the relative value of various individual lives. This, he believes, protects the dignity of all persons.

The principle of nonmaleficence is the foundation of what might be labeled as Ramsey's "conservative" position on the issue of abortion. Abortion is ethically wrong, he believes, unless it is performed as an unavoidable means for saving the life of the mother. Fletcher's rule that "no unwanted and unintended baby should even be born" is, for Ramsey, a clear example of instrumentally treating one human being, the fetus, as dispensable in relation to the "greater good" of the parents or the family.

By outlining the features of end-oriented and duty-oriented forms of ethical practices, exemplified by the theories of Fletcher and Ramsey, I am not implying these are the only styles of ethical practice that can legitimately bear the label "Christian," although in fact they are widely prevalent in both Christian and secular circles of contemporary ethical inquiry. It will be well, accordingly, to mention a third type of

Christian ethical inquiry represented by the American theologian, H. Richard Niebuhr.

Niebuhr's approach to ethical judgment begins with an analysis of "responsibility," and hence his ideas are often called "responsibility ethics."[8] If ends-oriented approaches attend primarily to supposed objectively absolute norms constituting Christian ethical practice, and if duty-oriented approaches attend to the absolute requirements of duty and obligation, Niebuhr's "responsible self" attends to what is the most fitting or suitable action to undertake in a given set of circumstances. While the Christian is under the absolute obligation to treat all persons according to the principles of agapeic love exemplified by the life of Jesus, we nevertheless do not live in a world in which we have choices between clear-cut good and clear-cut evil. In real life, under the conditions imposed by finitude, whatever is "good" *must* be intermixed with whatever is "evil." Thus, expressing love in our relations with human beings in a "sinful" world, in ways which do not cause injury to them, is simply not possible. Justice for one person or group of persons always creates injustice for others; cleaning up the environment of pollution will unjustly cost thousands of individuals their economic livelihoods; helping poor persons achieve meaningful existence beyond the level of poverty will always mean unjustly taking wealth from the rich. All action in a finite and ethically ambiguous world, even when motivated and guided by love, will necessarily issue in unintended injurious consequences to some person or group. In other words, in a sinful world, all human actions and decisions involve ethical compromise.

This is why, according to Niebuhr, the best anyone can do is take responsibility for this condition while doing the morally best one can, guided by the hope of causing as little injury to other people as possible. The "responsible self" is, therefore, the person attempting to apply the absolute demand to love all persons to the realities of the particular situation or context requiring a response, while knowing the impossibility of acting without causing some form of injury to others. Stated somewhat differently, the "responsible self" directs energy to expressing love realistically through the most appropriate action possible given the realities of the particular individual and social circumstances.

Niebuhr's more flexible approach to Christian ethical practice focuses more on developing desirable character traits and virtues than on commitment to an explicitly defined set of ethical principles guiding decision making. Since this approach places such great stress on an individual's inner disposition in place of abstract rules of conduct, generalizing about it becomes extremely difficult apart from reference to specific ethical issues. For example, according to Niebuhr, the realities of some circumstances might point to a positive decision to abort a fetus, while in another set of circumstances abortion would be morally wrong. There might even be circumstances when it is impossible to decide either to abort, or not to abort, a fetus. The realities of the living context requiring a decision must be the determining factor directing the specific forms of how love is expressed in specific ethical decisions. There are no objective ethical norms apart from concrete particular situations.

What I have described thus far, however, can also be applied to non-Christian ethical practice. There is nothing particularly unique in Fletcher's, Ramsey's, or Niebuhr's ethical views which is there simply because all three are professing Christians. The special character of the ethical practice of Christian faith derives from the assumption of the existence of a special epistemological connection between religious faith and ethical behavior not found in secular and non-Christian ethical perspectives. All religious Ways share this assumption to varying degrees. But Christian ethical thought usually assumes Christian faith supplies an individual with direct moral knowledge of what is ethically right and wrong unavailable to religiously noncommitted and non-Christian individuals. There are, of course, numerous ways this assumption has informed the ethical teachings of particular Christian theologians. But it remains the single assumption distinguishing Christian ethical thought and practice from non-Christian ethical philosophies.

For example, the secular utilitarian ethics of Jeremy Bentham (1748-1832) and the ethical assertions of Joseph Fletcher are both ends-oriented theories because both are concerned with the proper goals of an action. But whatever the specific content of Fletcher's understanding and application of *agapē* might be, "agapeic calculus" is certainly not the equivalent of Bentham's "pleasure principle," according to which an ethically good action is one maximizing the balance of bodily and emotional pleasure for the greatest number of individuals. It is Fletcher's religious faith and commitment to a Christian vision of reality that supplies the difference.

The question of what is and what is not "religious" about ethical principles is also an important problem for most religious Ways, but what is religious becomes an especially difficult question for the Christian Way because of the stress Christian faith traditionally places upon ethical practice. Christian theological reflection generally assumes that biologically and psychologically normal human beings have ethical capacities quite apart from specific religious experiences, insights, or commitments. All persons, that is, possess natural ethical endowments. Historically, this assumption has been of great importance in the history of Christian thought, because without it no one can be held accountable unless they are Christians.

But the point that Christian ethical theory stresses is that religious commitment makes a difference in ethical decision and practice. The exact nature of this difference, however, varies from theologian to theologian. For example, Fletcher is quite explicit about the relevance of Christian faith for ethical practice. He assumes that specifically Christian ethical practice motivationally differs from all other religious and secular ethical orientations. In so assuming, he incorporates the doctrine of the British moral philosopher, Stephen Toulmin, that ethics pro-

vides the *rationale* for choosing a particular course of
action as the "right" one, while religious faith provides the emotional impetus for actually choosing and
performing the morally right course of action.[9]   In
Fletcher's understanding, the basic problem of ethical
behavior is not knowing *what* is right, but being able
to do what is right. According to him, Christian faith
solves this problem.

Still other theologians, Karl Barth and Paul
Lehmann for example, believe Christian faith provides
direct moral knowledge of what is right and wrong, as
well as the emotional impetus for behaving accordingly.
In all probability, both Barth's and Lehmann's views
represent the most extreme versions of this idea:
Christian "revelation" supplies direct knowledge of
God's "commands," and this knowledge is simply not
available to non-Christians.[10]

The assertions of most theologians writing
about the ethical practice of Christian faith are not
as exclusivistic as Barth's and Lehmann's. The majority, like H. Richard Niebuhr, merely assume that Christian faith provides a special ethical sensitivity for
intuiting the right course of action in a given situation not immediately available to non-Christian persons. On the other hand, Paul Ramsey and many other
traditional Protestant thinkers have followed the Roman
Catholic "natural law" approach by positing two types
of ethical knowledge. One type is naturally available
to all persons regardless of religious faith and commitment because God has endowed humanity generally with
ethical sensitivity. The ethical knowledge grounded in

Christian faith, however, is more privileged and accessible only to religiously inspired individual Christians through special revelation.

THEOLOGICAL PRACTICE

Despite diversity of interpretation, the idea that faith grounded in love must be ethically exercised by Christians through social interaction with others, is an ancient theme of Christian teaching. Faith must, in the words of the author of the Epistle of James, "lead to action" expressing love to all persons. On this point, every Christian theologian, from the Apostle Paul to Paul Tillich, has agreed. But Christian practice does not only involve ethical commitment and action. Christian practice also involves the intellect, because faith, as a peculiarly human experience, involves the total human being. In other words, perhaps more than any other major religious Way, Christian faith is also practiced through the reasoned articulation of the implications of the experience of faith traditionally called "theology."

Because theology guides all other forms of Christian practice, the relation between faith and theology is so close that confessional systems of belief and opinion are often confused with faith by most practicing Christians. Even so, unlike the function of Buddhist doctrine conceived as a form of upāya, accurate propositional formulation of the experience of Christian faith historically has been a matter of supreme importance in Christian history.

Perhaps these statements will become more meaningful by reconsidering the generic nature of religious faith. Faith is, as I have suggested, not identical with belief in a set of doctrinal propositions or a body of theological opinions. It is not even belief in "truth," whatever this might be. Faith is "assent" (*credo*) to the truth as such, however it is named, in the dynamically personal sense of focusing total attention upon it with delight and engagement. "It is the exclamation mark in saying not merely 'yes' but 'yes!' to the truth when one sees it."[11] In respect to specifically Christian experience, faith is a personal, trustful, betting of one's life, a saying of "yes!" to the historical events surrounding the life and death of Jesus.

The "yes!" of faith always engenders practice. Faithful persons always act according to the truth to which they say "yes!"; ethically, the "betting of one's life" on the Christ event creates the intention of living one's life according to modes of action expressing love (*agapē*). But since faith is also a dynamic event involving the totality of a person's life, the intellect is also grasped and energized by the truth to which the "Yes!" of faith is given. Restated more plainly, there is always an intellectual dimension in the experience of faith, since it is necessary that we conceptualize and interpret the nature and meaning of the "truth" upon which we bet our lives before we can ethically practice betting our lives.

Theological reflection on the nature of Christian faith is what Thomas Aquinas and other Christian teachers have called "faith seeking understanding." To be faithful, theological conceptualization must seek to achieve the closest propositional approximation of the "truth" of the Christ event of which the human mind is capable. Certainly, the history of this perceived necessity undoubtedly includes the expansion of the early church beyond the semitic cultural traditions of Palestine into a world dominated by Greek cultural ideals. Successfully translating itself into this environment required reinterpreting Christian faith through the filter of Hellenistic philosophy, especially those traditions originating in Plato, Aristotle, and the Stoics. The Greek philosophers placed prime value upon clear, rational, abstract, propositional understandings of reality. This characteristic, once it became part of the Christian heritage, was never lost. Thus theology as a mode of Christian practice became possible only after the Christian Way established itself beyond the cultural and intellectual borders of Palestine. This process began very early in the history of the Christian Way, in fact some fifteen to twenty years after the death of Jesus, with the missionary work of Saint Paul--the first Christian to practice theology.

The Pauline understanding of faith is certainly not identical with believing certain opinions about the life, death, and resurrection of Jesus. Nor is faith identified with belief in the doctrinal formulations of Christian faith defined in the major creeds and confessions of the church. Not that there are no Christian denominations or individuals erroneously

identifying faith with belief in a collection of doctrines and creeds. But Christians are not called upon
to "believe" anything, as one, for example, "believes"
that the truth of mathematical or scientific propositions and opinions are either true or false descriptive
statements about physical reality. Rather, Christians
are called upon to *trust,* to bet their lives on, the
reality to which the creeds and confessions of the
Christian Way symbolically point. This is clear from
the root meaning of the Latin *credo,* "setting the heart
on." "Setting the heart on" means saying "yes!" to,
"taking refuge in," the sacred realities to which the
propositions of the creeds and confessions point, but
can never fully capture or completely communicate. The
Christian Way is always a way of salvation by faith,
not salvation by belief in propositional opinions about
God, Jesus, the Bible, or the church.

This conclusion can be easily illustrated
with reference to the Apostle's Creed, although any of
the major Christian creeds or confessions would serve
as well:

I believe in God the Father Almighty, creator
of heaven and earth; And in Jesus Christ His
only Son our Lord, Who was conceived by the
Holy Spirit, born of the Virgin Mary, suf-
fered under Pontius Pilate, was crucified,
dead and buried. He descended to hell, on
the third day he rose again from the dead,
ascended to heaven, and sits at the right
hand of God the Father almighty, thence He
will come to judge the living and the dead; I

believe in the Holy Spirit; The holy Catholic Church, the Communion of saints, the forgiveness of sins, the resurrection of the body, and the life everlasting.[12]

The words "I believe" are an English translation of the Latin *credo*. This modern English usage falsifies the original Latin meaning. That is, the Apostle's Creed does not call upon Christians to assent to the articles of the creed as true propositional statements about sacred realities. Rather, Christians are defined as persons who "set their hearts on" (*credo*) the realities to which the articles symbolically point and who govern their individual and social lives accordingly. The Apostle's Creed defines Christians as persons who trust, have faith in, accord their lives with, commit to, and bet their lives on "God the Father Almighty, Maker of heaven and earth, and in Jesus Christ his only Son our Lord. . . ." Christians are not called upon to "believe," in the modern sense of having an opinion about the truth of the propositional assertions, that God is an almighty father who created heaven and earth and that Jesus Christ is his only son who is at the same time our lord, and so on. No human being, in any religious Way, particularly the Christian Way, "believes" opinions and then has "faith." It is the opposite; we are first grasped by an apprehended truth and then we interpret the nature and implications of the truth that has grasped us. Creeds, confessional statements, and theological systems and opinions are intellectual responses to something prior to their articulation. They are not faith. They do not even conduce to faith. But they become expressions of faith when they are not confused with faith.

The distinction between faith and belief can be easily illustrated by Thomas Aquinas's theology. Thomas's attempt at theological synthesis is a particularly good example of how Christian theological reflection has traditionally conceived the difference between faith and belief, as well as their interrelation, because: (1) if any major Christian theologian ever took a rationalist view of the nature of faith, it was Thomas; (2) his system is a *summa,* meaning a systematic summary of the theological reflection of the Christian Way up until his own time in the twelfth century; and (3) his thought continues to play an important theological role in contemporary Roman Catholic and, in some degree, Protestant theology.

Thomas was a spokesman for that tradition of Western philosophical-theological tradition for whom humanity's highest personal achievements are attained through the use of the intellect. "Knowing" the truth, meaning rationally understanding whatever the truth is, especially true knowledge of the reality of God was, for Thomas, *the* final human beatitude. Not only faith, but all matters of human existence--from love to the physical reality of objects in the natural world--were understood by Thomas as objects of rational investigation. As a Christian theologian, he possessed "faith" as trust in the ability of the human intellect to arrive at clear, distinct, and rational apprehension of any form of truth, including the truths of theology.

But while Thomas taught a rationalist view of Christian faith, he also combined this with a "faith view" of the power of human reason to grasp truth. Knowledge, meaning conceptual understanding of reality obtained through the proper use of reason, not only is possible for human beings, but also possesses intrinsic value over and beyond any instrumental value. Knowledge is good in itself because it is self-authenticating. Wilfred Cantwell Smith has summarized this aspect of Thomas's theology as follows:

> Faith is an attitude to truth, and specifically to truth as conceptualizable, and more specifically still, to transcendent truth not yet discovered, not yet known.[13]

So while Thomas was aware that "truth," however it is named, ultimately transcends our present intellectual grasp, he also believed that human nature was so created by God to be aware of this fact, to dimly perceive there is more to truth than human beings have as yet rationally grasped. For the "object" towards which faith is directed is "ultimate truth" (*prima veritas*).

Thomas was also, however, an intellectual grasped by the Christian Way, meaning that for him truth and goodness were two sides of the same Christian coin. It is, accordingly, our love of truth, along with our giving allegiance to it (*credere*), that converges with love in general (*caritas*). Faith is not merely a dedication to truth, but an apprehending assent (*assensio*) to it, coupled with dedication to act in accordance with it. Faith is a positive relation to truth as such, not merely a belief in, or an opinion about, the validity of any particular rational formulation of truth. In other words, explicit belief is always secondary.[14]

The Latin term that Thomas chose to denote faith's relation to truth was *fides*, which carries the connotation of a mode or a way of knowing. But *fides* differs from other forms of knowledge, which Thomas denoted as *scientia,* by not being immediately and discursively demonstrable. The knowledge of faith (*fides*) is knowledge of another sort called *cognito*. Restated in more contemporary terminology, *scientia* designates rational, discursive knowing and understanding of the natural world, while *cognito* designates knowing a truth without complete intellectual understanding of it, an apprehending which is not yet a comprehending.[15]

The ultimate truth that human beings can apprehend, but never completely, through the exercise of reason, is God. We cannot know God, as God is, through the exercise of reason, nor as we shall finally apprehend God's essence in the final beatitude to which we are ultimately called, at which time we shall directly perceive God's full reality. Yet we do, although not completely, rationally apprehend God in the relationship of faith. The propositions of reason are, however, a means to a different end. They are human constructions, and to that degree they are artificial, even while serving as a means leading human beings to God. This is so because ultimate truth and reality—God in God's fullness—is "simple," while the human mind is so created by God to be unable to grasp God's total reality, or any other reality, in its simple form. To grasp reality, human reason must employ complex propositions about truth in order to mediate and represent truth's simplicity. And yet, while our minds must make do with these complex and elaborate propositions, no faith is involved when they do not direct our minds to God.

The relation between faith and propositional belief becomes even clearer as we consider Thomas's position on heresy. If faith is a personal orientation of the whole person to what is known to be right because it can be logically and coherently demonstrated to be so through the proper exercise of reason, heresy becomes a deliberate rejection of what reason clearly knows to be demonstrably true. The issue of heresy was not, for Thomas anyway, whether this or that propositional opinion *about* God or Christ or the church is "true," but whether a person's response to truth is "right." That is, heretics are persons who reject any article of faith, in the sense of not "taking refuge in it," which they know to be "right" even if they accept every other article of faith. But believing reasonably doubtful opinions and propositions about God, or having an ignorant understanding of a doctrine, is merely an "error."[16]

The propositional beliefs and opinions of Christians and non-Christians can be erroneous, but never heretical, in Thomas's understanding of the relation between faith and belief. His own systematic theology, his beliefs and opinions about the implications of what his faith (*fides*) made known to him through reason were those of a thirteenth century Christian that even he finally declared to be a "bunch of straw." But the faith he sought to articulate, the reality he experienced that engendered his theological reflection, was *not* a bunch of straw.

Distinctively Christian faith engenders the practice of theological reflection for all Christians, whether one is a trained academic theologian, a local pastor or priest, or a dedicated lay person. Thomas's particular understanding of the relation between faith and belief is an especially excellent illustration of this principle, but I could have just as well cited any major thinker in Christian history and made the same point. Ideally, the practice of theology energizes and guides the day-to-day practice of Christian faith. How Christians comprehend and rationally articulate the implications of their faith conditions how they practice their faith through worship and social-ethical relationships with others, as well as how they comprehend and relate to other religious Ways and secular world views in the contemporary world.

Consequently, when theological push comes to shove, the main body of Christian theological tradition agrees with Anselm's declaration, *credo et intelligam.* Translating these words by the standard "I believe in order that I may know" misrepresents Anselm's intended meaning, given the modern meaning of "belief" as "having an opinion." Christian faith is not "having an opinion" about that which we do not know or of which we are uncertain. Anselm's's statement may be more accurately translated, although not exactly literally, as

"I become involved in order that I may understand," or
perhaps "I take refuge in order that I may penetrate."
Any physician or chess player or artist or scholar or
administrator says as much if they are any good at what
they do. And this sort of involvement characterizes
the practice of theology as well--faith seeking under-
standing--the emphasis upon which sets the Christian
Way apart from all other religious Ways.

DEVOTIONAL PRACTICE

It is an abstraction, but nevertheless descriptively accurate, to characterize the Christian Way
as "theistic" and the Buddhist Way as "nontheistic."
Normally, Western philosophical thought reserves the
term "theism" to define a body of religious teachings
positing the existence of a transcendent power or powers grounding the existence of all finite entities, indeed without which there would be no finite entities.
This supreme reality, usually described in personalis-
tic language as creator, sustainer, and ultimately de-
stroyer of the phenomenal universe, is experienced as
particularly involved in the lives of human beings.

The Christian Way is also a monotheistic Way
that teaches all finite existence depends upon only one
transcendent sacred reality who not only creates, sus-
tains, and directs the processes of finite existence,
but who also decisively acts in history according to
specific events intended to establish the salvation of
all human beings. Employing more traditional Christian
language, God continually works in the realm of historical existence to achieve God's purposes, but has fi-

nally, once and for all, done so through the life, death, and resurrection of Jesus as the Christ. The Christian God is a powerfully transcendent sacred reality that cannot be limited by or reduced to anything finite. In other words, there is nothing in nature to which we can liken God, and doing so is "idolatry."[17] At the same time, however, God exercises power primarily through loving concern for the welfare of creation, and in particular for the human part of creation.

There are numerous definitions and defenses concerning the nature of Christian theism. But the general thrust of all of them is that however the reality of God is conceived, whatever the mode of God's creative relationship to the world is, whatever love or justice or the propositional formulations of orthodoxy are, and whatever the specific nature of salvation through Jesus the Christ entails, everything is dependent upon the sustaining power of God. Thus Christian practice does not emphasize self-disciplines of the sort meant to help Christians experience ontological union with whatever ultimate reality is however it is named, as in Buddhist practice. Christian practice is grounded in the act of responding to what Christians have experienced themselves receiving from God. The central form of this response expresses itself through the symbolic actions and language involved in worship; ideally all forms of Christian practice are simultaneously forms of worship, since all are intended to be expressions of gratitude for what Christians have received as unearned gifts of divine love. Thus understood, worship undergirds and energizes everything else comprising distinctively Christian practice.

"Worship" is a cover name for the heart of Christian practice. The Christian Way is a devotional Way, just as the Buddhist Way is primarily a meditative Way, even though contemplative disciplines also play an important role in Christian practice. Devotional practice creates the environment in which the reality of God can be encountered by the reality of the persons to the end of deepening and transforming all aspects of their lives. The specific practices of Christian worship—prayer, periodic public gathering for communal celebration, devotional reading of the scriptures, participation in liturgy, preaching, the celebration of festivals on holidays, baptism, the Eucharist—place the worshiper into direct contact with the reality of God. They are, that is, symbolic acts meant to open up persons to a sacred reality that Christians apprehend through Jesus as the Christ, a reality that can be "felt" but not directly touched, "seen" but not directly perceived, "heard" but not explicitly.

Understanding the specific role of Christian devotional practice requires understanding the generic nature of ritual. The history of religions has established that ritual activity is one of the oldest, most complex, and most persistent symbolic activities engendered by religious experience.[18] All religious Ways communicate their special world views through ritual patterns of behavior. In fact, any human action can take on a ritual character, thereby acquiring symbolic power capable of transforming individual and social life, because rituals are always symbolic paradigms dramatizing the central intent of a religious Way. Thus rituals martial visual and auditory symbols, along with intellectual and sensual images, into processes providing individuals with specific social and personal identity, a "structure of existence," to borrow a phrase from John Cobb, that creatively transforms persons into more completely real modes of being going beyond the simple givens of mundane experience. Through what is seen, said, and enacted, ritual expresses, as it creates, a psychic, social, and religious world for persons in such a way that rational reflection and social-ethical behavior become interdependently unified.

Through the specific ritual traditions of Christian devotionalism, ranging from the complex liturgical systems of Roman Catholicism and Greek Orthodoxy to the ritual silence of a Quaker meeting, the individual's Christian faith is affirmed even as it is created and renewed. Four facts concerning the symbolic power of ritual support this conclusion. First, all rituals confirm the social identity of individuals. Christian devotional practices socialize individual Christians into a "community of saints," through sharpening the differences between those who are members of this community and those who are not.

Second, because rituals sharpen an individual's social identity within the Christian community, increasing an individual's awareness of responsibilities to other human beings both inside and outside the community, Christian psychological identity becomes more sharply defined. Through being aware of the values, needs, and theology of the larger social order constituted by the church, the individual Christian's own self-identity is brought into clearer focus.

Third, ritual systems create a sense of historical identity. All ritual systems dramatically reenact a "sacred history" in which individuals participate as they undergo ritual practice. In the Christian Way, ritual systems allow past and present Christian persons to "participate" in the originating historical events which created Christian faith, as well as in the continuing ongoing history of the Christian Way. At this point, ritual links up with myth and story. Through ritual reenactment of the stories, myths, legends, and lives of significant Christian individuals, a Christian's own life is creatively transformed through a deepening of Christian self-identity. And if Mircea Eliade was correct, as I think he was, the periodic ritual reenactment of the founding events, the "myths" of the Christian Way, actually bring these "sacred times" of origins into the believer's contemporary "profane time," thereby rejuvenating time through sacralizing it.[19] In Christian language, devotional practice allows Christians to become contemporary with the founding events of Christian faith.

Finally, the ritual processes are profoundly paradoxical. Beyond the affirmation of an established social and personal identity, ritual may, and in fact often does, "transform" individuals by providing them with new identities beyond what even their particular religious community expects or desires. Viewed from the perspective of Christian experience, ritual occasionally gives Christians access to new modes of being and experience different from what a particular institutional form of the church accepts or expects as normally Christian. When this occurs--even if rarely--individuals may find themselves outside all institutionalized versions of the Christian community, while yet remaining authentically Christian in their faith and practice. Devotional practice, because of the symbolic power of ritual, creates the possibility for not only experiencing a renewed sense of personal self-identity going beyond the social and theological labels of Christian and secular institutions, but also encountering a transcending "other" experienced as a timeless cosmic reality that cannot be limited by any system. Christian devotional practice, in other words, often allows Christians to participate in what theologians have described as *communitas* (community), a personal relationship with God over and beyond what any institutionalized church doctrinally defines, and therefore usually expects.

Of course, not all Christians achieve this sort of personal liberation and self-transformation. Most probably do not, just as most Buddhists do not achieve enlightenment even if they practice meditation. But, in fact, the goal of Christian devotional practice remains the personal and social creative transformation of individual Christians. The meaning of "creative transformation" may differ from Christian to Christian, just as the meaning of "enlightenment," the Buddhist version of "creative transformation," differs from Buddhist to Buddhist. But it is devotional practice that engenders the uniquely *Christian* experience of self-transformation.

Even though creative transformation means different things to different Christians, there appears to be a unifying factor in all distinctively Christian devotional practice. The Christian Way proclaims all human beings possess everything they will ever have or require from God. No Christian is required to practice faith devotionally in order to seek anything from God, because devotional practice has nothing to do with achieving anything we do not already possess. Therefore, the only motivation left for undertaking devotional practice is gratitude for having received from God all that is required for meaningful human relationship with God. No Christian is "saved" by devotional practice, or any other form of religious practice. On the other hand, while devotional practice is not an instrumental device for achieving something from God that Christians do not already possess, devotional practice prepares the Christian to receive whatever transformative experience of the reality of God through Christ is possible through following the Christian Way.

MONASTIC PRACTICE

The practice of faith for most Christians means attempting to express love in social and ethical relationships, energized by whatever experience of God's presence can be sensed through devotional practices, as these are directed by whatever degree of theological understanding individual Christians have of the implications of their faith. In short, the ethical, theological, and devotional aspects of Christian practice are interdependent. Therefore, Christian practice does not normally involve isolation from worldly, secular life, but instead emphasizes perceiving and relating to the normal course of worldly events from the perspective of Christian faith. The Christian Way positively affirms life in the "profane" world, with all of its social, political, economic, and cultural concerns, as the arena where God most often confronts humanity. Accordingly, Christians are called upon to be "in the world, but not of the world." But there is more than one way of "being in the world, but not of the world"; one such way is monasticism.

The Christian monastic tradition, in varying degrees of rigor, requires withdrawal from the normal structures and involvements of secular life. But unlike the Buddhist Way, the Christian Way did not originate as a monastic movement. Unlike the Buddha, Jesus was not the founder of an ascetic monastic order over which he presided. Nor does the New Testament picture Jesus as a teacher of meditative self-discipline. In comparison with Theravada Buddhist tradition, where monasteries remain the most important religious institution, monasticism plays only a supportive institutional role in contemporary Roman Catholic practice, and hardly any at all in Protestant practice.

From the fourth to the sixteenth centuries, however, monasticism was the institutional center of the Christian Way. And in numerous important ways, the monastic ideal continues to play a vital role for significant numbers of modern Christians. Thus, because

the emphasis upon self-discipline is as important in
the Christian monastic heritage as it is in Buddhist
monasticism, and because the contemplative disciplines
that evolved within Christian monastic practice are in
many ways parallel to Buddhist meditational techniques,
it seems appropriate to discuss briefly this tradition
of Christian practice.[20]

Within the communal environment of Christian
monasteries and convents, monks and nuns cultivate
Christian faith through ethical, theological, and devotional practices in the same way all practicing Christians do, except with more rigorous, regulated, inten-
sified, secluded self-discipline. Monasticism, from
the German, *monadzein,* "to live alone", involves seclusion from temporal and secular concerns so that monks
and nuns can dedicate themselves exclusively to specifically religious pursuits. Among Western theistic religious Ways, Christian tradition provides the chief
and enduring examples of monastic life and training,
along with Sufi Islam. These examples are mostly found
in non-Protestant traditions--Roman Catholicism, Greek
Orthodoxy, Russian Orthodoxy, the Syrian Church, and
the Coptic Church. So even though monasticism is certainly not the central contemporary institutional expression of the Christian Way, and while Christian
forms of monastic discipline vary, all derive their
origins and authority from the sayings of Jesus in the
Gospels about poverty, celibacy, trusting obedience to
God, and caring service to others.

Consequently, Christian monks and nuns live
disciplined lives under the guidance of a monastic

"rule" governing their daily activities. While different orders emphasize different life styles--some purely contemplative, some dedicated to missionary service, some to educational and social service of various sorts beyond the walls of the monastery, some to complete isolation from the outside secular world--monastic practice attempts to regulate and discipline the total living environment of its followers. Specifically, life organized around a monastic rule seeks to simplify a monk's or a nun's life so that nothing interferes with his or her love and service to God and humanity. The explicit intention of this simplification is to surrender to the will of God to such a degree that the monk or nun actually wills what God wills. Again, the model for this goal is the picture of the perfect surrender of Jesus' will to the will of God, even to the point of accepting an undeserved death by crucifixion. The traditional cover term designating monastic practice, accordingly, is "the imitation of Christ."

The surrender of an individual's will to the will of God can most easily occur in isolation from the distractions of secular care and involvement. These distractions are systematically purged from the seeker's environment, at least as much as possible. To this end, monastic practice includes not only physical, mental, and emotional isolation from the normal biological, social, and cultural concerns governing the course of most people's lives, but also the practice of differing degrees of bodily asceticism, physical labor, prolonged periods of communal and private prayer, the study of theology, and the quest for personal transfor-

mation through "mystical experience."[21] Despite the
many changes over the centuries, these continue to be
the classical elements of Christian monastic practice.

Even though the quest for personal transformation through "mystical experience" is the central
goal of monasticism, not all Christian monks and nuns
seek or attain this goal. Nor does monastic theology
teach that mystical self-transformation is attainable
solely through self-effort. The term "mystical experience" refers to a special form of religious experience
possessing three interrelated qualities: (1) a "zero
point" experience of union in which individuals lose
all sense of separation between themselves and the object experienced; (2) specific disciplines very similar
to meditation that are taught and practiced in order to
achieve this experience which is called, in Christian
terminology, "contemplative prayer;" and (3) an experience which ultimately cannot be described because it is
regarded by those who have it as ineffable.

The experience of union is normally very
brief and usually, but not always, occurs more fre-
quently and easily after the initial zero point experience. Subsequent mystical experiences are not structurally different from the initial experience, and they
are usually apprehended as deeper, more profound variations of the insights gained during the first experience. But while the mystic is experiencing zero point,
there is no consciousness of the normal subject-object
dualities characterizing "normal" waking sensory consciousness.   Whether the mystic is a Buddhist or a
Christian, there exists no perceived distinction be-

tween the mystic and the object experienced. They become "one."

However, after mystics have experienced zero point, they normally interpret the meaning of what happened to them according to the special theology or world view under which they have been trained. Buddhists interpret their experience as a kind of "monistic" overcoming of all subject-object separateness between themselves and whatever realities are encountered in the experience of nirvāṇa. That is, Buddhists experience themselves as the absolute reality beyond name and form, so that enlightenment is interpreted as the metaphysical union between themselves and the Dharma. Buddhists seek to *become* what they experience during enlightenment, or perhaps more accurately, they discover there is no subject without object, no nirvāna without samsāra, that they *are* and always have been the Dharma looking at themselves.

But the theological tradition of the Christian Way teaches that God is an ultimate reality whose nature ontologically transcends anything and everything in the finite world. Accordingly, Christian mystics do not often interpret the zero point experience of unity with God as an ontological merging of their nature with God's nature. That is, Christian mystics do not often experience metaphysical unity with God. Rather, union with God is interpreted as a "psychological union," for want of a better descriptive term, in which the mystic's will is unified with the will of God. The mystic's *will* becomes the will of God while remaining metaphysically distinct from God--a form of unity with

God that Christian mystics have traditionally under-stood to be implied in Jesus' statement, "I and the Father are One." Thus Christian mystics seek to experience God's will as their own to overcome all separation between what they egotistically will and what God wills. The model guiding this quest for an inner attitude of perfect obedience to God was again the New Testament's picture of Jesus' will perfectly conformed to the will of God.

Christian monastic disciplines, therefore, interiorize the doctrines of Christian faith so that monks and nuns can experience the union of their wills with the will of God. The disciplined environment of monastic life, especially in fully cloistered orders such as the Trappists, is highly conducive to producing this sort of experience. For example, most Christians normally engage in prayer with varying degrees of intensity. But monastic prayer is a special kind of prayer called "contemplative prayer," intended to open the seeker to the possibility of a special type of encounter with God called the "beatific vision." This experience is the foundation of the merging of the mystic's will to the will of God. Here prayer becomes a contemplative technique very similar to some forms of Buddhist meditational technique.

There are many forms of contemplative prayer in Christian monastic practice. The best-known example of prayer used as a contemplative technique is the "Jesus Prayer," which originated in the Greek Church with the Hesychast movement: "Lord Jesus Christ, Son of God, have mercy on me a sinner." The Jesus Prayer is practiced much like Buddhist might meditatively practice a *mantra*. Through the constant repetition of the Jesus Prayer the seeker focuses total concentrated attention upon the sound and rhythm of the words, and the meaning of the sacred realities bound up with Jesus' relation to God. After a length of time, perhaps years, a sense of union with the sacred reality represented by "Jesus" may occur, sometimes in a vision, sometimes in mere silence.[22]

Other forms of prayer may be used as contemplative techniques, such as, the Lord's Prayer, the Rosary, the daily office during which standardized liturgies are performed by the whole monastic community, the silent contemplation of teachings and doctrines, the devotional reading of scripture, silent reflection on the events of one's life, or wordless contemplation of a visual or a mental image of Jesus.

It is important to understand that within the context of Christian faith, monasticism represents a discipline in which the seeker practices all the usual forms of Christian practice, except in a more intense, rigorous, and disciplined way. And while not all monks or nuns experience union with God, this is the explicit goal of Christian monastic practice. But Christian mystical experience is "Christian:" if it occurs, the mystic experiences zero point as a gift, not as the result of the personal self-effort, energy, and discipline that he or she has expended in its quest. Part of the Christian mystic's experience is awareness that the experience is merely preparation for union with God. Monastic discipline does not create union with

God. This comes as a gift of God's grace in spite of the mystic's self-efforts.

CONCLUDING OBSERVATIONS

All religious Ways structure the practice of faith through ethical, rational, and devotional modes of human action within a social-communal context. Faith without practice--or what Christians call "works"--in any religious Way is a "lifeless thing." Not that practice engenders faith; rather practice and faith mutually and simultaneously engender one another. One does not, indeed cannot, happen without the other.

This conclusion need not imply "faith" and "practice" carry the same meanings from religious Way to religious Way. From a generic viewpoint, faith may be expressed through ethical conduct, but the specific ethical expressions of faith and the specific roles of ethical self-discipline vary among religious traditions. All religious Ways require some form of rational practice. But there are important differences between "faith seeking understanding" in the ritual reenactments of tribal mythology in the religious Ways of so-called "primitive" tribes, and the highly complex and articulate theological speculations and abstractions of the Christian Way or the doctrinal formulations of the Buddhist Way guiding the practice of Buddhist meditation.

For purposes of interreligious dialogue, however, *differences* between how religious Ways practice faith remain much more important than similarities. Dialogue is not even a theoretical possibility, and mutual transformation cannot thereby occur, when we assume that the differences between the religious Ways of humanity are not more important than whatever they might share in common. Dialogue begins when both sides of the encounter recognize differences as important symbolic pointers to real experiences of encounter with the Sacred, however it is named. In short, Buddhist truth and Christian truth are real but different truths reflecting real but different encounters with reality-- the way things really are.

The fact that, for example, my Buddhist colleague ethically practices his faith differently than I do, coupled with the recognition that ethics plays a different function in the Buddhist Way than in the Christian Way, might indicate that my Buddhist colleague has experienced a dimension of the reality of the Sacred I have missed. If so, perhaps I should incorporate his insights and practices into my own religious practice.

Of course the opposite might also be true. I might discover that some aspect of Buddhist ethics is not especially relevant to my particular cultural-historical situation. But even this discovery does not imply the inferiority of Buddhist ethical self-discipline to Christian ethical practice. However, I can make neither positive nor negative evaluations of this sort unless I first focus on the differences between the Christian and Buddhist Ways, appreciate these differences, and recognize that these differences do not constitute contradictory truth claims, but different versions of truth. What Buddhists experience is really there to be experienced; what Christians experience is really there to be experienced. If this is so, Buddhist and Christians have much to share and learn from one another.

Accordingly, I shall close this chapter with a description of what I believe to be the fundamental structural differences between Buddhist and Christian practice. I hope to establish the comparative groundwork for the conclusions I wish to defend in the final chapter of this volume.

The essential characteristic of the various forms of Buddhist practice, conventionally grouped under the headings of *sīla* (moral causality), *jhāna* (meditation), and *paññā* (wisdom), is they are all expressions of *upāya* or "skillful means" designed to help seekers achieve the transformative exPerience of enlightenment. Consequently, Buddhist forms of practice are more in the nature of "techniques" or "methods" for achieving specific goals or ends than Christian forms of practice. This is true, however, only for beginners and novice seekers of enlightenment. Consequently, the Buddhist Way also teaches that after enlightenment, means and ends, practice and theory, technique and goal, become experientially unified. Stated in Buddhist language, practice itself becomes enlightened, thereby shedding all of its previous instrumental meanings. The enlightened Buddhist continues practicing, but for this individual practice does not achieve anything he or she does not already possess as an enlightened Buddhist; it merely serves to deepen the enlightenment experience. Like the accomplished master of any art, an enlightened Buddhist does not separate practice and goal. As accomplished pianists continue practicing, even when performing a concert, so that their skilled performance *is* their practice and their practice *is* their skilled performance, so for the enlightened Buddhists: practice *is* their enlightenment and enlightenment *is* their practice.

This understanding of the nature of practice is quite different from traditional Christian understanding. With the possible exception of Jodo Shinshu Buddhist practice, there is nothing in the traditions of Christian practice structurally comparable to Buddhist practice. The forms of Christian practice--ethical self-discipline, theological reflection, devotionalism, and even the contemplative disciplines and life styles of Christian monasticism--are never conceived as mere techniques the devotee should appropriate as a means for achieving anything from God. The practice of Christian faith does not demand the appropriation of techniques that achieve anything that the person of faith does not already possess. In fact, practicing the Christian Way to achieve anything from God is a sign of "unfaith," at least according to the mainline traditions of Christian tradition.

The structural differences between Buddhist and Christian practice become clearer as we compare the function of ethical practice in each Way. Ethical self-discipline possesses a dual role in Buddhist practice not present in Christian practice. For the Buddhist lay devotee, as well as for those Buddhists practicing meditation on a regular basis both within and without the monastic *saṃgha,* moral self-discipline through the practice of *sila* is a technique for achieving an end the seeker does not already possess. The guiding principle is the Law of Karma. Ethical practice for the majority of Buddhists is a means for achieving positive karmic merit in order to achieve more positive, happier future rebirths, rather than the achievement of enlightenment. Consequently, while enlightenment is never an unethical event for Buddhists who achieve it, just as salvation is never an unethical event for Christians, most Buddhists do not practice *sila* to achieve enlightenment, just as most Buddhists do not practice meditation. Rather, the goal of practice for most followers of the Dharma is happier rebirths. By doing morally good deeds, as delineated through the disciiline of *sīla*, Buddhists seek positive karmic merit.

But the seeker who actually achieves enlightenment through meditation experiences the ethical disciplines of *sila* quite differently. For enlightened seekers, the ethical values governing the practice of *sila* become internalized. Such enlightened ones are "spontaneously" compassionate (*karuṇā*), are lovingly kind (*mettā*), are sympathetically joyful (*muditā*), are equanimious (*upekkhā*). Such ethically perfected individuals no longer "practice" ethical self-discipline to achieve these ethical states; they become ethically perfected, naturally and spontaneously extending these ethical virtues through their actions toward all beings without exception. At this experiential level, "practice" loses all instrumental connotations for enlightened *arhats*, Bodhisattvas, and Buddhas. But for all unenlightened Buddhists, *sīla* remains a technique for achieving karmic merit.

Because Christian ethical practice assumes that nothing a person does carries any merit whatsoever, all connotations of "technique" are ruled out. The sole motivation for Christian ethical practice, as well as for all other forms of Christian practice, is simple gratitude for what God has already given as a gift. Therefore, Christians are normally instructed to be involved in the world through acts of love and compassion to others, such as seeking justice for the oppressed, feeding the poor, curing the sick, and generally anything human welfare and community, merely because these "works" are necessary and their doing is their own reward. Christian ethical practice must be guided by love "with no strings attached," and Christians are able to so practice, if only imperfectly, because they have been loved by God "with no strings attached."

Of course, not all Christians actually practice this ethical ideal, but it is the paradigm governing Christian ethical practice. And because Christian ethical practice does not carry the instrumental meaning of technique for achieving an end, many Christian participants in current Buddhist-Christian dialogue have assumed that sensitivity to ethical and social issues, especially in the modern secular world, is less fully developed in the Buddhist Way than in the Christian Way. Many Buddhist participants in the dialogue have agreed with this assessment, urging Buddhist encounter with Christian tradition as a way to ethically transform the Buddhist Way to deepen the relevance of Buddhist faith for life in modern, technologically advanced, secularized society. Whether these judgments accurately portray the character of Buddhist ethical practice remains, in my opinion, an open question.[23]

Finally, several issues coming into focus in Buddhist-Christian encounter regarding Buddhist meditation and Christian contemplation. Buddhist meditation remains the sole means by which enlightenment can be achieved. The connotations of "technique" continue as part of the meaning of Buddhist meditational practice, although this too disappears with the achievement of enlightenment. But Buddhist faith is primarily expressed through the techniques of meditation, because meditation is the only method for achieving of enlightenment.

As indicated, meditation is also practiced in the Christian Way, mostly in the environmental confines of Christian monasticism. Here, many Christians, primarily Roman Catholic and Orthodox, now believe they have discovered the essential point of encounter with the Buddhist Way. Are the contemplative practices of Christian faith similar to Buddhist meditational practice, and if so are similar experiential results achieved? Can the contemplative disciplines of the Christian Way be renewed through borrowing Buddhist meditative techniques such as *zazen* ("seated meditation") in Zen Buddhist practice? Many Roman Catholic theologians and contemplatives, as well as many Buddhist meditators, believe these questions should be the

main focus of Buddhist-Christian dialogical encounter.[24]

But there are other questions. Can Christian
contemplatives appropriate Buddhist meditational techniques meant to achieving *Buddhist* experiences, practice these techniques in a Christian monastic environment guided by the world view of theology, and still
achieve authentically *Christian* "enlightenment?" Are
world view, method, environment, and experience so
closely intertwined in the practice of any religious
Way that the meditative techniques of one tradition are
unable to engender what a different religious Way can
affirm as authentic transformative experience? When
Christian contemplatives appropriate Buddhist meditational styles, do they not also appropriate, if only
unconsciously, the Buddhist world view? And if so, is
not "Christian enlightenment" a compromised form of
Buddhist enlightenment? While I do not believe this is
necessarily a bad thing, this aspect of Buddhist-Christian encounter poses some rather interesting issues, a
fuller treatment of which I shall reserve for the final
chapter of this study.

Buddhist-Christian dialogical encounter also
occurs at the level of Buddhist and Christian theologi-
cal-philosophical practice. This aspect of Buddhist-
Christian encounter is the primary concern for most
Protestant participants in the dialogue. The issues
seem to center on the notion of selfhood in Christian
teaching in comparison with the Buddhist doctrine of
nonself. This issue is the topic of chapter seven.
But the comparative issues of selfhood versus nonself-

hood create further issues concerning Christian conceptions of God as opposed to apparent Buddhist agnosticism concerning all notions of deity. This topic shall be considered in chapter eight.

NOTES

[1]Also see Romans 4:3-5, 4:19-29, 14:1, Gal. 5:5, and I Cor. 13:13.

[2]Cf. Hermann Ridderbos, *Paul, An Outline of His Theology* (Grand Rapids. Mich.: Eerdmans Publishing Co., 1975), 171-74, 237-52; Gunther Bornkamm, *Paul* (New York: Harper and Row, 1969), 109-227; and Rudolf Bultmann, *Theology of the New Testament,* I (New York: Charles Schribner's Sons, 1951), chapt. 5.

[3]See Paul Feine, Johannes Behm, and Werner Georg Kummel, *Introduction to the New Testament,* trans. A. J. Mattill, Jr. (Nashville: Abingdon Press, 1966), 282-92.

[4]Edward Schillebeeck, *Jesus, An Experiment in Christology,* trans. Hurbert Haskins. (New York: Crossroad Publishing Co., 1981), 159.

[5]Alfred North Whitehead, *Process and Reality* (New York: Macmillan, 1929), 521.

[6]See Joseph Fletcher, *Situation Ethics* (Philadelphia: Westminster Press, 1966). This interpretation and analysis of Fletcher's conceptualization of Christian ethical practice is based upon my understanding of the notions of this particular work.

[7]See Paul Ramsey, *Deeds and Rules in Christian Ethics* (New York: Charles Schribner's Sons, 1967), for the most accessible statement of his "duty oriented" approach to Christian ethical practice.

[8]H. Richard Niebuhr, *The Responsible Self* (New York: Harper and Row, 1963).

[9]See Stephen Toulmin, *An Examination of the Place of Reason in Ethics* (Cambridge: Cambridge University Press, 1950).

[10]Barth's clearest and perhaps most forceful statement about the moral knowledge inherent in and unique to Christian faith is his *Against the Stream* (Edinburgh: Oliver and Boyd, 1956).

[11]Wilfred Cantwell Smith, *Faith and Belief* (Princeton: Princeton University Press, 1979), 118.

[12]The date and place of origin of the present form of the Apostle's Creed cannot be fixed with precision. There is considerable evidence of a date in the late sixth or early seventh century somewhere in southwest France. See John H. Leith, ed., *Creeds of the Churches* (New York: Doubleday, 1963), 22-26.

[13]Smith, *Faith and Belief*, 81. This analysis of the relation between faith and belief in Thomas's theology essentially follows Smith's analysis and conclusions. I am indebted to him for clarifying this aspect of Thomas' theology for me for the first time.

[14]All references to Thomas's major work, *Summa Theologiae,* are from the standard translation of the English Dominicans (22 vols.), 2d ed. (London and New York), 1912-1936, hereafter abbreviated *Summa Th.* See 2:2:4:2 and 2:2:4:5. Also see Etienne Gilson, *The Christian Philosophy of St. Thomas Aquinas*, trans. L. K. Shook (New York: Random House, 1956), 381-439.

[15]*Summa Th.*, 2:2:4:5, 2:2:2:9.

[16]*Summa Th.*, 2:2:5:4. Also see Smith, *Faith and Belief*, 87-88, 296-97, nn. 103-105.

[17]The earliest explicit proclamations of monotheism in the Bible are found in the following passages in Isaiah: 40:12-20; 41:1-5, 21-29; 43:17-28; 44:6-20; and 45:18-25.

[18]For excellent studies of the ritual process as a means of transformation in the lives of human beings, both within and beyond the context of the Christian Way, see Mircea Eliade, *Patterns in Comparative Religion,* trans. Rosemary Sheed (New York: World Publishing Co., 1963), 1-37, 388-488, 437-58; Victor Turner, *The Ritual Process* (London: Routledge, 1969); and Claude Levi-Strauss, *The Savage Mind* (London: Weidenfeld and Nicholson, 1967).

[19]This is a process that occurs in all religious Ways. On the relation between myth and ritual, see

Mircea Eliade, *Cosmos and History*, trans. Willard R. Trask (New York: Harper and Row, 1959), 1-48.

[20]See D. Knowles, *Christian Monasticism* (New York: McGraw-Hill, 1969) and George Zarnecki, *The Monastic Buddhism,* (New York: McGraw-Hill, 1973). For comparable studies of Buddhist monastic practice, see Nalinaksha Dutt, *Early Monastic Buddhism*, 2 vols. (Calcutta: Calcutta Oriental Series, 1945) and Holmes Welch, *The Practice of Chinese Buddhism, 1900-1959* (Cambridge: Harvard University Press, 1967).

[21]My understanding of mysticism is based on the following works: Ray C. Petry, ed., *Late Medieval Mysticism*, (vol. 13 of *The Library of Christian Classics*, eds. John Baillie, John T. Mc Neill, and Henry van Dusen (Philadelphia: Westminster Press, 1957); Agehananda Bharati, *The Light at the Center* (Santa Barbara, Ca.: Ross-Erickson, 1976); and W. T. Stace, *Mysticism and Philosophy* (Philadelphia: J.B. Lippincott, 1960).

[22]See William Johnston, *Silent Music* (New York: Harper and Row, 1974), 17-22, for the similarity between the Jesus Prayer and the Buddhist use of *mantra* techniques of meditation.

[23]See my "To John Cobb: Questions to Gladden the Atman in an Age of Pluralism," *Journal of American Academy of Religion 45* (June 1977), 753-88.

[24]In fact, this seems to be the main preoccupation of Roman Catholic participants in the Buddhist-Christian encounter. See William Johnston, *The Still Point* (New York: Harper and Row, 1971); Thomas Merton, *Mystics and Zen Masters* (New York: Dell Publishing Co., 1969); and Joseph J. Spae, *Buddhist-Christian Empathy* (Tokyo: Institute for Theology and Culture, 1980), 197-242.

CHAPTER SEVEN
Buddhist and Christian Paradigms of Selfhood

Then, O Bhikkus, all body, whether past, present, or future, personal or external, coarse or subtle, high or low, far or near, should be understood by right knowledge of its real nature--"This is not mine; this I am not; this is not my soul."

Mahāvagga 1.1.38

Jesus said to his disciples, "If anyone wishes to be a follower of mine, he must leave self behind; he must take up his cross and come with me. Whoever cares for his own safety is lost; but if a man will lose himself for my sake, he will find his true self. What will a man gain by winning the whole world at the cost of his true self?

Matthew 16:25-26, *New English Bible*

THE PARADOX OF HUMAN SELFHOOD

The most complicated issues of current Buddhist-Christian dialogue (complicated because they express the core assumptions of each religious Way's world view) emerge when the Buddhist doctrine of nonself is confronted by traditional Christian conceptions of selfhood. Christians are easily confused when they are instructed by Buddhists regarding the nonselfhood of human nature, while Buddhists remain mystified by traditional Christian conclusions about selfhood. The major differences, it seems, between the Buddhist and the Christian Ways originate here: in Buddhist emphasis upon meditative self-discipline versus Christian emphasis upon worship; in Gautama the Buddha's being the model of human perfection through self-effort versus Jesus the Christ's being the model of total abdication of self in obedience to God; in Buddhist "salvation through works" versus Christian "salvation by faith through grace"; in Buddhist struggle for enlightenment versus Christian anticipation of eternal life in the Kingdom of God; in Buddhist compassion versus Christian love; in what appears to be Buddhist ethical and social disinterest versus Christian ethical and social activism.

Unfortunately, most of these contrasts are treated rather stereotypically by representatives of each Way. To be sure, Buddhist-Christian experiential and conceptual differences are real. And yet while real, they need not be interpreted as contradictions. Nor are Buddhist-Christian teachings and practices necessarily in competition. The experienced realities to which their respective teachings about selfhood point are there to be experienced by either Buddhists or Christians. In short, what Buddhists experience through meditative insight as nonselfhood, and what Christians experience as denial of selfhood in relation to God revealed through Jesus as the Christ, are realities that can be experienced by anyone willing to undergo the requisite self-discipline. Neither Buddhist nor Christian teachings are illusions.

However, ignoring the differences between Buddhist and Christian selfhood teachings in the hope of discovering some common denominator is not particularly useful. Nor is it particularly useful to place Buddhist and Christian conceptions in competition with one another because of their differences, assuming commitment to one Way's view as "truer." A more appropriate approach, a more dialogical approach, recognizes the differences between Buddhist and Christian conceptions of human selfhood as more interesting than their similarities, and accordingly more informative. Each Way illuminates truths hidden by the other's particular teachings and practices. Stated more plainly, the Buddhist doctrine of nonself prevents Buddhists from apprehending dimensions of human experience more comprehensively revealed to Christians through Christian conceptions of selfhood. Similarly, Christian teaching blinds Christians to the realities of human selfhood more adequately expressed through the Buddhist doctrine of nonself. Both Ways are right, and both are wrong because both are one-sided.

Accordingly, Buddhists and Christians need to "pass over" into one another's teachings and experiences of selfhood to appropriate whatever their own distinctive teachings have excluded from their awareness. Demonstrating the truth of this thesis, however, requires thoroughly comparing and contrasting the essential structural meanings of the Buddhist doctrine of nonself (Pali: *anattā*: Sanskrit: *anātman*) with the essential structural meanings of Christian selfhood.

It might be useful to think of concepts of selfhood as paradigmatic models of the experience of self-identity through time. Hence a description of the Theravada and Mahayana versions of the doctrine of nonself, followed by a similar descriptive account of traditional Christian views of selfhood, should illumine the evidence for my contention that the Buddhist doctrine of nonself ignores realities emphasized by tradi-

tional Christian notions of the self; likewise, traditional Christian portrayals of the self ignore realities of the experience of self-identity through time
more coherently articulated by the Buddhist doctrine of
nonself.

Two notions require further explanation:
"the experience of self-identity through time" and
"paradigm." By "self-identity through time" I mean the
consciously subjective bipolar sense that human beings
have of their own existence. We see ourselves as enduring centers of our own experience through the course
of our individual and social histories. For example,
when looking at a photograph taken of me ten years ago
and comparing it with two other photographs taken of
me, one just after my birth on March 23, 1939, and the
other three months ago for a passport, I immediately
experience myself as an "I" or enduring self labeled
"Paul Ingram" who, although the subject of much change
through time, has not changed. The infant in the oldest photograph is "I"; the ten year old photograph
bears an image of "me"; the recent passport photograph
is a picture of "me." Not that changes have not occurred. I am no longer the infant, I am no longer the
thirty-four-year-old adult male leaving his father's
house to assume a new teaching position in the Pacific
Northwest; I am not even the same person I was when my
passport photograph was taken three months ago. And
yet, in spite of the obvious changes that have occurred, I, at least, perceive different forms of an apparently unchanging "me" remaining self-identical
through "my" time.

More often than not they remain unexamined while we interpret the meaning of our experiences through them. They may even be totally unknown to us, and they are also "unprovable." Yet without them we can ascertain nothing legitimately bearing the label "knowledge." Paradigms are, consequently, crucial for any field of disciplined inquiry, whether in the study of physical phenomena or in the study of religious experience. This chapter, therefore, is about the traditional Buddhist nonself paradigm and the traditional Christian self paradigm as tacitly operating models through which Buddhists and Christians have apprehended the meaning of the experience of self-identity through time.

THE THERAVADA NONSELF PARADIGM (ANATTĀ)

The earliest scriptural reference to the doctrine of nonself, the Anattālakkhaṇa-sutta (Sanskrit, Anātmakakṣaṇa-sutta) or "Discourse on the Marks of Nonself," sets out the Buddhist nonself paradigm in interrelationship with the two other "marks" (lakkhaṇa) of existence, "impermanence" (anitya) and "suffering" (duḥkha). As one of the marks of existence, the doctrine of nonself is so intertwined with the doctrines of impermanence and suffering that separating it from these two marks deprives the nonself paradigm of all of its distinctively Buddhist meanings. Similarly, the Buddhist nonself paradigm requires the world view articulated by the doctrine of dependent co-origination (pratītya-samutpāda) to maintain its distinctively Buddhist conceptualizations of the experience of self-identity through time.

Etymologically, the word *anattā* consists of the negative Pāli prefix *an* and *attā* (Sanskrit, *an* and *ātman*)"[3]. Most often translated as "nonself" or "non-soul," the doctrine of *anatta* explicitly and utterly rejects all theories of substantially permanent self or soul entities remaining self-identical through time. There existed in India during the Buddha's lifetime a number of *ātman* theories positing the existence of substantial souls or self-entities that were subject to change or becoming but which themselves did not change or become. In contrast to these notions, collectively labeled "eternalist" views of the self by subsequent Buddhist teaching, the Buddha taught his own distinctive nonself doctrine.[4] In his view, belief in a substantial unchanging self-entity of any kind was the root cause of humanity's deepest and most obstinate delusion because it represented the fundamental form of clinging (*taṇhā*), of which all other forms of clinging are simply expressions.

The Theravada Buddhist Way faithfully maintains its allegiance to the Buddha's nonself paradigm in its doctrinal formulation of *anattā*. When Theravada Buddhists, supported by the techniques and experiences of meditation, analytically examine what we conventionally label as "self" or "person" (*puggala*), nothing identifiable as a an enduring self-entity is encountered. Supported by meditative experience, therefore, the analytical arguments articulating the Buddhist nonself paradigm become extensions of the Buddhist world view conceptualized by the doctrine of dependent co-origination. Once more, applying dependent co-origination to Buddhist notions of human nature conceived through the doctrine of nonself, the *nydana* or "spoke" or "link" in the chain of interdependent causal factors employed is *nāma-rūpa*.

Nāma, literally "name," but often too simply translated as "mind," is a collective noun denoting the psychological, perhaps non-physical, dimensions of existence. *Rūpa*, or "form," but often translated as "matter," "body," or "corporeality," denotes the physical dimension of experience. Taken together, which they must be according to the Buddhist world view, *nāma-rūpa* defines the organic psycho-physical unity of all "things" and "events" constituting the universe at any moment of space-time, including those psycho-physical events called "human beings" or "selves" or "persons."

Buddhist teaching does not interpret the *nāma-rūpa* relationship dualistically. "Name" and "form" are interdependent, each integrated with the other, creating the other. Or as the Buddha is reported to have said, "Form goes on when supported by Name (*nāma*), and Name when supported by Form."[5] All "things" and "events" existing at any moment of space-time consist of numerous expressions of name and form relationships. But the name and form relationship most often analyzed by Theravada Buddhist thought is human selfhood.

Buddhagoṣa's metaphor likening name and form to a blind man and a cripple, who being helpless when separate, can support one another when they agree to work together, wonderfully illustrates the bearing of

the name and form relationship on the Buddhist nonself
paradigm.   The crippled man agrees to ride on the
shoulders of the blind man while directing the way as
the latter carries him.

> As a pair are mind and body both
> To one another a support;
> As soon as one of them dissolves,
> The other too does disappear. . .
> As men are able with a ship
> To cross the waters of the sea,
> Just so, supported by his body,
> The mind keeps going on.
> And just as with the help of men
> The ship may cross the mighty sea,
> Just so supported by the mind
> The body may be keeping on.
> As men and ship transverse the sea,
> Depending on each other's help,
> So are the mind and body too,
> Each other they support and help.[6]

But neither "mind" nor "body" is a substantial entity.
Even "mind," often identified by non-Buddhist philosophies with the enduring self or center of an individual's existence, is a perpetually fluctuating process.
For,

> this that we call mind, that we call con-
> sciousness, arises as one thing, ceases as
> another, whether by day or by night. Just as
> a monkey faring through the woods, through
> the great forests, catches hold of one
> branch, letting it go, seizes another; even

so that which we call mind, consciousness,
that arises as one thing, ceases as another,
both by day and by night.[7]

In short, we are not bodies possessing a
mind, nor are we minds that can exist apart from the
physiological processes of bodily existence. Whatever
"we" are is neither *nāma* nor *rūpa* in separation, but a
perpetually changing set of interdependent "mind-body"
interrelationships. Yet there exists no entity remaining self-identical through time that "has" these interrelationships. We *are* these interrelationships at any
single moment of space-time.

This conclusion achieves added depth when
viewed according to the theory of the five *skandha* or
"heaps" or "aggregates." All individual "entities,"
including human beings, consist of five ever-changing,
interrelated "heaps:" (1)*rūpa*, (2) *vedānna*
("sensation"), (3) *sañña* ("contact"), (4) *saṃkhārā*
("mental activity," but perhaps best conceived as
"volition"), and (5) *viññana* ("consciousness"). What
we call a self is reduced by the five *skandha* to a series of complex psychosomatic relationships comprised
of form, sensations, feelings, (both physical and emotional), perceptions, unconscious mental states, and
conscious mental activity expressed as "mind" (*nāma*).

Since no *skandha* is permanent, or indeed can
even exist independently from the other four, neither
can any particular form of their relationship be permanent. Therefore, "individuals" composed of particular
skandha relationships too are impermanent. Whenever
the five *skandha* come together at a certain time, and

when what is thereby formed is given a "name," it becomes a "name and form" processive event. But when the
five *skandha* disintegrate the very next instant, there
is no "name and form" entity. There is only the next
set of instantaneous *skandha* relationships.

Thinking of the five *skandha* as "forms of energy-events" provides a good metaphor for grasping the
implications of this aspect of the Buddhist nonself
paradigm. For the five *skandha* are "empty" (Pāli:
suññata) of substantial, permanent self-entities remaining identical through the processes of these five
interrelationships. Relating to the Buddhist nonself
paradigm, what we call a "self" or a "person" is in reality merely a collection of energy-events constantly
assuming various impermanent forms, but "empty" of sub-
stantiality. We are, in other words, "empty" non-
selves because:

> Whatever there is of corporeality, feeling,
> perception, mental formations, whether past,
> present, or future, one's own or external,
> gross or subtle, lofty or low, far or near,
> this one should understand according to real-
> ity and true wisdom: "This does not belong to
> me. This I am not. This is not my Self."[8]

Finally, the nonself paradigm, as one of the
three marks of existence, is always conceived in relation to the other two marks, "impermanence" and
"suffering." The "fact" of nonselfhood is experientially corroborated by the "fact" of universal impermanence, which, because Buddhist teaching stresses the
transient character of the five *skandha*, leaves abso-

lutely no room for any sort of substantially enduring self-entity. Throughout his life, the Buddha constantly reminded his followers of the impermanence of all phenomena. Once, to drive this point home, he held their attention in a rather earthy way:

"There is no materiality whatever, O Monks, no feeling, no perception, no formations, no consciousness whatever that is permanent, everlasting, eternal, changeless, identically abiding forever." Then the Blessed One took a piece of cow dung in his hand and he spoke to the monks: "Monks, if even that much of permanent, ever lasting, eternal, changeless, individual self-hood, identically abiding forever, could be found, then living of a life of purity for the complete eradication of ill would not be feasible."[9]

The Theravada nonself paradigm remains utterly loyal to the Buddha's instruction.

THE MAHAYANA NONSELF PARADIGM (ANĀTMAN)

Our sense of who we are, or sense of "self," Gautama saw, originates in our conscious experience of our self-identity through time. Our memories of our individual and social pasts, along with our present anticipations of our futures, bind us to our ideas about the past and the future. For viewing our individual pasts and futures as our "own" implies we are permanent self-entities enduring from our pasts towards our futures. Thereby, we ourselves create the sources of our suffering, the specific forms of which we undergo in ways expressive of the particular characteristics of our clinging to our conceptions of our selves as permanent self-entities enduring through time.

According to Gautama and subsequent Theravada teaching, however, we are not self-entities subject to a succession of past experiences and future anticipations. Our sense of enduring self-identity is not an objectively given reality about which beliefs can be entertained. Rather, enduring, permanent selfhood exists only in being believed, as a mental construction. In other words, reality, meaning "the way things really are," is a flux of happenings possessing no enduring substantial entities to which events "happen," including human self-entities. There exists no "I."

The Mahayana nonself paradigm continues, while in many ways expanding and deepening, the Theravada nonself paradigm. To the Theravada doctrine of the three marks of existence-suffering, impermanence, and nonself--the Mahayana version of the Dharma added a forth mark, "emptiness" (śūnyatā). According to Theravada teaching, "emptiness" primarily designates the impossibility of being a substantially independent self-entity. Mahayana doctrine expands this notion by using it to deny the possibility of a substantial self-entity within the *dharmas* or "elements" constituting existence at any moment of space-time themselves. Accordingly, what is mostly implied by Theravada teaching in this regard becomes explicit in the Mahayana Buddhist Way.

The scriptural source for the doctrine of emptiness is one of the earliest groups of Mahayana texts collectively called the *Prajñaparamita-sutras* [Discourses on the Perfection of Wisdom], some of which were in process of formulation as early as the second century. The doctrine of *śunyata*, is, therefore, one of the foundational teachings of the Mahayana Dharma.[10]

The "Wisdom Sutras," as they are often called, are dialogues between the Buddha and seekers of enlightenment at the stage of "coursing in the perfection of wisdom," a mental state of deep meditative concentration that nevertheless permits verbal discourse. The "perfection of wisdom" consists of directly apprehending the "emptiness" of all the elements (*dharmas*) comprising existence at any given moment of time, especially including that particular "element" that human beings mistakenly assume to be the self. Even *samsara* and *nirvāna*, both of which are also "elements" of existence in the Buddhist world view, are empty. So too are all the Buddhas and Bodhisattvas, as are the unenlightened beings whom they guide towards enlightenment. No ontological difference exists between the relative and the absolute because both are empty. What all "things" or *dharmas* are empty of is *svabhāva* or "own being," a technical term in Buddhist philosophy denoting (1) something existing through its own power independently of anything else, (2) because it possesses an invariant and inalienable mark or character, and thereby (3) possesses an immutably substantial essence.

The implications of the doctrine of *śunyata* for the Mahayana nonself paradigm were most systematically elaborated in two commentaries written by the philosopher-logician Nāgārjuna: the *Mūlamādhyamika-*

kārikās [Middle Length Stanzas] and the *Vigrahavyāvar-tanī* [Averting the Arguments].[11] That Emptiness is central to Nāgārjuna's understanding of the Buddhist and the subsequent Mahayana nonself paradigm may be illustrated by the following verses:

> 14. When emptiness "works," everything in existence "works."
>
> If emptiness does not "work," then all existence does not "work."
>
> *Mmk, 24*

> 70. All things prevail for him for whom emptiness prevails;
>
> Nothing whatever prevails for him whom emptiness [does not prevail].
>
> *Vv*

What all things are empty of is "own-being" (*svabhāva*). Roughly equivalent to what Western philosophy traditionally designates as "substance," own-being in Buddhist and non-Buddhist Indian philosophy refers to that which can be distinguished from its own attributes, characteristics, or relations. Most simply, own-being names a substantial "something" having attributes and characteristics standing in relation to other entities having attributes and characteristics while remaining unaffected by attributes and characteristics. Therefore, own-being conveys something like a substantially self-existent thing or entity whose existence is ontologically independent of its attributes and relationships. Nāgārjuna's assertion that all things are empty of own-being, therefore, is simultaneously a denial of any form of substance-attribute perspective as a true ontological portrayal of "the way things really are."

Nāgārjuna's major analysis of the concept of own-being occurs in chapter fifteen of his *Middle Stanzas*, entitled "Analysis of a Self-Existent Thing" [*Svabhāva purikṣa*], as Frederick Streng translates it. Own-being, Nāgārjuna declared, simply is impossible because:

1. The production of a self-existent thing by a conditioning cause is not possible. [For] being produced through dependence on a cause, a self-existent thing would be "something which is produced."

2. How, indeed, will a self-existent thing become "something which is produced"? Certainly, a self-existent thing [by definition] is "not produced" and is independent of anything else.

Mmk 15

Own-being, by definition "that which is self-existent," cannot be the effect of any form of causation. And if it cannot be the effect or product of any cause, it cannot come into being. But if again, by definition, own-being is ontologically independent of causal interaction, not only can it come into being, it cannot cease being either. Thus assuming the perspective of own-being, we see that *nothing* can either exist or cease existing.

3. If there is an absence of a self-existent thing, how will another existent thing come into being?

5.   If there is no proof of an existent thing,
       then a nonexistent thing cannot be proved.
       Since people will call the other-existence
       of an existent thing a "nonexistent thing."
              Mm 15

       Accordingly, if own-being were indeed the on-
tological reality of things, Nāgārjuna argued, the conceptual result is "eternalism," meaning that any sort
of change or becoming or process is in principle impos-
sible--a teaching that the Buddhist Way has always regarded as heretical. But arguing against the possibility of own-being is not identical with arguing for the
"nonbeing" of things, or in Nāgārjuna's language,
"other-existence." Other-existence leads to nihilism,
which the Buddhist Way also regards as an unacceptable
heretical teaching.   Thus because other-existence
(nonbeing) itself is a correlate of or relative to
"own-existence" (being), Nāgārjuna denied the very
terms by which any assertion of self-existence or
other-existence, of being or nonbeing, can be made. He
rejected, in other words, all world views and ontolo-
gies assuming either being or nonbeing as their fundamental categories.
       6.   Those who perceive self-existence and other-
              existence, and an existent thing and a non-
              existent thing, do not perceive the true na-
              ture of the Buddha's teaching.
       7.   In "The Instructions of Kātyāyana," both "it
              is" and "it is not" are opposed by the Glori-
              ous One, who has ascertained the meaning of
              "existent" and non-existent."

10. "It is" is a notion of eternity. "It is not"
is a nihilistic view.

Therefore, one who is wise does not have re-
course to "being" or "non-being."

Mmk 15

Nāgārjuna's arguments rejecting all ontolo-
gies and world views, established on the categories of
"being" and "nonbeing" as well as on the related distinction between substance and attributes, perfectly
coincide with the Theravada nonself paradigm.   If anything, however, his interpretation of the Wisdom Sutra's doctrine of Emptiness pushes the Theravada nonself paradigm to its most logically coherent extreme.
Simply stated, his negative claim was that all things
are empty of own-being.   But the positive implications
of his doctrine pushed the Theravada nonself paradigm
in a direction which most Theravada Buddhists found,
and continue to find, unacceptable.

What is positive about Emptiness?   If Emptiness means all things are empty of own-being, what is
positively true about empty things, entities, or
events?   The answer to this question is found in several passages in Nāgārjuna's writings:

27. The "being dependent nature" of existent
things: that is called emptiness."
That which has a nature of "being dependent"
--of that there is a nonself existent nature.
Vv

18. The "originating dependently" we call
"emptiness;" This apprehension, i.e., taking

into account [all other things], is the understanding of the middle way.
19. Since there is no dharma whatever originating
independently,
No dharma whatever exists which is not empty.
36. You deny all mundane and customary activities
when you deny emptiness [in the sense of] dependent co-origination.

Mmk 24

Things being empty of own-being, all things
are what they are and are not through dependent co-
origination. Emptiness *is* dependent co-origination.
However, dependent co-origination, while certainly a
central doctrine in Nāgārjuna's thought, possesses a
rather different meaning for him and for subsequent Mahayana tradition than for Theravada tradition. The
Theravada doctrine of dependent co-origination is really an atomistic theory of "elements" (*dharmas*) interdependently constituting existence at any moment of
space-time. And, unlike the "things" they constitute,
the Theravada "elements" do not lack "own-being." In
contrast, Nāgārjnuna's rejection of own-being is utterly explicit and absolute, and thereby his conceptualization of the Buddhist nonself paradigm radically
transforms earlier Theravada conceptualization of the
meaning of nonself.

Since Emptiness and dependent co-origination
are interdependent teachings in his concept of the Buddhist doctrine of nonself, dependent co-origination
cannot refer to the causal relationships among self-existent *dharmas* composing existence. On the contrary,

dependent co-origination must itself be a function of the conditions it comprises. That is, whatever "is" at any moment of space-time consists of conditions or relationships, and these too are dependently co-originated. Or, as Streng has interpreted Nagarjuna on this point:

> Considered in the context of emptiness, co-originating dependently loses its meaning as a link between two "things"; rather it becomes the form for expressing the phenomenal "becoming" as the lack of any self-sufficient reality.[12]

Since whatever "is" is dependently co-originated simultaneously with whatever "is not," self-existence is denied to everything, including Emptiness and dependent co-origination. Objects, events, "selves," do indeed exist, but not as self-existent objects. All entities are "events" of complex interrelationships, which is also saying they are dependently co-originated.

Nāgārjuna's interpretation of Emptiness and the implications of his interpretation for the the teaching of dependent co-origination comprise the core teaching of the Mahayana nonself paradigm. Every Mahayana school, in varying degrees of logical consistency, assumes his perspective as an axiomatic starting point for its own unique teachings and practices. Accordingly, what we usually call a "person" or a "self" represents merely a name we conventionally give to a momentary set of dependently co-originating relationships. But there exists no permanently self-existent

entity that "has" these relationships. For whatever
"we" are, "we" are empty, like everything else, of own-
being. The self is a momentary nonself, meaning a se-
quence of interdependent relationships possessing no
substantial ground in which these relationships inhere.
Stated somewhat poetically, there is no "I" that eats,
I am my eating; there is no "I" that loves or hates, I
am my loving or hating; there is no "I" that clings, I
am my clinging; there is no "I" that suffers, I am my
suffering; there is no "I" that attains enlightenment,
I am my enlightenment.

THE CHRISTIAN SELF PARADIGM

The Christian Way, in contrast with the Buddhist Way, has never formulated a clearly defined doctrine of human selfhood. Nevertheless, traditional
Christian teaching and practice assume a concept of human nature that, although not often articulated with
much detail, constitutes the Christian self paradigm.
Accordingly, I am concerned in this section with making
this tacitly assumed self paradigm explicit. The
Christian self paradigm originates in two interdependent, but at times contradictory, sources: the Bible
and the Bible as read through the traditions of Greek
philosophy. Specifying the central characteristics of
the traditional Christian self paradigm must begin with
analyzing these two sources.

Contemporary biblical scholarship has conclu-
sively demonstrated there are no dualistic assumptions
in the biblical images of human existence. Nor, in direct contrast, do the biblical images of human exis-

tence include notions of permanent, substantial self or soul entities that remain unchanged through time (in direct contrast with Greek and most Hindu notions of human nature). The biblical view of human existence is holistic and, borrowing a phrase from process philosophy, "processive."[13] A human being is pictured as a unity of "soul," "body," "flesh," and "spirit" simultaneously constituting the whole person. None of these constituent elements is capable of separating itself from the total structure of a person's reality. For since God created human beings entire, in humanity's entirety they must be "saved," "salvation" itself meaning "wholeness."[14] Thus the biblical images portraying selfhood focus on the ultimate fulfillment of the total life of all human beings, not on a substantially changeless part of this life called a "soul" or "self."

In many ways, the biblical images of selfhood have much in common with the Buddhist nonself paradigm.[15] However, the idea of a substantially immutable soul entity at the center of human selfhood is deeply ingrained in popular Christian imagination and most traditional theology. The reasons for this mostly involve the spread of the Christian Way beyond the limited cultural confines of Palestine to the wider and dominant culture of Hellenistic civilization. In the process, biblical images of selfhood, along with the biblical images of God, were translated into the predominant world view of first and second century Hellenistic civilization—a world view established on Greek philosoPhy, especially the philosophy of Plato and Plotinus. The mixture of biblical and Greek images

of the self subsequently created major problems
throughout Christian intellectual history, especially
in the formulation of authentically Christian notions
of selfhood reflective of biblical images of human nature.

Accordingly, several contemporary theologians
have written about the need to reject the notion of a
permanent soul because it is "dualistic" and unreflec-
tive of biblical notions of human existence, not to
mention of biblical revelation. Among the most vocif-
erous was arl Barth. "We must," he said,

contradict the abstractly dualistic conception of which so far we have summarily called
Greek, but which unfortunately must also be
described as the traditional Christian view.
According to this view, soul and body are indeed connected, even essentially and necessarily united, but only as two "parts" of human nature.

In general, the character and result of
this anthropology are marked by a separation
of soul over the body, a humiliation of the
body under the soul, in which both readily
become not merely abstractions but in fact
two "co-existing" figments--a picture in
which probably no real man ever recognized
himself, and with which one cannot possibly
do justice to the biblical view and concept
of man. It was disastrous that this picture
of man could assert and maintain itself for
so long as the Christian picture.[16]

In agreement with Barth, Paul Tillich also believed the importation of Greek soul theory was not only unbiblical, but superstitious, especially the concept of the soul's immortality:

> For the individual participating in Eternal Life, Christianity uses the two terms "immortality" and "resurrection" (besides "Eternal Life" itself). Of the two, only "resurrection" is biblical. But "immortality" in the sense of the Platonic doctrine of the immortality of the soul, was used very early in Christian theology, and in large sections of Protestant thought, it has replaced the symbol of resurrection. In some Protestant countries it has become the last remnant of the whole Christian message, but it has done so in the non-Christian pseudo-Platonic form of a continuation of the temporal life of an individual after death without a body. Where the symbol of immortality is used to express this popular superstition, it must be radically rejected by Christianity; for participation is not "life hereafter." Neither is it a natural quality of the human soul. It is rather the creative act of God who lets the temporal separate itself from and return to the eternal.[17]

The point of Barth's and Tillich's rejection of Greek notions of the soul, a rejection also shared by many other contemporary Roman Catholic and Protestant theologians, can be easily grasped by considering the biblical terms used to designate human existence.

Undoubtedly, the most descriptive word designating the Hebrew view of human nature is *nephesh*, often translated "soul" in older English translations of the Bible. A more accurate translation, however, is "life" in the generic sense of the force animating all living things. *Nephesh* has nothing to do with the ideas of immortality of a substantial soul entity remaining self-identical through time. For at death, the *nephesh* "goes out" (Gen. 35:18), meaning it ceases to exist. Nor is there any suggestion in the Hebrew scriptures of the survival of the *nephesh* of a living being whose "life" it was. Even the inhabitants of the Hebrew nether world, Sheoul, are not described as living beings but as *rephaim* or "shades," a condition which cannot really be called life because it is more like a state in which "nothing means anything anymore." The ancient Hebrews possessed no notion, in other words, of what happens after death other than that the "life" of a living being runs out.

The New Testament's equivalent to the Hebrew *nephesh* is *psychē*. Unlike Platonic and Aristotelian philosophy, where *psyche* designates a substantial, immortal "soul" associated with human rationality, the New Testament use of *psychē* mostly corresponds to the Hebrew meaning of the life force animating living beings. It denotes the quality of "vitality" or "aliveness." Thus *psychē* is "life" that can be cared for, loved, saved, judged, or lost. (2 Cor. 1:23; 1 Thes. 2:8; Rom. 16:4). In Romans 11:3, for example,

Paul quotes the Septuagint version of 1 Kings 19:10, "...and they steal my life" (psychē), where psychē without doubt means "life." Romans 16:4 gives exactly the same meaning. The "life" to which Paul was referring is the natural aliveness or "life force" that human beings share with all other living beings, in contrast to lifeless things called apsychos, a generic term meaning all inanimate objects.

Paul and other New Testament writers also employed psychē in the psychological sense as the center of human emotions, thought, and will. In this meaning, the psychē or "soul" can be deeply grieved or wonderfully exalted. (Matthew 26:38; Luke 1:46; John 12:27) It can be addressed and complimented on its possessions. (Luke 12:19) Psychē can also be used reflexively to describe emotions and expressions of the will in the sense of specific desires, abilities, or the determination of goals (Ephesians 6:6; Col. 3:23).

Finally, in a number of instances psychē is used in reference to an individual or a group of individuals. Many of these references are found in Acts. And in Romans, for example, Paul wrote of "every soul of man that works evil," where is psychē employed not only in the sense of "individual person," but also to mean the agent of evil actions. The use of "soul" in this context does not denote a "part" of a human being responsible for doing evil, but rather the whole person as capable of doing evil. An identical usage is repeated in Romans 13:1 without reference to evil. In 2 Corinthians 12:15 Paul mentions being "spent for your souls," meaning his gift of himself in service on their behalf as persons. Finally, "soul" can also refer to the psychological-moral unity of several individuals when qualified with the word "one." (Acts 4:32; Phil. 1:27)

Nowhere in the New Testament, it must be stressed, when *psychē* is employed to refer to individual human beings, does it denote a substantial soul entity "dwelling" or "entrapped" within the "body" (*soma*). The wholeness and unity of persons was further emphasized in Paul's "anthropology" by the manner in which he connected *psychē* with *sōma*, a term that he exclusively employed to designate the generic unity of a human being. Human existence was, for him, always "somatic" or bodily existence, and thus *sōma* is the most comprehensive term he used to describe human nature. In fact, so central was *sōma* to Paul's understanding of human nature that he even believed the resurrection occurred in bodily form, albeit a "spiritual body" rather than a physical body. (1 Cor. 15:50; 15:44-49) The only life possible for human beings, whether in this life or after, is somatic existence.

Because *sōma* does not refer to merely a person's physiology and its attributes, it is descriptive of the whole person--mentally, physically, and spiritually. In other words, we do not *have* a *sōma*, we are *sōma*, as Paul said in Romans 12:1: "Present your bodies (*sōma*)," meaning "yourselves," the totality of what we are, "as living sacrifices." Consequently, *sōma* designates whatever constitutes human nature as a unity, and therefore amounts to the same meaning as "self," although without substantialist connotations. The whole human self, everything together constituting a person as distinctively human, the New Testament designates as *sōma*.

This last point is deepened, interestingly enough, when we realize that nowhere in the New Testament is a corpse referred to as *sōma*. Paul in particular reserved soma as a designation for human beings because of the qualities of life (*psychē*) animating living existence. Somatic existence means being capable of making ourselves the object of our own thoughts and actions while simultaneously experiencing ourselves as subjects being formed by our thoughts and actions.

Now, since human beings are *sōma* capable of relating themselves to the environing world as subjects of their own thoughts and actions, there exist two possibilities for the kind of life one may experience. We may be at one with ourselves, so that our actions, thoughts, and emotions actually correspond to what we will. Or we may be so estranged from ourselves as to be at the mercy of "powers" and forces not under our control but of our own making. Paul believed being at the mercy of "powers" and forces not of our making but which determine our existence is the normal condition for all human beings because of the universality of sin.[18]

Paul called the totality of these objective "powers" estranging us from ourselves, each other, and God the "flesh" (*sarx*), and he believed the *sōma* of all persons is completely dominated by these powers. Thus he often referred to the "deeds of the *sōma*" as "life according to the flesh." No one is free from this condition, nor can anyone freely will to do whatever is good. Human existence, in a state of universal sinfulness, must be lived under the bondage to powers over which no one has control--powers such as lust, anger, desire, pride--all of which are forms of human egoism as well as objectively existing demonic beings seeking to control our lives.[20]

"The flesh," however, does not simply describe human natural endowments, which are in themselves neither good nor sinful. Rather, "the flesh" describes the attitude according to which we absolutize anything finite into an ultimate concern, cling to these entities, and thereby surrender ourselves to them rather than surrendering ourselves to God's demand that we love all human beings with "no strings attached." In other words, the things to which we cling in effect become our "deities", and the service we perform in devotion to the pursuit of such deities is "life according to the flesh." Paul concluded that under the conditions of universal sinfulness, this is the only possible way human life can be lived.

Finally, Paul and the rest of the New Testament writers followed Hebraic tradition in the use of the term *pneuma* or "spirit." In the Hebrew Scriptures, "spirit" is called *ruah*, literally "breath" or "wind," and to a large degree this usage is synonymous with "life" (*nephesh*). The same is true in the New Testament: "spirit" (*pneuma*) and "life" (*psyche*) are also to a large degree synonymous, although Paul reserved *pneuma* to describe God's spirit or the Holy Spirit.

As descriptive of human beings, "spirit" does not point to some higher faculty within an individual distinguished from his body and soul. But in distinction from psychē, pneuma most often denotes a form, expression, or "style" of life that a person expresses in his conscious behavior. And in this sense, Paul's use of "spirit" approximates some modern conceptions of consciousness--the conscious knowing, willing, and doing of actions, along with whatever conscious intentions motivate our actions. In this sense, an individual's actions may be motivated by several varieties of "spirit." For example, individuals can be described as either evil-spirited or good-spirited persons when their desires are consciously motivated by either evil or good intentions. Pneuma can also mean agreement between individuals, as when in 2 Corinthians 12:18, for example, Paul asks, "Did we not walk in the same spirit?" meaning "did we not agree?" "The spirit is willing, but the flesh is weak," the words of Jesus reported in Matthew, also illustrate Paul's use of spirit. Accordingly, the spirit of individuals may characterize good, bad, or indifferent qualities of their lives, depending upon their conscious motivations. In a similar way, Paul wrote of the "spirit of faith," the "spirit of the gentleness," the "spirit of the world," the "spirit of love," the "spirit of anger," and the "spirit of pride."

To summarize, the biblical self paradigm does not entail splitting human life into separate parts, sōma (body) and psychē (life or soul), with psychē conceived as a permanent self or soul-entity dwelling within a body and expressing itself through life and spirit. According to biblical tradition, a human being is a living unity of body, life, and spirit. Persons (sōma) are beings pursuing goals and desires while consciously experiencing and knowing themselves by what and to whom they relate. Or restated somewhat differently, our "self," what we are at any moment, is an interdependent unity of body, "soul" or life, and spirit apart from a permanent self or soul-entity possessing these "attributes." In similarity with the Buddhist nonself paradigm, this amounts to saying we *are* our relationships, our eating, our feelings, our desires, our actions, our history. How we relate to the world and others in the world, how we love, how we think, how we sin, how we judge, *is* what "we" are at that moment.

Modern biblical scholarship has completely demonstrated how unbiblical the traditional Christian self paradigm is, along with the failure of that paradigm's ability to express adequately the Christian experience of selfhood. Most contemporary theologians, and several modern theological movements, have questioned and renounced the traditional Christian self paradigm because it cannot be reconciled with either the Bible or the world view of modern physics and current psychological theory. Accordingly, there exists a growing awareness among sensitive Christians that if Christian faith actually requires belief in a substantial self-entity, or for that matter in a transcendent self-entity named "God," an unsolvable metaphysical and epistemological incoherency immediately emerges, not to mention serious religious difficulties.

The traditional Christian self paradigm involves a synthesis of biblical images read through Hellenistic spectacles, a reading beginning in the first century and continuing in many forms to this day. In numerous ways, the Homeric literature certainly reflects notions of the soul quite similar to biblical tradition. In this literature, for example, *psychē* is an insubstantial life force or "breath" that leaves the body at death through the mouth or a wound. It can appear as a ghost, but after a proper burial dwells in a shadowy, impersonal underworld called *hades*, a place very similar to the biblical *sheoul*. Thus the most ancient Greek conception of the soul bore no relation to human mental functions. But the Pythagoreans, and later Plato, expanded this notion by splitting *psychē* from the physical foundations of bodily existence and assigning mental functions to it. Plato also added *pneuma* as the life force, keeping the soul eternally animated even after the body dies. Accordingly Plato, Aristotle, and subsequent Hellenistic philosophical tradition interpreted the soul as a substantially permanent self-entity enduring through time, experiencing change but itself never changing. The soul, in other words, is immortal.

During the first four centuries of Christian history, when the Church was interpreting and spreading its message in the environment of Hellenistic civilization, the classical Greek notion of the soul was mixed with oriental influences, especially those depreciating the human body as composed of evil material "stuff," the limitations of which had to be overcome for human beings to achieve salvation. This led to a general tendency for Christians, both theologians and laity, to view human existence dualistically: the soul is eternal, good, substantial, and involved in the process of salvation, while the body in which the soul is "entrapped" is mortal, evil, a hindrance to the process of salvation, that must be overcome. To satisfy concern about the destiny of various human souls after death, doctrines were promulgated of hell as a place where non-saved souls are consigned by God for eternal punishment in the form of torture for their sins, purgatory as a place where sinful souls are temporarily punished for sin in preparation for entry into Heaven, and Heaven as an abode of eternal bliss and joy because the soul attains eternal life in the direct presence of God. Of course, various levels of sophisticated interpretation existed, and continue existing, in the application of these teachings to the lives of Christians. But in point of fact, none of these teachings has very much to do with the Bible precisely because all so profoundly distort biblical portrayals of selfhood. They also distort biblical images of God.

The traditional Christian self paradigm, therefore, may be defined as a contradictory mixture of biblical and Greek images. Portrayed as substantial self-entities, human beings are unchanging subjects of experience and behavior to which the word "I" refers. It is this "I" whose salvation is sought and that is held accountable for its deeds. The Christian Way continues revolving around this self paradigm even though most sensitive Christian thinkers now find it unacceptable; for surely this self paradigm profoundly misrepresents the biblical images of human selfhood. Nor does it adequately portray Christian experience of selfhood in relationship with the God that Christians trust was manifested in the life and death of Jesus of Nazareth.

CONCLUDING OBSERVATIONS

On the basis of the foregoing comparisons, at least three concluding observations emerge which should provide important topics for future Buddhist-Christian dialogical conversation. First, the Buddhist nonself paradigm, in both its Theravada and Mahayana versions, and the biblical self paradigm are remarkably similar. Both perceive human existence as a series of ever-changing relationships. Furthermore, there exists no substantially permanent non-changing center, no "I" to which these relationships "happen." For we are our re-lationships. Accordingly, there seem to be unexplored areas of common experience that provide direction for continuing Buddhist-Christian dialogue.

But while similar, the Buddhist nonself paradigm and the Christian self paradigm are not iden-tical, especially regarding what each paradigm implies about the role of God in the quest for authentic human selfhood. Now, the Buddhist nonself paradigm does not exactly deny the existence of God, provided that by "God" we do not mean a transcendent, substantial non-changing sacred entity remaining self-identical through time. But even if there are gods, these realities can have nothing to do with the achievement of enlightenment. Human experience of *duḥkha* is not God's problem, and, therefore, we must rely on ourselves, or more accurately, on our non-selves, to achieve enlightenment— a process requiring the meditative realization of our nonselfhood existing in an utterly processive universe in which there are no permanent entities of any sort to which to cling. Once realizing this, we stop clinging and thereby cease experiencing *duḥkha*. So even if there are gods, or, for that matter, a God as monotheistically conceived in the Jewish, Christian, or Islamic religious Ways, no deity can be of any help to suffering, clinging beings. For devotional reliance upon God merely represents one more form of ignorant clinging to permanency in an impermanent universe. In other words, devotionalism ultimately generates new and deeper forms of suffering.

Still, the biblical self paradigm, precisely because it does not involve notions of permanent selfhood, also implies non-substantialist images of God. The biblical god, of which the human self is an "image," is not a transcendent, substantial, non-changing sacred entity, but a "living God"—a god totally involved in the world God created and continues creating, and who, as a consequence, is positively and negatively affected by the world. In other words, God is not a self-entity any more than human beings are self-entities, although God is "eternal"—not, be it noted, "immortal." Consequently, "salvation," meaning a quality of relationship with God named "eternal life" by the New Testament, does not entail permanent self-entities achieving their "soul's" immortality in the presence of another immortal, unchanging self-entity named "God." For Christian salvation is something coming to human beings as a gift expressing God's continuing creative action in history. "We" cannot save ourselves, for finally and ultimately, what "we" are is conditioned by our relationship with each other as well as with God.

The theme of creation is not, of course, emphasized by the Buddhist Way. Nor is Buddhist enlightenment Christian salvation. Still, study of the Bible can do much to help Buddhists free themselves from the rather widespread stereotypical assumption that the Christian Way requires belief in substantialist notions of human selfhood and God. Clearly, this is not the case, and never has been. In dialogue with biblical images of selfhood, Buddhists can achieve a more accurate and less stereotypical understanding of Christian experience.

Second, drawing attention to the differences between Buddhist and Christian selfhood paradigms certainly does not imply the Buddhist nonself paradigm is in error while the Christian self paradigm is a mirror image of reality, or *vice versa*. Both may be true reflections of reality, "the way things really are," because both paradigms express differing yet valid interpretations of the bipolar structure of the experience of self-identity through time. In fact, I think this is the case; for the Buddhist nonself paradigm overstresses the experience of becoming at the expense of ignoring the experience of stability and permanency by explaining it away as a "delusion," and the Christian

self paradigm overstresses the experience of permanence
and stability while ignoring the experience of becoming. Both experiences are real and require, it seems
to me, a more integrative interpretation of the relationship than either the traditional Buddhist nonself
paradigm or the traditional Christian self paradigm
seems capable of developing separately. Buddhists
might be able to incorporate into the Buddhist nonself
paradigm insights regarding human selfhood which are
more adequately conceived through the Christian self-
paradigm without compromising the integrity of Buddhist
faith and practice. The result would be a more coherent
and balanced understanding of human selfhood. Likewise, Christians need to appropriate Buddhist insights
regarding change and becoming into the Christian self-
paradigm for the same reason--achieving a more coherent
and balanced understanding of human selfhood.[20]

Third, Christian dialogue with the Buddhist
nonself paradigm should be preceded by a lengthy dialogue with biblical images of human selfhood. Otherwise, the present distortions of the traditional Christian self-paradigm will continue, and thus prevent full
understanding of and appreciation for the realities of
the experience of selfhood more fully articulated in
Buddhist faith and practice.

In conclusion, Buddhist appropriation of
truths in Christian biblical images of selfhood would
create a different Buddhist Way from what the West or
the East now knows. I do not believe, however, this
Way would be less Buddhist. But I am also convinced
that the Christian Way would emerge from reappropriat-

ing the biblical self paradigm, along with truths of the Buddhist nonself paradigm, as a Christian Way different from what the East or the West now knows. I also believe that it would not be less Christian. On the contrary, faithfulness to the Dharma and faithfulness to Christ require Buddhists and Christians to to expose themselves consciously and critically to just this sort of mutual transformation.

NOTES

[1]Narada Thera, trans., *The Buddha and His Teachings* (Colombo: Vajiraramaya, 1964), 100.

[2]Thomas S. Kuhn, *The Structure of Scientific Revolutions* (Chicago: University of Chicago Press, 1962), chapts. 1-2.

[3]See "atta" in *Pali Text Society Pali-English Dictionary* (London: Luzak, 1959).

[4]There also existed views of the self that Buddhist tradition labeled "nihilistic." The general characteristic of these views was their denial of any center of selfhood in human existence, thus reducing human nature to a mere configuration of material forces or elements unguided by anything external to their own operating principles. A convenient Western label describing these views might be "materialism." Spelling out the details of either specific "eternalist" or "nihilistic" views of the self contemporary with Gautama is unnecessary here. But it is most important to notice Buddhist philosophy portrays Gautama's doctrine of nonself as a "middle way" between these two types of self theories.

[5]*Saṃyutta-nikāya* [Collection of Grouped Discourses] 11, 94 in Rhys Davids, trans., *The Book of Kindred Sayings* (London: Oxford University Press, 1952).

[6]*Visuddhimagga* [The Path of Purity], 18 in H. C. Warren, *Buddhism in Translations* (Cambridge: Harvard University Press, 1909), 185.

[7]*Saṃyutta- nikāya*, 25.5.

[8]Ibid., 22.95.

[9]Ibid., 22.96.

[10]See Lewis R. Lancaster, "The Prajnaparamita Literature," in *Buddhism: A Modern Perspective*, ed. Charles Prebish (University Park: Pennsylvania State University Press, 1975), 69-71.

[11]Passages cited from these texts are taken from the translation of Frederic J. Streng, *Emptiness: A Study in Religious Meaning* (Nashville: Abingdon Press, 1967), 183-227. Hereafter references to these texts will be abbreviated *Mmk* and *Vv* respectively.

[12]Ibid., 63.

[13]See Lewis S. Ford, *The Lure of God* (Philadelphia: Fortress Press, 1978), 45-70.

[14]My interpretations of the biblical views of selfhood are based on the following sources: Gerhard von Rad, *Old Testament theology,* 2 vols. (New York: Harper and Row, 1962); Gunther Bornkamm, *Paul* (New York: Harper and Row, 1971); Rudolf Bultmann, *Theology of the New Testament,* 2 vols. (New York: Charles Scribner's Sons, 1951); and Herman Ridderbos, *Paul, An Outline of His Theology* (Grand Rapids,Mich.: William B. Eerdman's Publishing Co. 1975).

[15]Lynn de Silva, *The Problem of the Self in Buddhism and Christianity* (New York: Harper and Row, 1979), 1-10, 75-90.

[16]Karl Barth, *Church Dogmatics* (Edinburgh: T. and T. Clark, 1961), vol.3, part 2, 387. Also quoted in de Silva, *The Problem of the Self in Christianity and Buddhism,* 76.

[17]Paul Tillich, *Systematic Theology,* (Chicago: University of Chicago Press, 1963), 3: 407-408.

[18]Anything, including attitudes, actions, or omissions separating a human being from God. See the article on "sin" in Keith Crim, ed., *Abingdon Dictionary of Living Religions* (Nashville: Abingdon Press, 1981), 694-695.

[19]Paul accepted the existence of demons, using his language, "principalities and powers." In so doing, he simply accepted the common world view of first-century Hellenistic civilization.

[20]Although it is not possible to undertake this task in this particular chapter, the philosophical vision of Alfred North Whitehead contains a number of

conceptions about the structure of the experience of self-identity through time that take into account both the experience of becoming and the experience of stability and permanency. Buddhist and Christian reflection could profit by employing a scheme like Whitehead's for clarifying what their respective selfhood paradigms ignore. This need not entail reducing the Buddhist Way or the Christian Way to Whitehead's categories. The point is that Whitehead's scheme could serve as a hermeneutical bridge between the Buddhist and the Christian conceptualizations of selfhood and thereby create the possibility for each Way's appropriation of insights from the other hidden by their own paradigms. Some of the writings of John Cobb illustrate this possibility. See, for example, his *Beyond Dialogue* (Philadelphia: Fortress Press, 1982).

CHAPTER EIGHT
The Question of God

It is indeed a fact that salvation cannot come from the mere sight of Me. It demands strenuous efforts in the practice of Yoga. But if someone has thoroughly understood this my Dharma, then he is released from the net of suffering, even though he never cast his eyes on Me. A man must take medicine to be cured; the mere sight of the physician is not enough. Likewise, the mere sight of Me enables no one to conquer suffering; he will have to meditate for himself about the [knowledge] l have communicated.

Aśvaghoṣa, *Buddhacarita*, 20[1]

"If you knew me you would know my Father too. From now on you do know him; you have seen him." Philip said to him, "Lord, show us the Father and we ask no more." Jesus answered, "Have I been all this time with you, Philip, and you still do not know me? Anyone who has seen me has seen the Father."

John 14:7-10, *New English Bible*

THE HUMAN EXPERIENCE OF SELFHOOD AND GOD

In spite of the numerous parallels between the Buddhist and biblical paradigms of selfhood, Buddhist and Christian conceptions of the self are not identical. The Buddhist nonself paradigm and the Christian self paradigm imply opposing conclusions about the nature of God and, indeed, about the nature of the Sacred in general, as well as about the function of God in the quest for what Buddhists call "enlightenment" and what Christians call "salvation."

Not that Theravada or Mahayana versions of the doctrine of nonself categorically deny the existence of God, provided God is not defined as a transcendent, substantial, nonchanging sacred self-entity, eternally enduring through time. The usual Western portrayal of Buddhist teaching and Practice as "atheistic" is inaccurate. But even if gods do exist, however defined, such beings can have nothing to do with anyone's achievement of enlightenment. The fact of *duhkha* is our problem, not God's problem, according to the Second Noble Truth. We must, therefore, rely solely on our own self-efforts through the disciplined practice of meditation. Even the God of Christian teaching cannot help suffering, clinging beings, because devotional reliance upon God represents merely one more form of ignorant clinging to the delusion of permanency in an impermanent universe. According to Buddhist teaching, devotion to a sacred entity named God, however conceived, merely engenders new and more intense experiences of suffering.

But opposition need not mean contradiction. The question of God most certainly divides Buddhists and Christians. However, the same question even divides Christians. To be sure, Buddhists find it difficult to remain Buddhist apart from nonclinging to God in their quest for enlightenment. And Christians cannot remain Christian apart from faith in God as encountered through the events of Jesus' life, death, and resurrection. Even so, much depends upon the meaning of the word "god." Accordingly, this chapter summarizes (1) the generic characteristics of traditional Christian doctrinal portrayals of God, (2) process theology's characterization of God, particularly in the thought of John Cobb, and (3) how process theology's characterization of God has been creatively transformed through dialogue with the Mahayana Buddhist doctrine of Emptiness (śūnyatā). My thesis is that process theology's dialogue with Mahayana versions of the Buddhist doctrines of nonself, impermanence, and dependent co-origination is the leading contemporary Christian example of the possibilities of creative transformation through interreligious dialogue.

It would be absurd, of course, to claim that process theology's conception of God is the only, or even the best, way of thinking about God available to Christians resulting from dialogue with the Buddhist Way. Nor should anyone assume that Buddhists will, or even should, easily appropriate process theology's conception of God into a possible doctrinal reconstruction of the Dharma. Only Buddhists can pass judgment here. Nevertheless, not only is process theology's reflection on the sacred reality Christians call God an approoximation of historically normative Christian meanings, but its characterization of God does not contradict Buddhist religious experience. Thus if Cobb and other process thinkers following his lead are correct, Buddhists and Christians can allow one another to be mutually transformed through converting the contradictions between the traditional Buddhist denials of God and traditional Christian affirmations of God into complementary polarities. Whether such a conversion of opposites will actually occur remains another question. I do think, however, it remains a possibility worth dialogical exploration.

SOME PRELIMINARY DEFINITIONS

In the previous chapter, I argued that the traditional Buddhist nonself paradigm and the traditional Christian self paradigm are, in separation from one another, inadequate descriptive accounts of the human experience of selfidentity through time. I also concluded that dialogue with Whiteheadian process philosophy might help both Buddhists and Christians to create more logically coherent conceptions of the experience of self-identity through time that harmonize the realities of human selfhood to which the Buddhist nonself Paradigm and the Christian self paradigm symbolically point. But I did not undertake this task myself, thereby leaving a very important issue of Buddhist-Christian dialogical encounter unresolved. Consequently, since the question of God is interdependent with the question of human selfhood, I must now clearly define what I mean by "subject," "person," and "self" before continuing further.[2]

According to Whitehead, the existence of any human being from conception until death (and perhaps thereafter) may be characterized as a series of unconscious and conscious "units" of experience. Every individual experiential unit in this series, which Whitehead called an "actual entity" or "actual occasion of experience," represents a series of subjective processes of "feeling" or "prehending" the entire "data" presented to it by its environing universe and synthesizing these data into a complex experiential whole. At the instant this synthesis is completed, the subjective immediacy of the actual occasion perishes.

Thereupon it immediately becomes an object to be unconsciously or consciously experienced by future actual
entities in this series. As an immediate process of
unconsciously and consciously experiencing and synthesizing, an actual entity is a "subject." As an object
to be experienced by future actual entities, it is an
"object," or in Whitehead's terminology, a "subject-su-
perject." According to this perspective, an individual
human life is a series of experiential units called
"actual entities," which become objects for subsequent
subjects in this series.[3]

Following Whitehead's lead, I shall use the
word "person" to denote a particular series of human
experiences[4] extending from the moment of conception
until death, considered as a whole. That is, "person"
refers to the totality of an individual's experiences
from conception until death. By "subject," I mean any
particular experiential unit or actual entity of a person's life, insofar as any particular actual entity
comprising that person's life is a process of "feeling"
or "prehending" the "data" of whatever entities constitute the universe objective to it. Finally, by the
word "self," I mean any particular subject of the on-
going life history of a person that is present, rather
than past or future. In other words, a "person" is a
series of "subjects," and a person's "self" is that
subject that at any given moment is contemporary, in
the sense of existing here-and-now. When a subject
that is here-and-now perishes, it loses its status as
the self of the person in question. The subsequent
subject evolves in its place, so that a person's "self"

consists of different subjects from moment to moment during that person's life history. But at any given moment of a person's life history, that person's self is always here-and-now, meaning always contemporary. The self is never past or future, except as an abstraction viewed objectively by other persons or by ourselves as we remember our past. But from the perspective of our own subjective experiences, we always experience our own selfhood as immediate and present.

Defining the self à la process philosophy constitutes a self paradigm descriptive of the experience of self-identity through time to which the Buddhist doctrine of nonself symbolically points. From the moment a person experiences enlightenment, the reality of the enlightened person's self, the "true Self" or "everyday mind" of Zen Buddhist teaching, is intuitively and nondiscursively apprehended as always here-and-now while simultaneously always changing. An enlightened person freely and creatively lives in the immediate present as the only moment of time there is. But inasmuch as the self is always changing, the enlightened person also apprehends the utter impossibility of clinging to any moment of the self's existence. Thus the enlightened ones, the Buddhas, experience the self, or in Buddhist language the nonself, as a kind of "groundless ground." That is, the self is a "ground" because it constitutes the enlightened person's point of departure for all experience and action in the world. More simply, "something," meaning the "self," experiences. But the self is simultaneously "groundless," because the self is never identically the same during any two instances of a person's existence. Again more simply, the self is also "nothing." We cannot, accordingly, cling to ourselves; we can only *be* ourselves from moment to moment during our personal life histories.[5] In the words of the Chinese Zen master Ummon (Chinese, Yün-mên, d. 949?): "Look! This world is vast and wide. Why do you put on your priest's robes at the sound of the bell?"[6]

The self, then, is whatever we are doing and undergoing as we are doing and undergoing it. For example, as I write these words on paper in my study, my self is the writing. As I gaze at a distant mountain while backpacking in the high country surrounding Mount Rainier, my self is the gazing and backpacking. As I love my family and my friends, my self is the loving. As I hate my enemies, my self is the hating. As I teach my courses at my university, my self is the teaching. As I eat and sleep, my self is the eating and sleeping. And *your* self at this moment is the reading of the words a whole series of my selves have written on this page. The self is a *process* of doing and undergoing.

But this definition of the self also describes the experience of self-identity through time to which the traditional Christian selfhood paradigm symbolically points. We *do* experience stability and order amidst the self's process of doing and undergoing, from the moment of conception until the moment of death. That is, we are the same *person* from moment to moment of our life histories, even though we are not the same *self* from moment to moment. The self we are at any mo-

ment of doing and undergoing, in other words, represents the present experiential culmination of everything we have ever done and undergone in the past.
What a person's self is now embodies everything that
person's self was from conception until the present.
Therefore, the experience that I am the same person today as I was when my father took that photograph of me
over forty years ago is not simply a delusion. But I
am not the same self today that I was when my father
took that photograph.

To summarize, as "persons" we experience stability and process simultaneously. Neither experience
is a delusion, even though we can be deluded in our understanding of the nature of these experiences. But we
never experience permanency. That is, the person named
Paul Ingram now writing these words on paper in his
study is a continuation of numerous past selves doing
similar writing and reflecting; the person named Paul
Ingram now loving his family and friends is a continuation of a series of past loving selves. In short, my
present self is a continuation and culmination of the
totality of past selves constituting the life history
of the person named Paul Ingram. Whatever my self will
become will be a continuation and a culmination of this
process until the person named Paul Ingram dies.

If the self paradigm I have described accurately reflects and coherently integrates Buddhist and
Christian conceptions of selfhood, the question now
arises about how that sacred reality Christians call
"God" might be conceived.

THE CONCEPT OF GOD IN PROCESS THEOLOGY

Process theology's conception of God is often called "dipolar theism" because God, according to Whitehead, possesses two interrelated and interdependent, but nevertheless distinct, natures. Whitehead believed God is a special type of actual entity whose existence during any moment of the temporal process of space-time is comprised of an abstract, essentially unchanging "primordial nature" and a concrete changing "consequent nature." As primordial, God's reality-- what God *is* from moment to moment remains eternal, absolute, independent, and unchangeable. That is, the primordial nature of God designates those abstract elements of the Sacred, however it is named, delimiting God as God at every moment of God's existence. According to Whitehead and subsequent process theology, traditional Christian doctrines of God have stressed the primordial character of God's existence while ignoring God's "consequent nature."

God's consequent nature is temporal, relative, dependent, and ceaselessly changing. For like every other actual entity comprising existence, God's existence always remains interdependent with, and hence relative to, everything occurring in the universe. In other words, the consequent nature of God was Whitehead's way of describing God's existence as simultaneously affecting and being affected by every thing and event in the universe from moment to moment of the temporal process.

In summary, then, God's primordial nature describes God's unchanging, abstract, enduring self-iden-

tity through time as God. The primordial nature of God
I understand to be parallel to what I have defined as
"person." God's consequent nature, however, describes
what God becomes as God interdependently interacts with
every element of the universe from moment to moment of
space-time. The consequent nature of God I understand
to be parallel to the "self" as a single momentary experiencing actual entity comprising the life history of
a human person. Accordingly, the consequent nature of
God describes God's *becoming,* while the primordial nature describes God's *being.* Thus God is an entity,
like all actual entities according to Whitehead's world
view, in process of interrelational and interdependent
becoming with everything in the universe.

Whitehead's dipolar theism and the processive
selfhood paradigm I described in the previous section
of this chapter entail serious philosophical and theological opposition to many traditional meanings of the
word "God" assumed by Western philosophical and theological speculation. Historically, Christian theology
has assumed several connotations in its portrayal of
God that are inconsistent with Whiteheadian dipolar
theism and process conceptualizations of selfhood.
Anyone supposing these connotations must remain normative for Christian teaching about God should be fore-
warned that process theologians are reflecting on a
different reality.[8]

God as Universal Controlling Power. This
characterization of God suggests, in varying degrees of
sophistication, that God controls every occurrence in
the universe. Assuming this perspective, traditional

Christian thought has tended to portray God as a powerfully deterministic being responsible for everything,
including those events that human beings usually experience as "good" and "evil." The problem is that conceiving God in this way makes incoherent the Christian
teaching that human beings are morally responsible for
their actions and are thereby accountable for their
"sin." At the same time, God is transformed into an
arbitrary, immoral, unresponsive entity, an image of
deity quite contrary to biblical tradition as well as
to Christian experience. God conceived as a universal
controlling power is also contrary to Buddhist teaching
and experience.

God as Universal Moralist. In its more
unsophisticated and popular versions, this characterization of God represents God as a transcendent divine
lawgiver and judge who has arbitrarily proclaimed a set
of ethical standards and moral rules, who keeps records
of humanity's failures to follow these rules, and who
punishes individuals and communities accordingly. More
sophisticated versions suggest God's ultimate concern
is the progressive development of humanity's ethical
standards and moral behavior. But even this version
makes primary for God what always remains secondary for
humane human beings. It also severely limits the importance of human beings as the only beings, so far as
anyone knows, capable of ethical attitudes and behavior.

Nor is the image of God as cosmic moralist a
requirement for Christian faith and practice, for this
image finds no support in important segments of the

biblical images of God as love, which, as Whitehead once said, is "always a little oblivious to morals." This image also contradicts Buddhist teaching and practice, especially the doctrines of *karma* and dependent co-origination.

God as Unchanging Absolute. The source of this concept of God in Western philosophical and theological speculation is classical Greek philosophy's identification of "perfection" with "immutability." When Augustine linked these two notions with "impassibility," Christian theology stressed that God must remain completely unaffected by finite things and events, as well as lack all emotional response. In other words, under the influence of Greek philosophy, traditional Christian teaching represented God as an unchanging, absolute, ultimate reality unrelated to the entities comprising the universe. All things and events are, on the contrary, related to God because traditional Christian theology assumes that an adequate description of the universe requires reference to the universe's dependency upon God. But the universe's existence has no bearing on the reality of God, for God is wholly and ontologically independent of every thing and event comprising the finite universe. So the God-universe relation remains purely external to God, for the universe contributes nothing to God. In other words, divine influence upon the universe is never conditioned by divine responsiveness to unforeseen, self-determining activities by things and events existing in the universe. This characterization of God, accordingly, is not only contrary to biblical images of the living God's relationship to the universe, but is also contrary to the Buddhist teachings of impermanence, nonself, and dependent co-origination.

God as Sustainer of the Status Quo. This conception of God characterizes all theistic religious Ways, and in fact is another means of portraying God as an unchanging, absolute, moralistic controlling power. God as cosmic moralist suggests God as unchanging absolute suggests that God has established an unchanging natural and moral order in the universe. God as controlling power suggests that the present natural and social order, whether experienced by human beings as good or as evil, is all that can or should exist, since God wills its existence. From this perspective, therefore, religious faith and practice most often mean preserving the social and political *status quo* is all that is possible for human life. But this understanding remains contrary to biblical tradition, as well as to Buddhist teaching and practice.

God as Male. In Western cultures, as well as those Asian cultures under the influence of the West, religious and political movements of liberation among women have starkly disclosed just how deeply traditional language about God is onesided in the teachings of all religious Ways. Although no religious Way is free from masculine sexism, traditional Christianity, in thought and practice remains, along with Judaism and Islam, an especially masculine-oriented religious Way. Not only have the orthodox creeds defined the three "persons" of the Trinity as male, for example, but God's masculinity has also been stereotypically reinforced by the traditional characterizations I have thus far described. That is, Christian theological reflection represents God as totally active, controlling, independent, and wholly lacking receptiveness and responsiveness to the universe. Indeed, for nearly two thousand years, Christian theological language has represented God as the stereotypical archetype of the dominant, inflexible, unemotional, independent (read "strong"), idealized Western male. Such a God seems quite unrelated to either masculine or feminine features of human experience. It is also in profound tension with the picture of Jesus' relation with and language about God in the Gospels.[9] God portrayed as a dominant male, consequently, does not seem to be theologically necessary for distinctively Christian faith and practice. This portrayal is also contrary to the Buddhist doctrines of impermanence, nonself, and dependent co-origination.

Of course, even though contemporary Christian process theologians reject these five features of traditional Christian portrayals of God, there are also important diversities among process theologians. The point requiring emphasis, however, is that the Buddhist doctrines of impermanence, nonself, and dependent co-origination as supported by the practice of meditation also entail explicit rejection of all portrayals of God involving any or all of these five characteristics. If Christian thought *must* conceive God as a masculine, moralistic, unchanging, substantially absolute, cosmic power controlling every thing and event in the universe, whose only relationship with the universe is sanctioner of the *status quo*, then Christian dialogue with the Buddhist Way cannot even begin. There can only be Buddhist-Christian monologue on the question of God.

The issues arising for Buddhist-Christian dialogue on the question of God are among the most complicated and serious. Can God be conceived in such a way that the distinctive features of Christian religious experience are maintained without closing Christians off from the insights of Buddhist teaching and practice? Do the Buddhist doctrines of impermanence, nonself, and dependent co-origination necessarily mean the rejection of all concepts of deity? Contemporary process theology remains convinced that the answer to the first question is "yes" and to the second question is "no." As John Cobb has concluded,

> *Christian faith is not essentially bound up with the God who is seen primarily as Creator-Lord of History-Lawgiver-Judge* and who has so long dominated the Christian sensibility and imagination of the West. What Christians know in Jesus is something quite different, and something which speaks more of full humanity than of repression, more of hope than of nostalgia or fear. The One who is met in Jesus is the God who suffers with us and for us more than the God who demands and judges from on high.[10]

The rationale for this conclusion requires specification.

First of all, and perhaps most obviously, much depends upon what the word "God" means. If a religious Way can only be defined in terms of the forms it has assumed in the past, then Buddhists and Christians are trapped in their traditional isolation from one another. But the history of religions clearly reveals the religious Ways of humanity are evolving processes rather than static entities. Like all living things, religious Ways are either processes of change or they are "dead religions."

To illustrate, one of the classic means by which Christian theology has represented God as a universal controlling power is by attributing to God the qualities of "omniscience" and "omnipotence." As omniscient, God knows every event in the universe directly, without mediation, as these events have occurred, are presently occurring, or will occur. As omnipotent, God knows everything there is to know in the universe because God determined every thing and event in the universe before they occurred.

Three representative medieval versions of the doctrines of divine omniscience and omnipotence appear in the theologies of Thomas Aquinas, Martin Luther, and John Calvin. Aquinas muted the deterministic implications of these doctrines, unsuccessfully, because he wanted to defend human freedom and thereby protect the church's teaching that human beings are morally responsible for their actions. But Luther's doctrine of predestination as foreknowledge and, even more so, Calvin's doctrine of double predestination pushed the notions of divine omniscience and omnipotence to their furthest logical conclusions. Accordingly, Luther and Calvin sacrificed human freedom in order to emphasize God's providence in the world. Both wanted to safeguard against human pride even as they incoherently taught human responsibility along with divine omnipotence and omniscience.

The notion that God knows the universe--the doctrine of divine omniscience--and that this knowledge is unchanging and absolute is interdependent with the notion of God's omnipotence. The most consistent connection between God's knowledge of the universe and God's power in the universe as its creator in Protestant theology occurs in Calvin's teachings. Even before God created the universe, he wrote, God determined every event in the universe, including which human beings were to be consigned to hell and which were to be granted salvation. Having determined every event in the universe in advance, before there was a universe, nothing happens without God's knowing it.

Thus God is pictured in traditional Christian theology as an absolute controlling power whose existence is ontologically independent of the universe God created. The logic underlying this aspect of the traditional Christian portrayal of God, in all of its variations, expresses the ancient notion of God's "simplicity." That is, because God is a "simple essence" or substance, all of God's attributes are ontologically identical. This in turn means God's knowledge of events is identical with God's determination of events. The reverse is also true; God's determination of events is identical with God's knowledge of events.

Biblical images are extremely ambivalent about representing God as the absolute controller of the universe. One reason, perhaps, is the lack of explicitly articulated doctrines of God in biblical literature. Certainly, the Bible does not characterize God as all determining. But the biblical images of God as creator and sustainer of the universe, when interpreted through the categories of Greek philosophy, tended to rule out the possibility of human freedom and responsibility in traditional Christian portrayals of God even as theologians argued that human beings are free and responsible agents.

Process theologians portray God's nature quite differently than traditional Christian thought. For Whitehead, God's relation with the universe centered on God's provision of an "initial aim" for every actual entity. By "initial aim," Whitehead meant an initial impulse, in the beginning felt conformally by a new actual entity at the beginning moment of its process of becoming, to actualize the best possibility open for it, given the concrete environmental circumstances of its situation. But this initial aim does not automatically become an actual entity's aim for itself. Every actual entity, along with the initial aim God provides for it, also possesses its own internal "subjective aim," which may or may not conform to the initial aim it has received from God. Any actual entity may choose to conform to the initial aim provided for it by God, but is under no divine compulsion to do so; an actual entity may also choose from among other possibilities open to it, given its immediate environmental context. In short, freedom is an ontological fact for all actual entities constituting the temporal process of existence.

The religious implications of this understanding of divine creativity, according to process theology, are numerous. First of all, God seeks to "persuade" each actual entity, including that species of actual entity which is the human self, towards the best possibilities open to it for its own existence. However, God does not, because God cannot, totally control an actual entity's self-actualization. Accordingly, divine creativity, like human creativity, always involves risk. Things and events may evolve in ways contrary to God's initial aim for them. Second, God's lack of complete control of events in the universe means that the occurrence of evil is not incompatible with God's love for all things and events. And finally, but perhaps less obviously, because "persuasion" rather than "control" best describes God's way of doing things, persuasion is the way human beings should seek to accomplish their ends. So even though traditional Christian thought does indeed characterize God as "love," love is normally subordinated to God's power, so that the traditional emphasis upon God's controlling power remains the dominant element of Christian theological reflection.

Contrary to the traditional Christian view, process theology unifies God's power with God's love. They are polar opposites characterizing the same sacred reality. That is, process theology describes God's loving character in terms of God's "consequent nature."

Doing so harmonizes not only with most of the New Testament's images of God, but also with human experience.
When we really love others, we do not seek to control
them. Nor do we coerce them into conformity with our
preconceived standards with promises of rewards or
threats of punishment. On the contrary, we try to persuade those whom we love to actualize for themselves
the best possibilities open to them, given the concrete
particularities of their existential situations. We do
this by providing an environment conducive to opening
them up to new, intrinsically attractive possibilities.

Traditional Christian theological reflection
also connects the image of God as controlling power of
the universe to the image of God as cosmic moralist.
Thereby God is characterized as *primarily* interested in
the development of moral behavior and ethical attitudes
among human beings. This has tended to imply that
creaturely enjoyment is not among God's primary concern
for his creation. Accordingly, since the time of St.
Augustine, most Christians have perceived enjoyment as
something God at best tolerates, but most often opposes.

Clearly, the most striking example of this
trend is the way in which Christians have tended to
view sexual relationships between human beings. The
pleasure of sexuality is tolerated as long as it is
concomitant to the primary biological function of sexuality, the reproduction of offspring. But this view
remains only an extreme example of the general Christian attitude towards human enjoyment, an attitude
which has historically tended to create rigidly life-

less forms of Christian practice in serious tension with, if unsupported by, humanity's natural attitudes towards enjoyment. But Jesus, called by some "glutton and drunkard" (Matt. 11:19; Lk. 7:34), could be quoted by the author of the Gospel of John as saying, "I came that they might have life, and have it abundantly" (John 10:10). The Christian Way, however, historically has not supported the evolution of communities encouraging the enjoyment of life. More to the point, when connected with images of God as controlling power of the universe, the image of God as cosmic moralist *must* imply human enjoyment is not a high priority for God, given the fact of universal human suffering. For if God is in complete control of every thing and event in the universe, then the sufferings of human existence, as well as the inequalities of human suffering, *must* be regarded as methods by which God promotes proper moral and religious attitudes among his creatures--attitudes not especially conducive to the enjoyment of God's creation.

Process theology, however, interprets God's fundamental aim--in Whitehead's words, God's "subjective aim"--as the promotion of every finite actual entity's enjoyment. That is, God provides every actual entity with an "initial aim" expressive of God's subjective aim that every actual entity "enjoy" the fullest "satisfaction" possible for it. In less Whiteheadian language, God influences every actual entity, including the human self, to achieve whatever it can achieve for itself that is intrinsically good. Nevertheless, because God is not in complete control of the universe, divine love is not contradicted by the enormous amount of intrinsic evil--"disenjoyment"--present in the universe. Actual entities are free *not* to incorporate God's initial aim for their maximum enjoyment and satisfaction into their individual subjective aims.

Process theology teaches that enjoyment is God's primary concern even for those entities incapable of developing moral attitudes. Religiously, this means God intends all human beings to enjoy themselves fully and completely in ways not inhibiting the enjoyment of other human beings and life forms. Restated more positively, God intends our enjoyment to increase the enjoyment of other living beings through the transformation of our immediate subjectively experienced enjoyment into the intention to contribute to the future good of all beings.

Because traditional portrayals of God characterize God as sanctioner of the status quo, the concern for order is a matter of great importance in the Christian Way. For images of God as sanctioner of the status quo are interrelated to images of God as cosmic moralist. To cite only one example, the connection between obedience to God and submission to a particular institutionalized system or social order has always found support among Christians because of the notorious verses of Romans 13, where the Apostle Paul wrote that we should "be subject to the governing authorities" because "they have been instituted by God." Anyone "who resists the authorities resists what God has appointed." Paul, in these verses, presupposes that God exercises direct control over at least the major features of the universe. In turn, this view of God's control over the universe further strengthened one of the historically dominant trends of Christian thought and practice: the political and social status quo *must* be upheld and defended, no matter how unjust it may be, as "God's will" for a universally "sinful world."

Challenging the image of God as sanctioner of the status quo, Whitehead understood God as the source of unrest in the universe. In his words, "The pure conservative is fighting against the essence of the universe."[11] By "essence of the universe," Whitehead meant that actual things and events, as opposed to abstract things and events, are processes of becoming, and that the source of these processes is God's primordial nature, which he also called the "Divine Eros."

God's primordial nature, Whitehead wrote, is God's "actual entertainment of all ideals, with the urge to their finite realization in their due season." But not all possibilities can be realized simultaneously, and this is why process is necessary.[13] Nor can any ideal possibility be attained or repeated indefinitely without losing its freshness, its novelty and zest. Accordingly, God's primordial nature is the divine "lure" or "goad" toward increased novelty in the universe stimulating all actual entities, including the human self, to attain ever new possibilities after old ones are no longer capable of giving zest to the enjoyment of being actual.[14]

But "process" is not synonymous with "chaos," because order is an essential ingredient for the maximization of an actual entity's enjoyment. God is the source of order in this sense, not in the sense of being a sanctioner of the status quo. Citing an example from Whitehead's writings, the richness of human experience can only occur because of the existence of physiological and psychological order within our bodies. "It is by reason of the body, with its miracle of power, that the treasures of the past environment are poured into the living occasion."[15] However, *excessive* order inhibits enjoyment as much as excessive lack of order. Order remains especially essential for that form of process called the human self. But order must not be dominant. In Whitehead's words, "The art of progress is to preserve order amid change and to preserve change amid order."[16]

According to Whitehead, God is the source of order in the universe in two senses. First, order in his world view represents the present dominance of an ideal possibility that in the past was a novel element in the world. Hence God is the source of novelty because of God's primordial function as the lure or goad leading every actual entity towards new possibilities for its existence. Second, neither moral order nor novelty is intrinsically good. Rather, order and novelty are instrumental to the one intrinsic good, which Whitehead believed is the enjoyment of intense experience. In his words, "God's purpose in the creative advance is the evocation of intensities. The evocation of societies [of actual entities] is purely subsidiary to this end."[17] This means "order" and "novelty" are merely the instruments of God's subjective aim of lur-

ing every actual entity to the most intense maximum enjoyment for which it is capable.[18]

Consequently, God's creative relation to the
universe is an "adventurous" love that takes risks by
luring the things and events comprising the universe
toward greater novel intensities of experience. This
is the function of God's primordial nature. But there
is also the responsive side of God's love for the universe, expressing God's consequent nature. "This adventure embraces all particular occasions but as an actual fact stands beyond any one of them."[20] In other
words, God's consequent existence is also an adventure,
because the novel enjoyments created by God's primordial nature for all things and events are divine experiences providing material for God's own enjoyment as
well. So God's life is an adventure because it continually involves risk. In concert with all finite actual
entities, in other words, God's life grows, becomes,
and changes as God affects and is affected by what God
experiences. As Whitehead summarized it in his well-
known series of antitheses describing God's dipolar existence:

It is as true to say that God is permanent
and the World fluent, as that the world is
permanent and God is fluent.

It is as true to say that God is one and
the World many, as that the World is one and
God many.

It is as true to say that, in comparison
with the World, God is actual eminently, as

that, in comparison with God, the world is actual eminently.

It is as true to say that the World is immanent in God, as that God is immanent in the World.

It is as true to say that God transcends the World, as it is that the World transcends God.

It is as true to say that God creates the World, as it is that the World creates God.

GOD AND EMPTINESS (ŚŪNYATĀ)

Whitehead believed his process world view, which he also called the "philosophy of organism," was congenial with some forms of eastern philosophy and religious Ways. He was particularly interested in the parallels he perceived between his thought and the Buddhist Way.[22] For this reason, contemporary process theologians, most notably John Cobb, are now expending much intellectual energy encountering the Buddhist Way.

By now, it should be clear that both Buddhist teaching and Whitehead's philosophy agree in their denial of the category of substance. Equally evident is that both are process world views. But Whitehead's "philosophy of organism" was in many ways consciously shaped by Christian teaching. Equally evident, Buddhist teaching draws conclusions from its denial of the category of substance that are religiously far removed from either Whitehead's philosophy or Christian process theology. Most Western philosophy, for example, has defined the self, in numerous variations, as an enduring entity because of its assumption of the category of substance. Accordingly, most Western philosophy generally, and traditional Christian theology specifically, continue conceptualizing the self as a permanent enduring subject of experience to which the first person English pronoun "I" refers. It is this self, this enduring "I" remaining self-identical through time, whose salvation is sought in traditional Christian teaching and practice.

Both Whiteheadian process theology and Buddhist teaching deny the existence of this self. As Cobb has written, the self we experience is not a unitary entity remaining self-identical through time. Rather the "self" denotes a strand of "momentary-here-and-now-experiences in the total flux of experience."[23] However, Buddhist doctrine teaches that mere intellectual acquiescence to this theory does not engender enlightenment, for persons merely believing the Buddhist doctrine of nonself continue behaving as separate, substantial selves. The failure to apprehend meditatively the existential truth to which the doctrine of nonself symbolically points is one of the causes of universal suffering (duḥkha).

Consequently, meditation is ultimately the only means by which we can undercut the delusion (māyā) of permanent, substantial selfhood. That is, meditation is a method (upāya) of stopping the intellectual interpretation of our experiences so that we may simply let our experiences be what they are--"empty" (śūnyatā) of all permanency whatsoever. Through meditatively realizing the emptiness of substantial selfhood, we become free from anxiety about our supposed past, future, or even present existence, because there exists no one about whom to be anxious.

From a view point external to the experience of a Buddhist meditator, the Buddhist world view posits the existence of a series of momentary strands of experiential units or events similar to what Whitehead meant by "actual entity" or "actual occasion of experience." A human being is a series of such experiential events. However, as subjectively experienced during the process of meditation, the human self is merely a here-now-momentary-event. Thus, from the Buddhist perspective, the internal subjective view point of the meditator is the real viewpoint because it is impossible for us to stand outside the stream of the experiential events constituting our selfhood from moment to moment.

All aspects of the foregoing analysis are quite intelligible to anyone deeply committed to a Whiteheadian version of process philosophy. However, Buddhists are not led by the experience of meditation to intellectual assent either to Whitehead's understanding of God or to any of the traditional Christian notions of God. For by the word "God," Buddhist teaching generally understands an ultimate ground of being, a substantial sacred self-entity underlying and relativizing the flux of phenomenal space-time events, while simultaneously transcending this flux. But Whitehead and process theology deny the existence of God understood in this way as well. Instead of an ultimate, substantially sacred self-entity remaining identical through time, Whitehead believed creativity to be metaphysically ultimate. In fact, "creativity" is the only "category of the ultimate" in Whiteheadian process thought:

"Creativity" is the universal of universals characterizing ultimate matters of fact. It is that ultimate principle by which the many, which are the universe disjunctively, become the one actual occasion, which is the universe conjunctively. It lies in the nature of things that the many enter into complex unity.[24]

That is, all actual entities, including God, are concrete instances of creativity. This in turn means creativity in Whitehead's view does not possess an imminent supertemporal reality because, as the "universal of universals," creativity possesses no independent existence apart from the existence of becoming actual entities. It exists only in concrete actual entities undergoing the process of becoming. So in place of a substantial, metaphysically ultimate being named "God," Whitehead believed God to be the chief example and formative element of the creative process undergirding the universe.

Therefore, even though Whitehead wrote about a primordially eternal nature of God--the divine reality as it unchangingly stands as God's envisagement of all possibilities ("eternal objects")--this dimension of God's nature is an abstraction from the actual processes constituting what God's nature is as "consequent." As consequent, God is never self-identically the same from moment to moment because of how God interacts with every thing and event in the universe. That is, God's consequent nature affects, even as it is affected by, every event in the universe at every moment of space-time, making God the chief example of the process that all finite actual entities undergo. Now even though the question of God is interrelated with the question of selfhood, and even though Whitehead's understanding of God is not found in Buddhist teaching, beings with functions analogous to God, called "Bodhisattvas," do appear in Buddhist literature. Thus the issue is, according to Cobb, whether the existence of a nonsubstantial, processive sacred reality named God is metaphysically and religiously an open possibility for Buddhist teaching and practice.

Cobb believes this possibility indeed exists, and he offers to Buddhists a very interesting rationale for this judgment. God's nature, he thinks, can be interpreted by Buddhists as the supreme and everlasting Empty (śūnyatā) One, in distinction from Emptiness as the metaphysically ultimate reality assumed by Mahayana interpretations of the doctrine of nonself. Buddhists might thereby reconceive God as a "Cosmic Buddha" without contradicting the doctrines of impermanence, nonself, and dependent co-origination. And in light of the fact that Mahayana tradition posits the existence of a Buddha that might easily be identified as a Cosmic Buddha named Vairocana (Japanese, *Birushana-butsu*) Cobb's suggestion deserves consideration. Vairocana Buddha is not a historical Buddha, but rather a personification of the essence or "suchness" of enlightenment itself. That is, all actual historical Buddhas, for example Gautama the Buddha or any Buddhist actually achieving enlightenment, are concretized historical instances of the universally generic truth of enlightenment as Emptiness personified by Vairocana. It seems indeed possible, consequently, to interpret Vairocana Buddha as a sort of universal "lure" goading all sentient beings toward enlightenment, for Vairocana is the "Buddha Nature" within all things and events. And since, according to the *Avataṃsaka Sūtra,* all things and events are concrete expressions of Vairocana's reality, and since all things and events simultaneously contribute to Vairocana's reality,[25] there appear to exist numerous parallels with Whitehead's dipolar conception of God. As the "lure" for the enlightened fulfillment of each actual thing and event in the universe at any moment of space-time, Vairocana functions in ways similar to Whitehead's description of God's primordial nature. But Vairocana's interdependent relationship with all things and events also suggests that this Buddha performs functions similar to what Whitehead described as God's consequent nature. In a parallel way, God, when viewed from the perspective of Buddhist thought, is "empty" of "self," insofar as "self" is conceived as an unchanging essence that can be preserved only by excluding its being influenced by its interaction with the universe.

But "similarity" does not mean "identity," and Cobb does not actually argue that Vairocana Buddha is an example of a Buddha or Bodhisattva that can be most easily perceived as metaphysically equivalent either to Whitehead's conception of God or to traditional Christian conceptions of God. Nor does Cobb conclude that Buddhists will, because of dialogical encounter with Christian process theology, appropriate a Whiteheadian conception of God coherent with Buddhist teaching and experience. Rather, he merely argues that when "God" is reconceived according to the categories of Whiteheadian process philosophy, (1) God becomes a metaphysically open possibility for inclusion in the Buddhist Way and, (2) process theology's own conception of God can be deepened and transformed through dialogical appropriation of the Mahayana Buddhist doctrine of Emptiness. In his view, God must be "empty" just as the human self is "empty," of what Nāgārjuna called "own-being" (Sanskrit, *svabhāva*). Lacking all substance, and thereby lacking a permanently self-identical character of its own, other than God's primordially abstract character, God, like all things and events, must be the ultimate instance of dependent co-origination.[26]

CONCLUDING OBSERVATIONS

Whitehead's conceptuality certainly lends itself to Cobb's reformulated Christian understanding of God. And surely, there are indeed elements in Whitehead's description of God's interrelationship with the universe that are quite similar to the way Buddhist tradition describes the functions of Vairocana. But whether Buddhists can accept these judgments remains another matter. In any event, Cobb's appropriation of the Buddhist doctrine of Emptiness into his reformu-

lated process conception of God seems remarkable because: (1) his on-going dialogue with Whitehead's
world view has allowed him to creatively transform several elements of the traditional Christian understanding of God into a conceptuality more adequately and coherently reflective of biblical images and Christian
religious experience; (2) his dialogue with the Buddhist Way has further creatively transformed his conception of God by enabling him to incorporate into it
insights to which the Buddhist doctrine of Emptiness
points; (3) his conception of God contradicts neither
the realities to which the Buddhist doctrines of impermanence, nonself, and dependent co-origination point,
nor the realities to which Christian teachings and
practice point; and (4) his suggestion of the metaphysical possibility of Buddhist appropriation of a process
understanding of God into its Dharma provides Buddhists
with an important dialogical access into an important
dimension of Christian teaching and experience which
has historically separated Buddhists from Christians.
Whether Buddhists can "pass over" into Christian teaching and experience in a way similar to the way in which
Cobb has passed over into Buddhist teaching and
experience remains to be seen.   But this should not de-
tract from the fact that his reformulated Christian
conception of God represents an example of how Christian thought can creatively transform itself through
interreligious dialogue.

        Still, the Christian Way does not apprehend
the sacred reality it names "God" apart from the historical figure of Jesus called the Christ.   Jesus was

not a process theologian. Indeed, he was no theologian at all. Nor did he know anything about Buddhist teaching and practice or Greek philosophy. Likewise, Buddhists apprehend the meaning of Emptiness not in some abstract Empty Cosmic Buddha such as Vairocana, but in the historical Gautama, after whom all other Buddhas and Bodhisattvas are modeled. Nor was Gautama a philosopher, much less a "process philosopher." The question becomes, can Christians, apprehending the meaning of "God" in Jesus, appropriate insights from the Buddhist Way relevant to christological understandings of God? And can Buddhists, whose faith and trust is not directed toward an abstract personification of Emptiness, gain access to the realities of the Sacred that Christians apprehend in the historical Jesus as the Christ? Is there anything in Buddhist faith and experience corresponding to a figure like Jesus as the Christ? These questions will be the foci of the next chapter.

NOTES

[1]Edward Conze, trans., *Buddhist Scriptures* (Baltimore: Penguin Books, 1959), 62.

[2]For many of the ideas in the following paragraphs, I am indebted to Jay McDaniel, "Zen and the Self," *Process Studies*, 10, (Fall-Winter 1980): 110-19.

[3]Alfred North Whitehead, *Process and Reality* (New York: Macmillan , 1967), 138-41, and *Adventures of Ideas* (New York: Free Press, 1967), 201-8.

[4]In Whitehead's terminology, a "person" is a "historical route" of actual occasions.

[5]The Buddhist scripture that most coherently supports my interpretation of the Buddhist doctrine of nonself is the *Flower Ornament Sutra* [Sanskrit, *Avatamsaka-sūtra;* Chinese, *Hui-yen-ching;* Japanese, *Kegon-kyō*]. The *Flower Ornament Sutra's* version of the Buddhist world view, as well as its nonself teaching, is in many instances parallel to Whitehead's world view and view of human selfhood. See Thomas Cleary, *Entry into the Inconceivable: An Introduction to Hua-yen Buddhism* (Honolulu: University of Hawaii Press, 1983).

[6]Zenkei Shibayama, *Zen Comments on the Mumonkan* (New York: Harper and Row, 1974), 122.

[7]For Whitehead's own discussion on God, see *Religion in the Making* (New York: The World Publishing Co., 1961), chapts 3-4; *Process and Reality,* 511-33, and *Adventures of Ideas*, 241-46. According to Charles Hartshrone, Whitehead's view of God is important because it "is the first view of God which technically accepts the living, personal, purposive, and therefore temporal, character ascribed to him by most religions, and which treats the relation of God to man as only a special though supreme case of the relation of any individual to any other, namely, the relation of action and reaction, reciprocal inclusion, mutual relevance. God includes us without abolishing our individuality and partial freedom, just as we include cells and electrons. Inclusion [through memory or perception] being made the basis of all relationship, the idea (which troubled William James and many others) that one mind

could include another only by a miracle ceases to seem persuasive." "The Compound Individual," in *Whitehead's Philosophy: Selected Essays, 1935-1970* (Lincoln: University of Nebraska Press, 1972), 61.

[8]See John B. Cobb, Jr. and David Ray Griffin, *Process Theology, An Introductory Exposition* (Philadelphia: Westminster Press, 1976), 19-41.

[9]See Rosemary Radford Ruether, *Sexism and God Talk* (Boston: Beacon Press, 1983), especially chapts. 1-2.

[10]John B. Cobb, Jr., *God and the World* (Philadelphia: Westminster Press, 1969), 37, emphasis supplied.

[11]Whitehead, *Adventures of Ideas*, 274.

[12]Ibid., 277.

[13]Alfred North Whitehead, *Modes of Thought* (New York: Macmillan Company, 1938), 53.

[14]Whitehead, *Process and Reality*, 35.

[15]Ibid., 516.

[16]Ibid., 515.

[17]Ibid., 161.

[18]Whitehead, *Adventures of Ideals*, 276.

[19]Whitehead, *Process and Reality*, 169.

[20]Ibid.

[21]Ibid., 528.

[22]Whitehead, *Adventures of Ideas*, 33; Whitehead, *Religion in the Making*, 66-72.

[23]Cobb and Griffin. *Process Theology,* 128.

[24] Whitehead, *Process and Reality*, 31. Also see Ivor Leclerec, *Whitehead's Metaphysics* (New Jersey: Humanities Press, 1965), 81-90.

[25]See Garma Chen-chi Chang, *The Buddhist Teaching of Totality: The Philosophy of Hua-yen Buddhism* (University Park: The Pennsylvania State University Press, 1971).

[26]John B. Cobb, Jr., "Buddhist Emptiness and the Christian God," *Journal of the American Academy of Religion*, 45 (1979): 22-25.

CHAPTER NINE
Buddhist and Christian Universalism

If, when I become a Buddha, all sentient beings in the
ten quarters should not desire in sincerity and trust-
fulness to be reborn in my Land, and if they should not
be reborn in my Land by thinking on me only ten times,
excluding only those who have committed the five irreversible actions and have slandered the Dharma, may I
not receive perfect enlightenment.

Larger Sukhāvatīvyūha [Larger Sutra on the Happy Land][1]

God loved the world so much that he gave his only Son,
that everyone who has faith in him may not die but have
eternal life. It was not to judge the world that God
sent his Son into the world, but that through him the
world might be saved.

John 3:16-17, *New English Bible*

THE INTENTION OF BUDDHIST-CHRISTIAN TRUTH CLAIMS

Buddhists and Christians more often than not
allege their distinctive teachings and practices to be
the completely valid, universally applicable means for
the salvation of all human beings. But neither the
similarities nor the differences between Buddhist and
Christian universalism in this regard originate in the
mere fact of Buddhist denial of a positive role to God
in the human quest for release from suffering (*duhkha),*
or in the Christian affirmation of the absolute necessity of trust in God for the salvation of human kind.
The source of Buddhist universalism lies in taking
refuge in the Buddha, the Dharma, and the Samgha as the
absolute prerequisite for the attainment of enlightenment.[2] While this claim in no way implies non-Buddhist

religious Ways are paths of spiritual blindness, Buddhists normally assume that specifically Buddhist teachings and practices are the only "skillful means" (up̄aya) available for the achievement of enlightenment.

Similarly, Christian universalism does not originate in the positive Christian affirmation of faith in God as the only means available for humanity's salvation, but rather in the teaching that God is known most completely through God's self-disclosure in the life, death, and resurrection of Jesus as the Christ. Neither does this claim necessarily imply the falsehood of non-Christian religious Ways or that non-Christian conceptions of God are erroneous, even though Christians have been historically less tolerant of other religious Ways than have Buddhists. But authentically Christian teaching explicitly asserts that God is most completely known through the historical events surrounding the life, death, and resurrection of Jesus of Nazareth, and thus faith in this God is the absolute prerequisite for what Christians call "eternal life."

Consequently, when Buddhists and Christians enter into dialogue, it is important for the participants not to underplay the radicalness of either Buddhist or Christian claims of universal validity. Christians should never be satisfied with a form of faith and practice that either neglects or falsifies the deepest dimensions of reality, and if the Buddhist Way can teach Christians about this, they should be grateful pupils. But neither should Buddhists neglect dimensions of reality more completely expressed in Christian teaching and experience.

As I noted in chapters one and eight, process theology, notably in the work of John Cobb, is the most consistently coherent contemporary Christian attempt to engage Christian universalism with Buddhist universalism. So serious is Cobb's commitment to dialogue with the Buddhist Way that he self-consciously seeks to "Buddhize" the Christian Way. Once more, for most process theologians, neither Buddhist nor Christian universalism need result in Buddhist or Christian monologue. But what can Buddhists appropriate from the Christian Way? Is it possible to "Christianize" Buddhist universalism, particularly at the point so widely separating Buddhists from Christians—the reality Christians apprehend through faith in Jesus as the Christ?

I previously noted Cobb's belief that it is not only possible, but imperative, in an age of religious pluralism to Buddhize the Christian Way. I described the essentials of his views in chapters one, seven, and eight in order to illustrate what I believe is the most radical Christian example now occurring of the creative transformation of the Christian Way through dialogue with the Buddhist Way. But while I remain deeply influenced, and indeed persuaded, by many of Cobb's conclusions, I have not sought to defend them. Nor shall I do so in what is to follow. But if, as he believes, "the heart of Buddhist truth is not contradictory to the heart of Christian belief,"[3] then Buddhists should be able to appropriate some of the major christological commitments of Christian faith without abandoning the wisdom of Buddhist teaching and practice. The question is, of course, why Buddhists should be interested in doing so.

Accordingly, in what follows I describe how and why Cobb believes the Christian Way can contribute to what he calls the "fulfillment" of the Buddhist Way. My intention for the moment is descriptive: I wish to describe the essentials of Cobb's theses to illustrate the possibilities of mutual creative transformation through interreligious dialogue.

Cobb's potential appropriation for Buddhists of Christian christological teaching centers on four claims, each one of which requires the other three to support its validity: (1) Buddhist universalism is most completely expressed in Pure Land teaching and practice, particularly in the Jōdo Shinshū [True Pure Land School] established by Shinran in the twelfth century in Japan; (2) the reality that Pure Land Buddhists name "Amida Buddha" is the same reality Christians name "Christ"; (3) if this is so, Buddhists can learn from traditional Christian christological reflection important characteristics of Amida Buddha to which they have not traditionally attended; and (4) the Buddhist Way can best advance itself in the modern world through recognition of the "decisive incarnation of Amida in the historical Jesus."[4] Comprehending the implication of Cobb's view for both Buddhist and Christian self-understanding requires detailed exposition of the content of each of these claims.

BUDDHIST UNIVERSALISM

As Cobb understands it, Buddhist universalism originates in Gautama the Buddha's aim to teach all sentient beings the means by which they might achieve enlightenment. He did so by explaining the cause of suffering and by proposing a "middle way" for achieving release from suffering not requiring superhuman, ascetic austerities. Nevertheless, most of the Buddha's followers, including some of those most intimately associated with him, discovered that in fact his way was extremely difficult because of the stress he placed on the exercise of their own disciplined self-efforts.

Standard Theravada teaching stresses that the achievement of enlightenment requires many lifetimes of rigorous, self-disciplined struggle. However, other Buddhists, even some among Gautama's immediate followers, remained critical of what they perceived was the elitism of what later evolved into the Theravada interpretation of the Buddha's Dharma. They criticized this elitism for removing ordinary seekers so far from the achievement of enlightenment. Because enlightenment was thought to be so difficult to achieve during one single life cycle, the Theravada Dharma was referred to by these Buddhists as the "small vehicle" (hīnayāna), while proposing their conception of the Dharma as the "great vehicle" (mahāyāna) capable of transporting all sentient beings to the "further shore" of enlightenment.

The Mahayana Buddhist Dharma maintained the primary Theravada focus on meditation as the sole means for achieving enlightenment. Furthermore, Mahayana meditational practice is highly varied, structured, and demanding, requiring lengthy periods of practice and personal self-discipline. Even so, most Buddhists do not meditate, even in the Theravada Buddhist world. Practicing Mahayana Buddhists most often engage in devotional practices meant to gain the help of the Buddhas and Bodhisattvas for their problems in this life cycle and to obtain a more positive rebirth in their next life cycle.

One particular Bodhisattva legend has evolved into the classical form of Mahayana Bodhisattva veneration. According to the *Larger Sukhāvatī-vyūha* [Larger Sutra on the Happy Land],[5] an Indian prince named Dharmākara took a series of forty-eight vows to achieve the wisdom of enlightenment so he could aid all other sentient beings in their quest for enlightenment. This prince, upon the attainment of enlightenment, was transformed into Amitābha Buddha (Japanese, Amida Buddha), the "Buddha of Infinite Light," and now resides in a Buddha Land called the "Happy Land" (Sanskrit, *Sukhāvatī*), or more commonly, the "Pure Land." All beings may achieve rebirth into this Buddha Land if they so desire through simple trust in Amida Buddha to effect their rebirth there at the time of death.

Therefore, even though Mahayana teaching stresses meditation as the most appropriate method for achieving enlightenment, most Buddhists practice the Dharma under the assumption that the vast majority of sentient beings require the aid of Bodhisattvas like Amida Buddha. "Hence," as Cobb accurately notes, "the Pure Land tradition in Mahayana Buddhism was important

as the expression of its concern for the universality
of salvation."[6]

In twelfth century Japan, two developments
occurred that Cobb believes pushed the devotional universalism of the Buddhist Way to its furthest, most coherent limits. First, Hōnen, the founder of the Jōdo
Shū [Pure Land School] tradition of Pure Land faith and
practice, concluded that although in past epochs of
world history, self-effort in the striving for enlightenment was necessary, in this present evil period
called mappō [End of the Dharma] it is now impossible.
Amida Buddha's vows to "save" all sentient beings apart
from human striving are the only possible means for
salvation. Secondly, as Honen's teachings were syste-
matized by Shinran's teachings, faith as trust in Amida
Buddha and nontrust in human self-effort was understood
as the only requirement for receiving Amida Buddha's
grace through which alone salvation was possible. In
many ways parallel to Luther's doctrine of "salvation
by faith through grace alone,"[7] Shinran concluded that
if salvation is universally available for all sentient
beings, its achievement cannot depend on human achievement and striving, but solely on Amida Buddha's "grace"
(Japanese, tariki or "other-power"). According to
Cobb, Shinran was "correct that the universal compassion of Buddhism could best come to expression through
his doctrine of salvation by grace through faith
alone," and therefore Shinran's teachings excluded religious practices conceived as self-disciplined methods
for achieving enlightenment. In this attitude too,
Shinran resembled Luther, for like Luther, Shinran per-

ceived monastic disciplines as irrelevant to salvation. And like Luther again, Shinran not only opposed monasticism, for identical reasons he also rejected the entire monastic tradition of the Buddhist Way.

But Cobb also thinks the universalism of Shinran's and Luther's teachings of salvation by faith through grace alone need not have necessitated the wholesale rejection of either Buddhist or Christian monasticism. In his words:

> Christians today know that although they are justified apart from special spiritual disciplines, they are free to practice those disciplines. The disciplines they are free to practice include Buddhist as well as traditional ones. They practice them not in order to be justified but because they want the depth and spiritual maturity that such disciplines can help to provide. There is nothing in Pure Land Buddhism to prevent encouragement of the important and effective disciplines developed in other schools such as Zen. What is important is that salvation not be understood in such a way that people are *driven* into these disciplines. The Pure Land Buddhist or the Christian is free to practice Zen meditation or not practice it. There is no obligation. Understood in this way, Pure Land thought and practice can rightly see themselves as the fulfillment of the Buddhist quest for universality.[8]

AMIDA BUDDHA AS CHRIST

Occasionally, Cobb notes, Christians use the title "Christ" inappropriately as a proper name for the historical Jesus, a usage that is historically and christologically very misleading. "Christ" is an honorific title given to Jesus of Nazareth because it expresses the way in which the earliest Christian community in Jerusalem theologically interpreted what they believed was his redemptive work among them. Since the earliest days of the Christian community, Christians have perceived Jesus as the "Christ" or "Messiah," that is, the "anointed one." Similarly, Pure Land Buddhists might appropriate "Amida" as a proper name for Dharmākara, but this too is misleading. For only after Dharmākara, through self-disciplined practice requiring many eons of rebirths, became an "enlightened one" did he become a Buddha named "Amida." In this sense, accordingly, "Christ" and "Amida" do not refer to the same sacred reality.

There exist, however, other layers of meaning in the names "Christ" and "Amida" for Christians and Buddhists. For example, Christians have often conceived of Christ as a preexistent sacred reality who assumed human form in the historical Jesus roughly two thousand years ago, and, after Jesus' death, "returned to the right hand of the Father." Perhaps analogously, Buddhists have often thought of Amida as a Buddha residing in a "Buddha Land" called the "Pure Land." And so interpreted from this perspective, Christ and Amida might name "divine beings" for Christians and Buddhists, while nevertheless naming quite different sacred realities. For Christ is conceived as a supernatural being subordinate to God, the main thrust of fourth century Arian christology, while Amida remains simply one Buddha among numerous Bodhisattvas and Buddhas residing in other Buddha Lands. It remains clear, however, that neither "Christ" nor "Amida" conceived in this fashion name the same reality.

The historical fact remains that the early church repudiated Arian "subordinationism" at the Council of Nicaea in 325. Consequently, Cobb argues, the mainline Christian teaching is that Christ

is not a creature, however exalted. Christ is God. But when we say Christ, we are not simply referring to God in general but speaking of God as everlasting Word, creatively and redemptively working in the world. This is the Truth which opens us to all truths. Similarly, in Pure Land Buddhist reflection, Amida did not remain one Buddha among others. Amida came to name instead the reality which is incarnate in all Buddhas. This raises the question whether Amida as that which is incarnate in all Buddhas and Christ as the creative and redemptive activity of God in the world names the same reality. I believe they do, but this must be shown.[9]

In explaining his thesis, Cobb appeals to Shinran's interpretation of the Mahayana Buddhist doctrine of *trikāya* or "three bodies" of a Buddha.[10] According to this ancient teaching, ultimate reality, the Dharma as manifested in every Buddha, is called *dhar-*

makāya or "body of Dharma." Another means of conceiving this notion is that all enlightened Buddhas express, are transformed by, and thus are particularized
forms of, the universal "suchness" of the absolute
Dharma. The concrete, historical form assumed by the
dharmakaya in individual human beings actually achieving enlightenment is called nirmāṇakāya or "manifest
body." All historical Buddhas, such as Siddhartha Gautama, are concrete historical manifestations of this
"body." But the "body" taken by the dharmakāya in the
numerous Buddhas and Bodhisattvas residing in their
Buddha Lands is the "body of bliss" or saṃbhogakāya.
According to Pure Land tradition prior to Shinran's
lifetime, Amida Buddha is merely one among many saṃ-
bhogakāya-forms of ultimate reality (dharmakāya) residing in his special Buddha Land called the Pure Land.

In Cobb's words, pre-Shinran Pure Land formulations conceived Amida as "subordinate to the Dharmakaya."[11] For the dharmakāya, as ultimate reality in
all of its "suchness," is "empty" (śūnyatā) of all
forms and Buddha manifestations. So Amida is a saṃ-
bhogakāya-form of ultimate reality, and therefore possesses the distinct, but limited, character of enlightened wisdom and compassion. In other words, the dharmakāya, beyond all forms and expressions, assumes an
upāya-form of saṃbhogakāya called "Amida Buddha" for
the sake of those persons unable to experience enlightenment for themselves through the practice of meditation. This represents, according to the oldest Pure
Land traditions, a concession to human weakness and
therefore should not be taken as the ultimate truth of

enlightenment. The deepest achievement of enlightenment, attainable only through the practice of meditation, bypasses the *saṃbhogakāya* manifestations of enlightened reality altogether, apprehending the eternal
dharmakāya as it is in all of its "emptiness."

This understanding of Amida Buddha--one which
subordinates Amida Buddha to the *dharmakāya* as one of
numerous *upaya*-forms of ultimate reality--was rejected
outrightly by Shinran. According to him Amida *is* the
dharmakāya. At this point, Cobb believes he has discovered a suitable Buddhist parallel to traditional
christology. Just as Christian doctrine teaches that
faith in Christ can only be existentially valid if
Christ *is* God, so Shinran taught that faith as trust in
Amida's Bodhisattva vows to save all sentient beings
can only be existentially valid if Amida *is* the *dharmakāya*. In this sense, Cobb argues, "Christ" names for
Christians what "Amida" names for Buddhists, or at
least for those Buddhists adhering to Shinran's understanding of Amida.

In further specifying what this conclusion
means for Buddhists, Cobb once more appropriates Whitehead's category of creativity. In many ways parallel
to the traditional Buddhist world view, Whitehead recognizes, Cobb says,

> that ultimate reality as creativity is beyond
> all forms since in principle it is suscepti-
> ble to any form whatsoever. In many respects
> his [i.e. Whitehead's] analysis of creativity
> corresponds to some Buddhist accounts of
> Dharmakaya, especially as Dharmakaya is ex-

plained in terms of dependent origination. But Whitehead believes that in actuality, although creativity is completely without any character of its own, it is never experienced apart from a primordial ordering of the infinite array of the pure forms or pure possibilities. . . .Thus what is wholly without character in itself has been primordially characterized by a decision that ordered what is possible for the sake of all creatures. Whitehead calls this character of creativity the Primordial Nature of God.[13]

Of course, as Cobb also recognizes, Shinran arrived as his specific Pure Land formulations quite differently than Whitehead arrived at his philosophical categories. Still, remarkable congruities do exist between Whitehead's and Shinran's understanding of reality. According to Cobb's interpretation of these congruities:

In Amida the Dharmakaya has a primordial character. This character is fully revealed in the vow of Dharmakara as the aim to save all sentient beings. There is for Shinran no access to an ultimate reality that is not characterized by this primordial vow.[14]

In other words, from the perspective of Whiteheadian process philosophy, subordinating the "primordial" aspect of ultimate reality (in Buddhist language, the *dharmakāya*) to the "consequent" aspect of ultimate reality (in Buddhist language, the *saṃbhogakāya*), appears unnecessarily arbitrary. Everything that we can actually experience or realize is ultimate reality with its primordial character. Or as Cobb, writes, "To regard ultimate reality in abstraction from this character as superior to ultimate reality as thus characterized seems to express an unnecessary prejudice."[15]

In summary, Cobb's arguments rest on his assertion that Whitehead's concept of the primordial nature of God addresses the same feature of ultimate reality as Shinran's teaching that Amida Buddha is the eternal *dharmakāya*. Once more, he believes, Whitehead's conception of the primordial nature of God and Shinran's conception of Amida Buddha as *dharmakāya* are remarkably analogous to Johannine and patristic conceptions of Christ as the Word of God or Logos. According to this tradition of Christian theology, Christ possesses a primordial character apart from which nothing exists, while simultaneously expressing a "creative-redemptive" character in Christian experience of the historical Jesus as the Christ.[16]

Accordingly, "Amida is Christ," meaning, "the feature of the totality of reality to which Pure Land Buddhists refer when they speak of Amida is the same as that to which Christians refer when we speak of Christ."[17] But this conclusion does not mean either Buddhist or Christian accounts of ultimate reality are completely accurate. But Cobb's analysis does imply that Christians can gain clearer knowledge about Christ through encountering what Jōdo Shinshū Buddhists have taught concerning Amida Buddha. Likewise, Buddhists are in a position to gain further insight about Amida

Buddha through encountering what Christians have taught concerning Christ.

WHAT BUDDHISTS CAN LEARN FROM CHRISTIANS

More accurately formulated, the issue is, what can Buddhists learn about Amida if they recognize Amida as Christ?[18] In responding to this particular problem, Cobb addresses two others: the sense in which the reality of Amida is personal, and the sense in which Amida is ethical.

Of course, the Pure Land teaching that Amida Buddha is a historical Bodhisattva actually transformed into a Buddha whose nature is characterized by enlightened compassion toward all sentient beings, expresses a religious personalism rare in non-Jodo Shinshu Buddhist teaching and practice. But Cobb also believes there exists a sense of the personal theologically important for main stream Christian teaching and practice which is missing from Jōdo Shinshū conceptions of Amida Buddha. Since for the Christian Way the question of personalism concerns the interaction between God and humanity, Christian teaching rests on the biblical image of God's creation of humanity in God's own "image." And if this conception is valid, God, like other human beings, can be addressed, especially in prayer, because God "hears" and responds to persons when so addressed. Again, according to biblical understanding, God is involved in the history of the world and responds to contingent human actions as these occur. Biblical images of God also suggest that God rejoices when sinful human beings repent and that God even knows when a sparrow dies.

According to Shinran's Pure Land teachings, Amida Buddha, while infinitely wise and compassionate, remains transcendentally unaffected by the ignorance and suffering of the sentient beings he vows to save. This means sentient beings are affected by Amida Buddha, while he remains passive and unchanging as the universe impinges on his experience. This element of Shinran's teachings is but one expression of an older traditional Buddhist theme. According to this theme, there exists a sharp contrast between *samsara,* the realm of dependent co-origination (*pratītya-samutpāda*), and the enlightened realm of *nirvāṇa.* Buddhas, according to this ancient normative tradition, totally transcend the world of suffering samsaric existence, and therefore they can only function as models for human beings to imitate in their own quests for enlightenment.

This tradition was greatly modified in the Mahayana version of the Dharma, especially in the teachings of Nagarjuna. He, and most of the subsequent Mahayana tradition, rejected the older Theravada teaching of two "realms of existence" called *samsara* and *nirvāṇa. Nirvāṇa* equals *saṃsāra,* according to Nagarjuna, so that there exists no samsaric realm of dependent co-origination ontologically distinct from an enlightened realm called *nirvāṇa,* for both are "empty" (*śūnyatā*). This teaching, in turn, means the meditative realization of the ontological nature of the samsaric realm of becoming and suffering *is* the achievement of enlightenment. Understood from this perspective, the Buddhas, including Amida Buddha, are not divine beings existing beyond the phenomenal world; they are beings who have perfectly realized the true nature of this world, and thereby are also simultaneously affected by every event experienced by all sentient beings even as all sentient beings are affected by them.

The upshot of this analysis is not that personal characteristics are completely absent from traditional Mahayana conceptions of the Buddhas and Bodhisattvas. Rather, from the perspective of traditional Christian concern for the personal, Cobb believes Buddhist concern for the personal is underdeveloped because of the monistic ontology assumed by Mahayana Buddha and Bodhisattva veneration. For him, the issue emerges from the teaching that the saṃbhogakāya is incarnated in every Buddha and Bodhisattva. He asks:

Should it [the saṃbhogakāya] not have the same duality of relations? At least in Christian experience and teaching it has seemed appropriate to believe that the One that gives gracious character to ultimate reality also responds perfectly to all that happens in the world. It is hard to see that anything would be lost to Buddhists if they assimilated from the Christian knowledge of Christ the conviction that our lives are in this way of importance to Amida.[19]

Perceiving a de-emphasis of the personal in the Buddhist Way, Christians have traditionally criti-

cized Buddhist teaching and practice for an alleged un-
derdevelopment of social and political consciousness.
Some contemporary Buddhists even acknowledge the need
to sharpen Buddhist ethical and social sensitivity
through dialogue with the Christian Way.[20] Agreeing
with this general Christian perception of the Buddhist
Way, Cobb maintains that the difference between Christian ethical and social activism and the lack of Buddhist emphasis in these matters is quite marked. But
to accurately understand how he and other Christian
thinkers have assessed the Buddhist Way in this issue,
it is important to understand what is *not* being said.

First of all, the point is not that Buddhist
cultures and societies have failed in the socialization
of human beings. On the whole, Buddhist societies
probably function more humanely, are less overtly aggressive, and are morally more highly evolved than most
Western societies defining themselves as "Christian."
Second, the Buddhist Way has created humane forms of
community because its teaching and practice strongly
discourage attitudes of violence and greed. Buddhist
tradition has always opposed exploitation of the weak
and underprivileged. Buddhist societies have also, on
the whole, been less violent than Christian societies.
And, finally, Buddhists are generally more tolerant of
religious diversity than Christians. At least Buddhists have historically not waged wars "for the sake
of the Buddha" to the degree Christians have waged wars
against nonchristians, not to mention against one another, "for the sake of the Gospel." There is no question that Buddhist teaching and practice encourage per-

sonal kindness and social generosity as much as do Christian teaching and practice. Finally, Buddhist individuals assume as much social responsibility with as much fortitude, self-discipline, and commitment as do Christians.

What, then, does Cobb think is lacking in the ethical-social traditions of the Buddhist Way?

> What is lacking is a trans-social norm by which society is judged. Even this must be stated with care. Buddhist humanism does provide a check against the tendency to value people only in terms of their social role in relation to others. . . .But this potential principle of leverage is rarely thematically developed. On the whole, Buddhism does not encourage attention by its adherents to critical evaluation of social and political programs of social protest. This seems to be because the mode of relation to individuals to trans-social reality, namely, to Emptiness or to Amida, does not direct them to a judgment of social structures and their historical roles.[22]

For Christians, Cobb thinks, this represents a very serious matter because Buddhist teaching and practice appear to possess little explicit sense of a transcendent norm according to which historical existence can be meaningfully understood and the "rightness" of ethical decisions be measured. In other words, the Buddhist sense of history leaves little room for emphasizing ethical and social issues as matters of

ultimate importance because the monistic assumptions of
Buddhist teaching and practice devalue historical existence. The realm of samsaric existence, conceived in
the categories of dependent co-origination, impermanence, and suffering, so devalues historical existence
in the world that "enlightenment" means "release" from
personal involvement in the world. Viewed from this
perspective, ethical concerns and social problems are
transformed into issues of secondary importance. The
everyday world of ethical and social decision-making in
which unenlightened persons must live must be tran-
scended, rather than ethically and socially transformed.

Christian ethical and social teaching derive
from the notion that God is the creator of the world,
and is continually acting in the world's history as the
arena in which God establishes the salvation of all of
humanity. Furthermore, God's ultimate act of creation
is the incarnation of God into human history through
the life, death, and resurrection of Jesus as the
Christ. History, thereby, becomes the stage upon which
God initiates and completes the drama of salvation.
God meets humanity *in* historical existence; historical
existence is not, therefore, a "realm" to be tran-
scended by human beings, for it is the only "realm" in
which we can encounter the reality of God. Finally,
according to the Christian view, history itself will be
eventually transformed into the "Kingdom of God." For
these reasons, unlike the Buddhist world view, the
Christian understanding of history encourages realistic
appreciation of both the actualities and of the possi-

bilities for meaningful human existence. Accordingly, Christian practice emphasizes possibilities for discerning God's call to salvation within historical events, while Buddhist practice, on the contrary, focuses only on the future enlightenment of individuals who must transcend the realities of historical existence.

This is why, Cobb believes, a "Christianized Buddhism" has much to contribute to the creative transformation of Buddhist ethical and social teaching and practice.[23] One means of Christianizing the Buddhist Way might involve recognizing that "Amida Buddha is Christ," a recognition that could lead Buddhists to interpret involvement in historical existence more positively as the arena where an individual's quest for enlightenment embraces the struggle for ethical goodness expressed in the search for social justice.

THE CENTRALITY OF CHRIST

Christian recognition that persons can know and trust God apart from Christian faith has, in spite of the doctrine of no-salvation-outside-the-church or explicit-Christian-belief, played a role of utmost historical importance. Indeed, the early church's teaching about the Logos was conceived as a means of comprehending how wise and virtuous non-Christians could be guided by the same sacred truth that Christians believed they apprehended in Jesus as the Christ. Cobb believes this teaching can be utilized in the contemporary context of modern religious pluralism as a means of demonstrating how at least some Buddhists within the doctrinal context of Jōdo Shinshū tradition also experience faith as trust in the same Logos that Christian teaching affirms in the historical Jesus of Nazareth.[24]

The theological difficulty with this idea, however, rests precisely on Christian recognition of the incarnate Logos in a particular historical figure named Jesus of Nazareth. Are there any reasons consistent with traditional Buddhist doctrine and religious experience for accepting Christian teaching about Jesus? More specifically, is there a rationale consistent with historic Jōdo Shinshū faith and practice impelling it to appropriate biblical history and the centrality of Jesus within this history? "Clearly," as Cobb understates it, "this would be a major development within the history of religions. . . ."[25]

But how and why? Cobb recognizes the immense difficulties of his views. For example, Shinran did not teach his followers to direct faith to Amida Buddha because of his own personal experience of Amida's saving grace. Nor did he offer empirical rationalizations justifying his reinterpretation of traditional Pure Land teaching and practice. Rather, the immediate context of Shinran's conception of faith presupposed the general Mahayana Buddhist confidence in Bodhisattvas possessing the ability, compassion, and wisdom to act in the way he believed Amida acted in vowing to establish the salvation of all sentient beings. Shinran grounded his Pure Land teachings, in other words, on what he believed was an historical event in the remote past--the "original" forty-eight Bodhisattva vows of the Indian prince, Dharmakara, and his subsequent self-

transformation into Amida Buddha and his creation of
the Pure Land.

Until very recently, however, and only under
the influence of Western methods of historiography,
Buddhists have expressed little interest in either
identifying or distinguishing historical fact and legend. The point of all of the numerous Bodhisattva
legends is to help Buddhist seekers meditatively experience their own present, immediate realization of the
Dharma, not of providing factual historical information
about past events. Accordingly, and in similarity with
other forms of Mahayana Bodhisattva veneration, the
story of Dharmakara provides Pure Land Buddhists with
confidence in the salvific power of his Bodhisattva
vows apart from questions of historical fact. Thus the
question of whether there even existed a human being
named Dharmakara who became Amida Buddha does not even
arise in Pure Land Buddhist teaching and practice.

However, what Westerners, especially Christian theologians, call "historical consciousness" is
now part of the intellectual and emotional framework of
modern Asians. The issue of the truth or falsehood of
the traditional scriptural accounts of Buddhist stories
now arises as often as it does in the West with respect
to the historical truth or falsehood of biblical stories. Whenever this occurs, Gautama the Buddha emerges
as a clearly historical person, and corresponding efforts can be made to distinguish his "original teachings" from later interpretations. Viewed from the perspective of modern Western historiography, consequently, Dharmakara and Amida Buddha, in fact all Bod-

hisattvas and Buddhas other than Gautama, can only be understood as mythic-legendary figures possessing no relation to empirical-historical reality.

Pure Land Buddhists, for whom historical consciousness has emerged as the starting assumption of their self-understanding of modern existence, possess several options--options that Christians have known since the Renaissance. Insisting that a mythic or legendary story is as good as a historical story because the point is the encouragement of faith is one option. But choosing this option undercuts belief in the gracious character of sacred realities symbolized by such figures as Amida Buddha. In other words, Buddhists may, as did Hōnen, argue that the attainment of faith here-and-now depends upon repetition of Amida's name in the *mantra*-formula called *nembutsu*, not on the historical accuracy of the stories about Dharmākara. This option may or may not be valid. However, as Shinran himself was aware, this option presupposes a different world view from that presupposed by his teaching of salvation by faith through absolute "other-power" alone.

Another option might be to take the authority of the historical Gautama the Buddha as the foundation for believing in the other-power of Amida Buddha's grace. The difficulty here, of course, is the lack of evidence that Gautama ever heard of a Buddha named Amida. Also, Gautama's own teachings and practices were diametrically opposite to Shinran's conception of "other-power."

As a third option, Pure Land Buddhists might base their faith in Amida's grace in the events surrounding the life and teachings of Shinran himself. For instance, Jōdo Shinshū Buddhist temples normally enshrine an image of Shinran, along with Amida, to which they pay homage. Once more, Shinran's teachings continue functioning as the standard against which the rightness or "orthodoxy" of Jōdo Shinshū teaching and practice is measured. In this way, Shinran might provide an historical foundation for faith in Amida's grace.

This option too, however, is problematic. Cobb summarizes the issue this way:

> Whereas the authority of a Zen master may be his own experience, Shinran did not present himself this way. He pointed away from himself to that Other-Power in which he placed his faith on the basis of authoritative tradition. To take Shinran seriously from an historical point of view, one must examine the validity of the tradition to which he appeals and the accuracy of his interpretation. Such a critical historical investigation is bound to raise problems for believers.[26]

In other words, explicit belief in the graciousness of Amida Buddha or of Christ as ultimate sacred realities *must* presuppose specific opinions about the actual course of historical events. In Pure Land thought and practice, beliefs about the graciousness of reality, symbolized by Amida Buddha as the *saṃbhogakāya*, play the primary role of importance, whereas

Christian faith and practice presuppose beliefs about the actual course of historical events. But in the Buddhist Way in general and the Pure Land Buddhist Way in particular, "we deal with a circle in which both aspects are needed. Both circles center in the graciousness that characterizes ultimate reality, and both have depended for their convincing power on recounting stories believed to be true."[27]

From the perspective of Christian theological reflection, in other words, the problem with Buddhist thought is the crisis of the relation between history and faith. Two hundred years ago, Christian interpretations of the founding events of Christian history became highly doubtful.[28] And as Christian accounts of the meaning of the events of Christianity's own history became more doubtful, Christian beliefs about God and the world view associated with these beliefs also became suspicious. Christians responded in several ways to this challenge.[29] The most valuable and theologically important response was replacing the first and second century accounts of the stories of Christian history with a historically more accurate account. In Cobb's words:

> That task will never be finished. . . . [but] little doubt remains that there *is* an historical story to tell and that its deepest meaning can be understood as just as supportive of belief in the graciousness of God as the mythical story could ever have been.[30]

Jōdo Shinshū has not yet worked through the crisis of the relationship of history to faith in Amida

Buddha. In the modern world of religious and secular pluralism, this crisis must be squarely faced before any religious faith can be meaningful and helpful to its adherents. If Jōdo Shinshū must face this crisis, then in many respects this Buddhist tradition must encounter more severe difficulties than those encountered by the Christian Way because its foundations are even further removed from the course of concrete historical events. Of course, Gautama the Buddha provides a historical foundation, but he plays only a secondary role of importance in Pure Land tradition to faith in Amida Buddha, a Buddha *without*, be it noted, a "historical body" (*nirmāṇakāya*).

Even so, there exists nothing in the Buddhist world view necessitating establishing the historical foundations of Pure Land faith and practice in either Indian or East Asian history. The Buddhist Way presents itself as a universal religious Way. Accordingly, Buddhist teaching and practice require the inclusive comprehension of all things and events, which in today's modern world must include world history, a history embracing not only the history of Israel and the events of Jesus' story, but also the history of India and the events of Gautama's story:

> The history that supports the Christian understanding of the graciousness of God supports equally well the Jodo Shinshu understanding of the wisdom and compassion that characterizes ultimate reality. It provides also the grounds for a desirable expansion of the Pure Land understanding of Amida.[31]

Cobb also admits, however, that it is unlikely, perhaps even inconceivable at the present time,
that Jōdo Shinshū Buddhists can appropriate Christian
history or Christian *understandings* of history to support the development and renewal of their own faith.

But there exists no reason in principle why
Buddhists cannot internalize the Palestinian
as well as the Indian past. It is in Palestine, rather than in India, that history,
when it is sensed as centering in Jesus, provides the strongest basis for believing that
we are saved by faith through grace.[32]

CONCLUDING OBSERVATIONS

Simply stated, Cobb's thesis that Christ is
Amida Buddha implies that Buddhists can deepen their
faith and practice by dialogically appropriating historical and ethical consciousness from Christian experience and teaching. For if it is true that Christ and
Amida Buddha are different names for an identical sacred reality, as Cobb believes is the case, then Buddhists, especially Pure Land Buddhists, are existentially in a religious context conducive to comprehending and appropriating Christian understandings of this
sacred reality. Because Cobb's views of Buddhist historical and ethical consciousness in comparison with
Christian experience and teaching were originally published in an essay entitled "Buddhist Emptiness and the
Christian God" five years before he united these views
with his notion that Christ is Amida Buddha in *Beyond
Dialogue*, the remainder of this chapter clarifies his

understanding of what Buddhist dialogue with the Christian Way can contribute to Buddhist self-understanding in a religiously plural world. I reserve a fuller critique of Cobb's analysis for the following, and concluding, chapter of this study, where I shall also try to bring the material of each of the previous chapters of this study to their resolution.

Cobb's arguments rest on his observation of parallels between Whitehead's conception of creativity and the Mahayana Buddhist doctrine of dependent co-origination (pratītyasamupt-pāda), interpreted according to Nāgārjuna's conception of "emptiness" (śūnyatā). Emptiness, he says, entails "a dissolution of Being in which there is a dissolution of metaphysics into the language of things and of mysticism into the sheer immediacy of the world."[34] That is, the meditative experience of Emptiness leads us to become more immediately and consciously aware of the universal flux of things and events rather than allowing us to transcend this flux.

> The serenity and spontaneity attained by realizing Emptiness do not lead away from awareness of what is occurring in one's world or reduce effectiveness of action. On the contrary, Buddhist meditation has been cultivated successfully for the sake of greater effectiveness in normal life.[35]

Thus the realization of Emptiness allows us to immerse ourselves totally in the processes of historical existence, to respond to these processes more adequately, and to appreciate them at every moment of our experience.

Difficulties occur, however, when we ask whether the meditative experience of Emptiness allows for the development of what Cobb calls "the principle of rightness." By "rightness" he means something like "propriety," "appropriateness," or "good judgment" as forms through which "rightness" is expressed.[36] Underlying these general terms is the ethical distinction between what is and what ought to be. The "principle of rightness" refers to judgments that some actions or states of affairs are better than others, and is thereby associated with the drive to actually shape the historical process to accord with these judgments. As employed by Cobb, the "principle of rightness" becomes a means of distinguishing between the Buddhist concept of Emptiness and the Christian concept of God.[37] Thus, he argues, Emptiness, as the "metaphysical ultimate" that he also identifies with Whitehead's concept of creativity, must be distinguished from "the principle of rightness" precisely because Emptiness calls for total immersion in the present moment as "the only moment there is."

Even though traditional Christian conceptions of God have often associated God with a metaphysical ultimate reality and the "principle of rightness," Cobb thinks "whenever biblical faith is primary, God must be identified with the principle of rightness rather than with the metaphysical ultimate."[38] This distinction sharply opposes Mahayana Buddhist and Christian conceptions of ultimacy. Emptiness is thereby linked to a spontaneous meditative absorption in a moment of space-time. Christian notions of God, in contrast, require us to conceive of the spatial-temporal process as possessing a directional quality characterized by a moral purpose not totally present in every moment of space-time. Even though Buddhist images of compassion and devotion express a certain practical blurring of the distinction between Buddhist and Christian ethical teachings and practices, Cobb concludes that at the level at which each religious Way interprets the nature of ultimacy the distinctions remain relevant. As he understand this situation, Emptiness permits the spontaneous nonjudgmental embrace of the causal process at every moment. But in focusing on the moment, the concept of Emptiness dissolves a distinction that for Christians is ultimately important. Without distinguishing between what is and what ought to be, and apart from awareness of the claims of "rightness," it becomes impossible, according to traditional Christian experience and teaching, to act purposefully in history.

In most instances of the Mahayana Dharma, accordingly, Emptiness--or perhaps more accurately, Emptying--is stressed in Buddhist teaching and practice. This is why Cobb remains convinced that what Mahayana Buddhists mean by Emptiness is not the focus of biblical tradition. For the biblical images of deity portray God as neither an empty sacred reality nor as a process of emptying. In all of the Bible's numerous images of the sacred reality Christians name God, God is represented as "the principle of rightness." As such, God becomes the source of the distinction between what is and what ought to be among human beings, as well as the demand for righteousness in human relationships.

It is important to note that Cobb does not claim, however, that the Buddhist Way lacks the principle of rightness or that traditions originating in the Bible are wholly devoid of what Buddhists experience as Emptiness. But he does claim that the biblical traditions, and in particular Christian teaching and practice, do not emphasize Emptiness. Nor does the Buddhist Way stress a transcendent principle or source of rightness by which to distinguish what is from what ought to be. To repeat, Cobb emphatically does not believe that Buddhists are less ethical than Christians:

> Much can be said of the horrors worked in history by those who have intended to serve righteousness, and among my Buddhist friends there are those who have become Buddhists because of their revulsion against the Biblical focus on righteousness and its negative consequences.

Hence, "the principle of rightness," and therefore historical consciousness and ethical self-discipline play differing religious functions in biblical tradition and the Christian Way than in most traditions of the Buddhist Way. In the Christian Way, "the principle of rightness" characterizes its experience of ultimacy; in the Buddhist Way, it does not.

Cobb believes this represents a serious deficiency in the Buddhist Way, at least from a Christian perspective. As Christians can deepen their awareness of the biblical images of God through dialogical appropriation of the Mahayana Buddhist doctrine of Emptiness into Christian teaching, so Buddhists can deepen their consciousness of historical existence and ethical practice through dialogical appropriation of the principle of rightness into Buddhist teaching. His conclusion that Christ names the same sacred reality that is Amida Buddha becomes, he believes, a door: through it Buddhists may dialogically appropriate that which is more systematically and coherently emphasized in the Christian Way. The validity of Cobb's conclusion will be among the issues considered in the next, and concluding, chapter of this study.

NOTES

[1]The Japanese title of this sutra is *Muryōjukyō,* and the Chinese translation used by Shinran may be found in an excellent *kambun* edition in *Shinshu Shōgyo Zenshō* [Collected Works of the Pure Land School] (Kyōto: Kōkyō Shōin, 1955), 1: 1-47. The passage I have translated is the Eighteenth Bodhisattva Vow, also called the "Original Vow" (Japanese, *hongan*) of Amida Buddha, the "Buddha of Infinite Light" (Sanskrit, Amitābha Buddha).

[2]John Ross Carter, ed., *The Threefold Refuge in the* Theravada *Buddhist Tradition* (Chambersburg, Pa.: Anima Books, 1982).

[3]John B. Cobb, Jr., *Beyond Dialogue* (Philadelphia: Fortress Press, 1982), 120.

[4]Ibid., 121.

[5]For an English translation of this text, see E. B. Cowell, ed., *Buddhist Mahayana Texts* (New York: Dover Publications, 1969).

[6]Cobb, *Beyond Dialogue*, 122.

[7]See my study, "Shinran Shōnin and Martin Luther: A Soteriological Comparison," *Journal of the American Academy of Religion* 39 (December 1971): 447-80.

[8]Cobb, *Beyond Dialogue*, 123. Also see *A Christian Natural Theology* (Philadelphia: Westminster Press, 1965), 282.

[9]Cobb, *Beyond Dialogue*, 124.

[10]For good introductory expositions of the *trikaya* doctrine, see Edward Conze, *Buddhist thought in India* (Ann Arbor: University of Michigan Press, 1967), 195-237 and Richard H. Robinson, *The Buddhist Religion* (Belmont, CA.: Dickenson Publishing Company, 1970), 49-70.

[11]Cobb, *Beyond Dialogue*, 125.

[12]See my study, *The Dharma of Faith: An Introduction to Classical Pure Land Buddhism* (Washington, D.C.:

University Press of America, 1977), 82-88, and Alfred Bloom, *Shinran's Gospel of Pure Grace* (Tucson: University of Arizona Press. 1968), 27-44, for Shinran's interpretation of the *trikaya* doctrine.

[13]Cobb, *Beyond Dialogue,* 126.

[14]Ibid.

[15]Ibid., 127.

[16]See John 1:1-14 and C. K. Barrett, *The Gospel According to St. John* (London: Seabury Press, 1958), 125-141.

[17]Cobb, *Beyond Dialogue,* 128.

[18]Ibid., 129.

[19]Ibid., 131-132.

[20]See, for example, Masao Abe, "God, Emptiness, and the True Self," *The Eastern Buddhist* 2 (November 1969): 15-30; Robert A. F. Thurman, "Guidelines for Buddhist Social Activism Based on Nāgārjuna's *Jewel Garland of Royal Counsels,*" *The Eastern Buddhist* 16 (Spring 1983): 19-51.

[21]Cobb, *Beyond Dialogue,* 132.

[22]Ibid., 133.

[23]Ibid., 136.

[24]Ibid., 137.

[25]Ibid.

[26]Ibid., 138. The problems confronting religious faith arising from modern historical-critical methodologies are present in all religious Ways. See Van A. Harvey, *The Historian and the Believer* (Philadelphia: Westminster Press, 1966).

[27]Cobb, *Beyond Dialogue,* 139.

[28]See Harvey, *The Historian and the Believer*, chapt. 1 for detailed analysis of the theological issues created for Christian faith by the rise of modern historical criticism.

[29]Peter L. Berger has developed a typology for comprehending Christian responses to modernity's challenge to Christian faith in a religiously plural world. He calls these traditional responses the "deductive possibility," the "reductive possibility," and the "inductive possibility." Cobb's theological approach to historical criticism, modernity, and religious pluralism is a clear example of what Berger means by the inductive possibility. See *The Heretical Imperative* (New York: Anchor Books, 1979), chapts. 3-5.

[30]Cobb., *Beyond Dialogue*, 139.

[31]Ibid., p. 140.

[32]Ibid.

[33]*Journal of the American Academy of Religion* 45 (1977): 11-25.

[34]Ibid., 14.

[35]Ibid., 16.

[36]Ibid., 17.

[37]Distinctions that I attempted to clarify in chapter eight of this study.

[38]Cobb, "Buddhist Emptiness and the Christian God," 27.

[39]See John B. Cobb, Jr., "Response to Eckel and Thurman," *Buddhist-Christian Studies*, 5 (1983): 38. This essay is Cobb's reply to M. David Eckel, "Emptiness and the Historical Process: A Historian's Response to the Image of Mahayana Buddhism in the Works of John Cobb and George Rupp," and Robert A. F. Thurman, "Beyond Buddhism and Christianity," both of which were published in the same issue of *Buddhist-Christian Studies*," as Cobb's reply, 7-19 and 21-35, respectively.

CHAPTER TEN
Conclusion in Process

Herein, monks, the yoeman farmer gets his field well ploughed . . . puts in his seed . . . lets the water in and turns it off very quickly. These are his three urgent duties. Now monks, that yoeman farmer has no such magic power, or authority as to say: "Let my crops spring up today. Tomorrow let them ear. On the following day, let them ripen." No! It is just the due season which makes them do this. Now the monk has no such magic power or authority as to say: "Today: let my mind be released from the *asavas* [impurities] without grasping, or tomorrow, or the day following."

> *Aṅguttara Nikāya* [Gradual Sayings] 1.219[1]

He said, "The kingdom of God is like this. A man scatters seed on the land: he goes to bed at night and gets up in the morning, and the seed sprouts and grows--how he does not know. The ground produces a crop by itself, first the blade, then the ear, then the full-grown corn in the ear: But as soon as the crop is ripe, he plies the sickle, because harvest time has come.

> Mark 4:26-29. *New English Bible*

INTERDEPENDENT BECOMING AND THE NECESSITY OF DIALOGUE

Everything must change because all things and events are processes of interdependent relativity. This view of existence is neither peculiarly Buddhist nor Whiteheadian. Nor have I concluded something peculiarly Christian, even though Buddhist teaching and Whiteheadian process philosophy appear to mirror the biblical record of how human beings have experienced their own and God's self-identity through time.

Just how the process of interdependent becoming should be best characterized is, of course, open to debate. But *that* the structure of existence entails processes of interdependent becoming appears universally confirmed by human experience. All things must interdependently change or they are dead, including the special religious Ways of humanity. The Buddhist Way must remain incomplete even for practicing Buddhists; the Christian Way has never been "once and for all delivered to the saints" (Jude 1:3), even for practicing Christians. Therefore, absolutizing the Buddhist Way into a permanent, unchanging religious structure represents a form of clinging *(tanhā)* to permanence in an impermanent universe. The karmic result is "suffering." Likewise, absolutizing the Christian Way into a once-and-for-all superior unchanging Truth according to which all persons must be saved constitutes an idolatry.

I have throughout this study reflected on the contemporary process of interreligious dialogue between the Buddhist Way and the Christian Way, as well as the effects this dialogical encounter may be having on the faith and practice of those Buddhists and Christians most existentially engaged in this enterprise. Hence in each of the preceding chapters I identified some of the important issues now emerging from contemporary Buddhist-Christian encounter, but without extensive comment about how these issues might be resolved. My goal in this final chapter is to declare my own "conclusions in process" about these issues. The quotation marks surrounding the words "conclusions in process" are intentional. Existence in a universe of processive relativity means that no complete resolutions, no final truths, no ultimate ends are ever attainable. There are no guarantees other than there are no guarantees.

That we inhabit an open-ended universe is one important common lesson in the Buddhist and New Testament versions of the parable of the sower.[2] The sower plants his seed, spending long hours working on the land, anticipating a bountiful harvest. But while his labor is necessary, there exists no guarantee that his crop will not fail. Even if there is a harvest, it might not be the bumper crop the sower desires or expects. And yet there can be no harvest at all without his backbreaking labor. So precisely because of the intensity of the sower's labor, in other words, there are sufficient grounds for hopeful anticipation of a future bountiful harvest. Still, all the sower can do is prepare the soil, work, and wait, because his crop will or will not grow according to its own internal rhythms, its own internal processes--processes with which the sower can cooperate, but never master.

Anyone reflecting on the process of Buddhist-Christian dialogue must necessarily be in a position similar to that of the farmer in the parable of the sower. No one can predict the final outcome of Buddhist-Christian dialogical encounter with any certainty. Not only is this particular dialogue still in process, but interreligious dialogue is itself a process with its own natural rhythms and structures. We can expend much intellectual energy cooperating with these rhythms and structures, but we can neither control nor predict their final outcome. Still, for those

laboring in this field of inquiry, reasonable grounds
exist for identifying general trends, new directions of
thought, emerging issues and possibilities for creative
transformation, and more comprehensive methods for
thinking about perennial religious questions. Most important, the process of dialogue is grounds for hopeful
anticipation of the emergence of new, less parochial,
more integrative experience of the Sacred far beyond
what contemporary traditional forms of Buddhist and
Christian faith and practice can, at present, either
acknowledge as a possibility or recognize as a legiti-
mate way of structuring human existence.

ADDRESSED TO CHRISTIANS

In chapter two I described the historic pattern of Christian theological reflection on its encounter with non-Christian religious Ways. I focused
this discussion on the Roman Catholic tradition of no-
salvation-outside-the-Church and the Protestant version
of this doctrine, no-salvation-outside-of-explicit-
Christian-belief. I then concluded that these twin
doctrines are neither conducive to interreligious dialogue, nor consistent with biblical images of Christian
faith, nor consistent with the historical precedent of
the church's earliest experience of dialogue with Hellenistic culture.

In principle, there can be no dialogue between Christians and non-Christians until Christians
renounce the doctrine of no-salvation-outside-the-
Church or explicit-Christian-belief. Not only do these
teachings prevent honest encounter with non-Christians,

as well as the creative transformation of Christians, they also constitute an idolatry contrary to historic Christian faith and practice. Absolutizing the symbols of the Christian Way into final representations of truth about the Sacred substitutes the symbols of Christian faith for the object of Christian faith. Thus, rather than pointing to the sacred reality Christians name God manifested in Christ, Christian symbols and institutions become māyā-forms, that is, "delusions," which Christians have trained themselves to substitute for the sacred reality to which they point. To the degree this occurs, Christians prevent themselves from encountering the Sacred. Not that Christian symbols are erroneous. But these symbols are transformed into delusions when mistaken for ultimate sacred truths by the doctrine of no-salvation-outside-the-Church or explicit-Christian-belief.

Because Christian faith and practice cannot be reduced to trust in belief systems, institutional structures, and liturgical forms, Christians are free to engage in the adventures and risks of "passing over" into the religious Ways of non-Christian persons. In support of this contention I described the ancient precedent of the early church's dialogical encounter with Hellenistic culture during the first three hundred years of Christian history. I also pointed to Saint Paul's teaching of salvation by faith through grace alone as an important theological justification for engaging in the risks of interreligious dialogue.

But one issue requires consideration for Christians now seriously engaged in dialogue with Buddhists. In chapters four and five I described how Roman Catholic participants in the contemporary dialogue with Buddhists have been most interested in "practice" (*praxis*)," mostly Buddhist meditative practice. The goal of Catholic dialogue with the Buddhist Way, so far, appears to be the incorporation of Buddhist meditative techniques for purposes of renewing contemplative discipline both within and outside the institutional context of Catholic monasticism. The theological interests motivating Karl Rähner's, Hans Küng's, and William Johnston's encounter with the Buddhist Way are specific examples of the Roman Catholic emphasis on *praxis*.

However, Catholic interest in Buddhist meditative practice has severely hindered serious theological and philosophical encounter with Buddhist teaching (*theoria*), which in turn has hindered, if not prevented, the creative transformation of Roman Catholic theological self-understanding. The primary source of Catholic lack of openness to creative transformation in dialogue with Buddhist teaching lies in the continuing theological and institutional influence of the doctrine of no-salvation-outside-the-Roman-Catholic-Church. If nothing contradicting the Church's theology or institutional structure can be valid, then the possibility of seriously considering the Buddhist world view as a truthful apprehension of reality does not even arise. Accordingly, the major assumption guiding most Roman Catholic dialogue with the Buddhist Way appears to be that Buddhist meditative techniques can be divorced from the Buddhist world view and appropriated in order to deepen Catholic contemplative life and experience.

Contemporary Protestant dialogue with the Buddhist Way, however, tends to focus its energy on Buddhist theory divorced from Buddhist *praxis*. The theologies of Tillich, Moltmann, and Cobb represent the most influential forms of this style of dialogue. The classical Protestant emphasis on the doctrine of justification by faith through grace alone is the source of Protestant theological interest in dialogue, especially as this doctrine is read through the notion of no-salvation-outside-of-explicit-Christian-faith. One historic effect of Protestant emphasis upon God's grace alone apart from human self-discipline is the drastic diminishing of the importance of practice (*praxis*). Accordingly, Protestant theologians usually remain more interested in how the traditional categories of Christian theological reflection can be reformulated through the appropriation of Buddhist ideas and philosophical conceptualities. In short, it seems there exists little Protestant interest in appropriating Buddhist religious *praxis* for purposes of creatively transforming Christian religious life and experience.

But can *theoria* and *praxis* be so sharply bifurcated? According to the Buddhist world view, they cannot; doing so is artificial and constitutes a profound misrepresentation, and therefore a misunderstanding, of the Buddhist Way.[4] Some traditions of the Christian Way also teach that *theoria* and *praxis* are polar sides of the same religious coin--they are both absolutely necessary in the structuring of Christian experience. The unity of teaching and practice, *theoria and praxis,* to which I alluded in the introduction of chapter five, was also described by William James in his classic work, *The Varieties of Religious Experience*, over eighty years ago.[5] As James discovered, the kind, quality, and intensity of religious experience--any religious experience--is conditioned by whatever particular practice we undertake as directed by the religious world view we espouse as we practice a specific religious Way.

The implications of the unity of *theoria* and *praxis* for future Buddhist-Christian dialogue are, I believe, immensely important. The techniques of Buddhist meditational practice, for example, were developed by Buddhists for purposes of internalizing the Buddhist world view. The specific kinds of experiences Buddhists achieve through meditation are what the Buddhist world view teaches the meditator to desire and expect to experience. Experiences contrary to the Buddhist world view are not likely to occur; even if they should, they are not likely to be recognized as authentic *Buddhist* experiences by either the meditator or other practicing Buddhists.

Consequently, the issue for Roman Catholic participants in their dialogue with the Buddhist Way may be formulated thusly: when Buddhist practices of meditation, such as *zazen*, are appropriated into Christian traditions guided by Roman Catholic doctrine, are the resulting experiences authentically Catholic? Is the relationship between *theoria and praxis* so interdependent that intentionally appropriating another reli-

gious Way's disciplines of practice means unintentionally appropriating much of that Way's world view? It
appears to me that Roman Catholic dialogue with Buddhist *praxis* has been quite uncritical at this point.
Not that change in the Catholic form of the Christian
world view would necessarily be an undesirable result
of its dialogue with Buddhist *praxis*. But Catholic dialogical passing over into the Buddhist Way would undoubtedly engender more rational creative transformation of Roman Catholic doctrine should it include intentional, critical appropriation of both Buddhist meditation and elements of the *theoria* guiding Buddhist
praxis. But for an unpredictable time to come,
Catholic encounter with the Buddhist Way will undoubtedly remain monological because of its one-sided emphasis upon Buddhist practice.

Protestant dialogue with the Buddhist Way
stresses the opposite pole of the unity of *praxis* and
theoria. Protestants seem generally more willing to
appropriate elements of the Buddhist world view in
their quest to reformulate Christian theology into
categories more relevant to human existence in this
present age of modern secular and religious pluralism.
The clearest example of this interest is the process
theology of John Cobb. However, the Buddhist conceptualities appropriated by Protestant theologians are usually divorced from their context in Buddhist religious
practice. As a result, Protestant encounter with the
Buddhist Way is as one sided, and therefore as divorced, from the experience of Buddhist persons as is
Catholic understanding. Protestants have simply ig-

nored the experiential dimensions of the Buddhist Way--
a dimension that can only be comprehended through the
practice of this Way's forms of meditation guided by
its unique world view. If one of the theoretical goals
of interreligious dialogue is empathetic understanding
of religious Ways other than our own, then Protestant
nonconcern for Buddhist *praxis* represents a serious inconsistency in its encounter with the Buddhist Way. As
most Protestant thinkers have explicitly affirmed, the
final purpose of interreligious dialogue is the mutual
creative transformation of those participating.   If
this is so, then contemporary Protestant theological
interest in Buddhist teaching divorced from Buddhist
practice constitutes a serious, and I think unnecessary, inconsistency in its encounter with the Buddhist
Way.   Unnecessary limitations are imposed on the process of creative transformation operating in the
Protestant Christian Way.

ADDRESSED TO BUDDHISTS

            In the conclusion of chapter three, I ob-
served how neither the Theravada nor the Mahayana versions of the Dharma evaluated non-Buddhist religious
Ways as realms of spiritual darkness.   No idea comparable to teaching with the Christian doctrine of no-
salvation-apart-from-the-Christian-Way evolved within
the Buddhist world view.[6] Instead, Buddhist interpretation and assessment of non-Buddhist religious Ways
was guided by its conception of *upāya*.   Accordingly,
those teachings and practices that could be assimilated
into the Buddhist Way as a "skillful means" of

preparing non-Buddhists for the practice of explicitly Buddhist ethical and meditational self-discipline were eagerly assimilated. By skillful teaching, the Buddhist Way creatively transformed itself from the very beginnings of its history far beyond the probable original teachings of Gautama the Buddha. Even so, traditional Buddhist interaction with non-Buddhist religious Ways was not uncritical, but, on the contrary, highly selective. Those teachings and practices that could not be creatively transformed according to the Buddhist world view--for example all notions of permanent selfhood or deity--were rejected outrightly as falsehoods not conducive to the attainment of enlightenment.

However, as I also observed in the concluding section of chapter one, contemporary Buddhist encounter with the Christian Way seems somewhat inconsistent with the historic pattern of the Buddhist Way's traditional dialogical response to non-Buddhists. For the incentive, interest, and leadership in Buddhist-Christian dialogue has almost completely originated from the Christian side of the encounter. Thus Buddhist-Christian dialogue currently runs the risk of becoming a Christian monologue.

There are certainly valid reasons for this state of affairs. The historical association of the Christian Way with political and economic ideologies according to which Western nations justified their colonial and economic exploitation of Asian cultures is one important source of Buddhist mistrust of Christian motives for dialogue. Another factor is the close ontological connection of Buddhist faith and practice with its traditional world view--a world view leaving little room for the sacred reality that Christians have traditionally worshiped as God. Assimilating any idea of God into Buddhist teaching and practice, particularly theologically normative Christian conceptions of God, would so alter the Buddhist Way that it might cease being recognizable as "Buddhist." In other words, Buddhist faith, practice. and experience is more clearly tied to an explicit ontology than is Christian faith, practice, and experience. Philosophically, therefore, it seems more difficult for Buddhists to dialogically pass over into the Christian Way than for Christians to dialogically pass over into the Buddhist Way.

At present, it is not easy to perceive how the Buddhist Way has creatively transformed itself through its contemporary encounter with the Christian Way because Buddhist conversations with Christians, with few exceptions, have largely been monologues. Surely dialogue and creative transformation are processes that ought not, in fact cannot, be forced upon Buddhists from the outside by Christians. But just as surely, dialogue and creative transformation are just as desirable and necessary for Buddhists as they are for Christians in this modern epoch of religious and secular pluralism. Indeed, historically, Buddhists have thought it desirable to pass over into non-Buddhist religious Ways guided by the "philosophy of assimilation" inherent in the concept of upāya.

Consequently, as one who is not a Buddhist but who nevertheless has been transformed by Buddhist faith and practice, I offer the following suggestions to my Buddhist friends and colleagues. Buddhists might, with little difficulty, systematically apply the concept of *upaya* to its encounter with the Christian Way. But in so doing, Buddhist interest and energy should be directed to all aspects of the Christian Way, not merely to Christian ethical and social practice. No religious Way is reducible to merely ethical and social interests. Buddhists might learn and appropriate much from Christian conceptions of history, for example. Likewise, certain forms of Christian devotional practice might be of interest to Buddhists, particularly Pure Land Buddhists. Processive concepts of selfhood and God might also provide focus for Buddhist assimilation of Christian interpretations of the experience of self identity through time. Christian contemplative discipline and monastic life could easily become a focus of Buddhist dialogical encounter as well.

Consciously applying its "philosophy of assimilation" to its dialogue with the Christian Way as a whole might energize the process of creative transformation in Buddhist faith and practice in directions never before imagined by faithful Buddhists. Non-Buddhists, of course, cannot predict just how this process will evolve and what results will be attained, for Buddhists themselves must engage in it, attaining whatever they can for themselves. After all, if the Buddhist world view accurately describes "the way things really are" in this universe of interdependent change, then whatever form the process of creative transformation assumes in Buddhist faith and practice, even should the Buddhist Way be creatively transformed beyond all present recognizable forms, would not necessarily be contrary to the Buddhist vision of reality. Indeed, even creatively transforming the Buddhist Way into such a totally new form of religious faith and practice that its followers could no longer wear the label "Buddhist" would not be contrary to the Buddhist world view.[7]

SELFHOOD, GOD, AND EMPTINESS

The key conceptual and experiential differences between the Buddhist Way and the Christian Way originate in how Buddhists and Christians have traditionally interpreted the human experience of self-identity through time. The Buddhist nonself paradigm and the Christian self paradigm are so different, in fact, that unless Buddhists and Christians discover a means of resolving the conceptual differences between these paradigms, the present Buddhist-Christian dialogue will be stalemated and further mutual creative transformation will become impossible.

In chapter seven, I described in some detail the Theravada and Mahayana versions of the Buddhist nonself paradigm, biblical images of selfhood, and the traditional Christian self paradigm. While in many ways similar to biblical images of selfhood, the Buddhist nonself paradigm and the traditional Christian self paradigm are mutually exclusive interpretations of the experience of human self-identity through time.

Because of this exclusiveness, I argued, both paradigms foster incomplete, one-sided, and ultimately incoherent conceptions of the human experience of self-identity through time. That is, the Theravada and Mahayana versions of the Buddhist nonself paradigm accurately describe our experience of change, impermanence, and interdependent becoming while ignoring, by explaining away as a delusion, our experience of constancy, stability, and duration. In other words, *that I change and that* I am impermanent is emphasized in the Buddhist nonself paradigm at the cost of ignoring the personal "I" that changes. Every thing and event must change: but paradoxically, the Buddhist nonself paradigm ignores the things and events that must change.

However, because of its underemphasis on our experience as stable, enduring selves existing through time, coupled with its neglect of our equally real experience of becoming, change, and impermanence, the traditional Christian self paradigm is likewise an incoherent account of human experience of self-identity through time. The source of this incoherency lies in traditional Christian theology's appropriation of Greek philosophy's category of substance--the principle conceptual vehicle through which Christians have for two thousand years attempted to transmit biblical images of human selfhood into the specific doctrines guiding Christian faith and practice. Not only has this attempt failed to account for humanity's experience of self-identity through time, it has also spawned conceptions of God that remain in serious tension with the biblical sources of Christian faith and practice. And since the substance categories of traditional Christian theology are also one of the sources of Christian theological exclusivism and religious imperialism, of which the doctrine of no-salvation-outside-the-Church or explicit Christian belief is a clear example, Christians have trained themselves to avoid openly encountering and understanding non-Christian persons.

If impermanence and interdependent becoming amidst stability and permanence are bipolar expressions of humanity's experience of selfhood, just as *yang* and *yin* are bipolar opposite expressions of one reality that the Chinese named the Tao, then a different selfhood paradigm integrating both Buddhist and Christian experiences of self-identity through time seems necessary. Such a reconceived paradigm would benefit Buddhist-Christian dialogue because it would facilitate mutual Buddhist-Christian "passing over" into one another's world views, practices, and experiences. But apart from a reconstituted selfhood paradigm, further Buddhist-Christian dialogue will probably not evolve much beyond the simple sharing of ideas between the more liberally collegial representatives of each religious Way.

I described a possible selfhood paradigm in chapter eight that I believe accurately integrates the insights of both the traditional Buddhist nonself paradigm and the traditional Christian self paradigm. In formulating this paradigm, I appropriated some of the categories of Alfred North Whitehead's process philosophy and established three interdependent distinctions: "person," "subject," and "self." By "person,"

I mean a particular series of human experiences extending from the moment of an individual's conception until
death. Or, restated somewhat differently, a "person"
is the totality of his or her experiences extending
from the moment of conception until the moment of
death. A "subject" is any particular experiential mo-
ment--in Whitehead's language, an "actual entity"--com-
prising an individual's life experiences, insofar as
any specific unit of experience of a person's life is a
process of "feeling" or "prehending" the "data" of
whatever entities comprise the universe objective to a
subject. And by "self" I mean any particular present
"subject" of a "person's" ever-changing, impermanent
life-history.

Accordingly, as individual "persons," human
beings are a series of interconnected "subjects"--in-
terconnected by what Whitehead called "prehension."
And a person's "self" is that "subject" that at any
given moment is contemporary because it exists here-
and-now. When a contemporary here-and-now subject perishes, it ceases to be the "self" of an individual
"person." But a person's subsequent "subject" evolves
in its place, becoming the new "self" of that person.
Thus a person's "self" is never permanent, because at
any given moment of a person's life history, the contemporary subject that is a person's self is always
here-and-now.

The upshot of this paradigm is that the stability and continuity that a person named Paul Ingram,
for example, experiences is constituted by a historical
series of "subjects," which, when contemporary, are

Paul Ingram's "self" at that moment, but which immediately perish after that moment to be replaced by another "self," *ad infinitum,* or at least until Paul Ingram dies. The self of an individual person named Paul Ingram, or the self of any individual person, is whatever a contemporary here-and-now momentary subject of that person is experiencing and undergoing at that here-and-now moment. In other words, a "person" experiences stability and processive becoming simultaneously because a "person" is a life-long series of experiencing, perishing "selves." Neither the experience of stability nor the experience of becoming is a delusion. But because we are "persons," we never experience permanency, since "persons" are a continuation of numerous past selves until death.

If the selfhood paradigm I have summarized, and more fully described in chapter eight, coherently integrates Buddhist and Christian interpretations of the experience of self-identity through time, then what are some of the implications for Buddhist-Christian mutual creative transformation through dialogue? I suspect there are at least three.

First, Christian experience and conceptualization of selfhood and Christian experience and conceptualization of the Sacred are co-determinate; *how* Christians have experienced human selfhood and God are interdependent features of the Christian world view. Likewise, Buddhist experience and conceptions of non-selfhood and the ways in which Buddhists have conceptualized the Sacred—whether named the Dharma, Buddha Nature, or Emptiness—are co-determinate: *how* Buddhists

have experienced nonselfhood and the Sacred are inter-
dendent features of the Buddhist world view.

Consequently, normative Buddhist teaching and
practice continues emphasizing the nonpersonal, dynamic, processive, impermanent character of existence
while simultaneously deemphasizing the personal, stable, and transcendent character of existence. Mahayana
teaching about the Emptiness of all things and events
at every moment of space-time represents the most extreme example of this emphasis in the Buddhist Way.
According to Mahayana philosophy, the "emptiness" of
nonself mirrors the "emptiness" of the whole of reality, so that ultimate reality at every moment of space-
time *is* Emptiness.

But in opposition to the Buddhist world view,
traditional Christian teaching and practice continues
to stress the personal, stable, non-changing, transcendent character of existence while deemphasizing the impersonal, dynamic, processive, nonsubstantial character
of existence. Consequently, Christian experience,
teaching, and practice focus upon worship and devotion
to God in whose image the human self is permanently
"made," and who is conceived as dualistically transcendent to the universe "he" created *in illo tempore*.

Of course, the Sacred conceived as a person-
alized object of devotion is an important element in
the Buddhist world view, especially in that version of
the Jōdo Shinshū Way established by Shinran. But Jōdo
Shinshū teaching seems contradictory to the central
"monistic" assumptions of the normative Buddhist world
view, and indeed may even seriously contradict this

world view. Nor does Christian teaching and practice completely lack stress on the totally other, impersonal, nonknowable, ineffable character of the Sacred, of which the human self is represented as a mirror image. But this tradition is found mostly in Christian mysticism, a tradition, be it noted, that is not usually regarded as normative by most Christians and is viewed with suspicion in most Protestant theological circles.[7]

However, as I argued in chapter seven, neither the Buddhist nonself paradigm nor the traditional Christian selfhood paradigm should simply be written off as delusions. Both paradigms express one-sided, incomplete interpretations of the human experience of self-identity through time. Therefore, neither the Buddhist Way's conception of Emptiness nor the Christian Way's affirmation of God are delusions. Rather, "Emptiness" and "God" may very well be two names for different, incomplete experiences of human encounter with the Sacred.

Second, if "Emptiness" and "God" indeed represent different Buddhist and Christian names for one sacred reality, then notions similar to John Cobb's suggestion that God can be reconceived as the supreme, everlasting Empty One might possibly do much to bridge the conceptual gaps between the Buddhist and Christian Ways.[8] Or, as translated through the categories of Whiteheadian process philosophy, reconceiving God's self-nature as Empty might be a metaphysical possibility for inclusion in Buddhist teaching and practice precisely because God as the Empty Sacred Ultimate Reality contradicts neither the Buddhist world view nor Christian religious experience. Buddhist appropriation of some sort of processive understanding of God is, of course, a task Buddhists must perform for themselves should they perceive sufficient reason for doing so.

But while appropriating some sort of process conception of God into Buddhist faith and practice does not necessarily contradict Buddhist teaching, it would surely engender the process of creative transformation within the Buddhist Way in, as yet, largely unexplored directions. Not because, as Cobb argues, Emptiness designates a "metaphysical ultimate reality" for Buddhists while God designates a "religious ultimate reality" that Cobb characterizes as "the principle of rightness" against which Christians must measure their responses to God and to other human beings.[10] Indeed, Emptiness and God may very well represent two different "ultimates" emphasized in Buddhist and Christian teaching respectively. But if twenty-five hundred years of Buddhist experience of nonself and Emptiness are not a complete delusion, but rather express truthful insight about "the way things really are," and if almost two thousand years of Christian experience are likewise not a complete delusion, but also express truthful insight about "the way things really are," then sufficient reason exists for exploring the very real possibility that Emptiness and God symbolize different conceptualizations of the experience of human encounter with one sacred reality. What Christians name "God" may be the same sacred reality Buddhists experience as Emptiness or the Dharma. One reason for Buddhist exploration of this possibility might be to create the possibility for deepening Buddhist consciousness of the historicity of all things and events, thereby allowing Buddhists to respond more coherently to the contemporary political, social, economic, and ecological issues posed by modern religious and secular pluralism.

Finally, if "Emptiness" and "God" are Buddhist and Christian names for one sacred reality, then Christians, through appropriating the concepts of Emptiness and nonself, can shed the substance categories of traditional theological reflection. So doing might engender possibilities for developing not only conceptual categories for reconceiving God that correspond more adequately to biblical tradition and Christian history, but also for developing theological categories more consistent with modern historical and scientific consciousness.

I previously suggested how Whiteheadian process philosophy has already served as a bridge to Christian reformulation of its conception of God and selfhood in the process theology of John Cobb. While process theology certainly is not the only contemporary Christian movement capable of creatively transforming Christian faith and practice through dialogue with the categories of Buddhist philosophy, this theological movement, more than any other "style" of modern Christian thought, has been the most serious, systematic. Christian dialogical response to the Buddhist Way. Indeed, I suspect process theology's encounter with the Buddhist Way constitutes the single most important theological paradigm for contemporary Christian encounter with all non-Christian religious Ways.

But Christians do not experience a sacred reality named "God" so generically. What Christians experience as God is the Sacred encountered in the historical events surrounding the life, death, and resurrection of Jesus as the Christ. Likewise, significant numbers of Buddhists experience the caring, nurturing, gracious character of Emptiness as the Dharma through symbolic personifications of the Sacred called "Bodhisattvas." The most completely evolved expression of this aspect of Buddhist experience is Jodo Shinshu teaching. But what can dialogue with Christian teaching about God manifested in Jesus as the Christ contribute to deepening Buddhist experience and understanding of the gracious, compassionate, and wise character of Emptiness personified as Amida Buddha?

JESUS AS THE CHRIST AND AMIDA BUDDHA

The topic of chapter nine was John Cobb's assessment of what Buddhists can dialogically appropriate from Christian christological teaching.[10] Assuming a "logos christology," the thesis around which everything in Cobb's understanding of Jōdo Shinshū Buddhist tradition revolves is that the reality Pure Land Buddhists name "Amida Buddha" is the same reality that Christians name "Christ."[11] If Cobb's understanding is correct, he argues, Buddhists can deepen their apprehension of the personal, gracious, caring character of Emptiness personified by Amida Buddha. And in the process, the role of historical consciousness, and thereby of ethical and social consciousness, in traditional Buddhist faith and practice might be transformed beyond its present role in the Buddhist Way.[12]

Although I disagree with his assessment of Buddhist ethical and social consciousness,[13] I find not only Cobb's thesis persuasive, but also his defense supporting his thesis as well. Since I have described Cobb's position in chapter nine, resummarizing his conclusions at this juncture would be redundant and serve no useful purpose. But the validity of the rationale behind Cobb's assertion of the identity of Christ and Amida requires clarification. He points to two key distinctions in the evident parallels between Jodo Shinshu teaching about faith in Amida Buddha and Christian reflection about faith in God revealed through Jesus as the Christ.

First, Buddhists conceptualize the object of Pure Land faith and practice, Amida Buddha, much differently than Christians characterize God. Most obviously, Christian thought understands God as an eternally existing, ontologically transcendent sacred reality. That is, there never was--and never will be--a time when God ceases to exist, because God possesses neither a "beginning" nor an "ending." By contrast, "eternity" is not a quality of Amida Buddha's nature. He is one among numerous "Bliss-body" (saṃbhogakāya) forms of the eternal dharmakāya that all particular Buddhas manifest in their natures. Furthermore, according to Pure Land mythology, there was a time when Amida Buddha existed only as a potentially realizable

goal of the Bodhisattva practices of the monk Dharmakara.

Nor is Amida Buddha an omnipotent, omniscient
creator of the universe, upon whose will every thing
and event depends for its existence. Amida Buddha is
not conceived as a creator, a judge, or a sacred reality structuring "his" purposes into the world, but
rather as a personification of totally nonjudgmental
compassion (karuṇā). Moreover, the realm of samsaric
suffering is the creation of no Buddha, and the universe possesses no inherent purpose that sentient beings must achieve because a Buddha wills it so. The
universe simply "is"; "salvation" means somehow transcending this universe by freeing oneself from the Law
of Karma binding ignorant beings to the recycling processes of rebirth in the realm of pratītyasamut-pāda.

Consequently, anything similar to the christology of the Christian Way is completely foreign to
True Pure Land Buddhist teaching. Amida Buddha is, as
far as can be determined by Western traditions of historiography, a legendary human being-become-savior.
But according to Christian teaching, Christ is God. It
is through this God-man named Jesus the Christ that God
defeated the powers of sin and death for all human beings through Jesus' death and resurrection. Since Jesus the Christ is simultaneously God and human, God's
defeat of the power of sin and death through the historical Jesus are also victories for humanity, or at
least for that portion of humanity whose faith in
Christ allows them to participate in this victory.

Christology, therefore, becomes the source of Christian struggle for justice and community through active participation in the political and economic structures governing human existence in the world. By contrast, Amida Buddha functions only through the modes of nonjudgmental, loving compassion (*karuṇā*). Amida Buddha never judges, and his "grace" or "other-power" is offered to all sentient beings so that eventually sentient beings will achieve enlightened rebirth into Amida Buddha's Pure Land.

But since, according to Christian teaching, humanity stands guilty before God because of sin, God judges humanity as worthy of only divine wrath and punishment, unless, be it noted, God's love grants grace to *some*, not all, human beings. In other words, Christian teaching assumes that without divine judgment there can only exist human indifference to evil and injustice in the world. Accordingly, the Christian God judges in order that divine love (*agapē*) might save some human beings. However, salvation is universal, according to True Pure Land Buddhist teaching. But in normative Christian teaching, salvation, while offered to all, is available to only a select few persons whom God "elects" to receive God's grace.

The second distinction follows from what I have noted in the preceding paragraphs. *How* "other-power" is understood to operate in True Pure Land teaching and *how* grace is understood to operate is traditional Christian teaching are quite different. *Tariki*, "other-power," signifies a process whereby Amida Buddha transfers a portion of his own infinite merit, acquired because of his personal self-efforts in his quest for enlightenment, to all sentient beings, who have no possibility of earning their own merit in the present "Latter Days of the Dharma" (Japanese, *mappō*). When Amida Buddha "transfers" a portion of his merit to an individual, the karmic chain binding that person to the recycling process of birth and death is broken because Amida Buddha's merits *become* that person's merits. It is this process that Shinran, and subsequent True Pure Land teaching, called "other-power." By this process, human beings are nonjudgmentally given the necessary merit for effecting their rebirth into the Pure *as enlightened Buddhas*, independent of their own self-efforts (Japanese, *jiriki* or "otherpower").

According to Christian teaching, particularly in the Pauline, Augustinian, Lutheran tradition, grace operates quite differently. Grace is a process whereby God *imputes* righteousness to an individual even though no person, because of sin, can ever become righteous through any form of self-effort or "work." That is, instead of regarding an individual's lack of righteousness and thereby judging that person accordingly, God judges that individual *as if he or she* were righteous, *as if he or she* really deserved salvation. God *imputes* righteousness to those who in fact always, in themselves, remain unrighteous even after receiving God's grace.

According to Shinran's and subsequent True Pure Land teaching, therefore, Amida Buddha's merits actually become an individual's merits. Consequently, that person *really becomes* worthy of rebirth into the Pure Land. But according to Christian teaching, on the contrary, God *imputes* righteousness to an individual through grace, so that salvation is awarded to that individual as *though* that person really merited God's gift of grace. However the righteousness that God imputes to a person does not become that person's righteousness.

It is precisely these distinctions between Pure Land and traditional Christian, particularly Protestant, teaching about the object of faith and the manner in which other-power and grace function in creating the salvation of human beings that point to amazingly similar experiences of faith in Pure Land Buddhist and Christian experience.[14] Neither tradition reduces faith to mere belief in or intellectual acceptance of doctrines and other sorts of propositional statements about their respective objects of faith. According to Christian teaching, faith is a saving relationship that God establishes with a Person through the power of grace apart from all human self-effort. From the human side of this relationship, faith is experienced essentially as trust in the promises of God made known through the scriptures and the teachings of the Church. Christian faith is, in other words, a responding trust in the graceful power of God's love and reliance upon this love, coupled with lack of trust in all human contrivances to earn God's love and consequent gift of salvation. But, one does not "decide" to trust God, for even the ability to trust God is created in a faithful person through God's grace.

True Pure Land Buddhist teaching and normative Christian teaching are in full agreement at this point. No one "decides," because no one can decide, to "trust" Amida Buddha's "other-power." According to Shinran, faith is a gift given to a person regardless of, perhaps in spite of, that person's physical, mental, or moral condition. Faith is also a prerequisite for "salvation," meaning rebirth into Amida Buddha's Pure Land as an enlightened Buddha. So the granting of faith through Amida Buddha's "other-power" and "salvation" are synonymous terms for Shinran and most subsequent True Pure Land teaching.[15]

To summarize: the fact that True Pure Land Buddhist teaching and Christian teaching, particularly in its Protestant expressions, differ (1) in their world views, (2) in the meaning of salvation, (3) in their understanding of the nature of the object of faith, and (4) in their understanding of how "grace" and "other-power" operate to bring persons to faith, reveals only more clearly the similarities in each tradition's experiences of faith. For the doctrinal formulations of the experience of faith as trust in True Pure Land teaching and Christian teaching are so parallel to one another that it is reasonable to assume, with John Cobb, that in spite of conceptual differences, both traditions point to the same sacred reality. In other words, "Christ and Amida name the same reality."

One possible implication of the view that Christ and Amida name the same reality is that Shinran's Pure Land teachings and subsequent Jōdo Shinshū tradition provide Christians with an experiential entry point for "passing over" into Buddhist exerience not normally available in Christian encounter with the more meditative forms of Buddhist practice such as the Zen, Theravada, or Tibetan Buddhist tradition. Systematically entering into this facet of Buddhist experience might not only deepen Christian apprehension of the ways in which Buddhists have encountered and experienced the Sacred, but it might also help Christians rid themselves of the unnecessary and unbiblical religious imperialism underlying traditionally graceless Christian absolutism and parochialism, while simultaneously renewing Christian faith and practice. In other words, knowing that another religious Way embodies an important tradition in which faith is experienced and doctrinally conceived in ways structurally parallel to significant traditions of normative Christian teaching and practice should help Christians comprehend the heart of the Christian Way more fully. For here is "hard evidence" supporting the ancient Christian teaching that "God has not been without witnesses" in all religious Ways.

Finally, Buddhists also possess an experiential entry point into Christian experience. Perhaps Buddhists have even more to gain from "passing over" into Christian conceptions of faith than Christians have in dialogue with Buddhist conceptions of faith. For Shinran's doctrine of faith through other-power possessed no historical precedents in traditional practices of Bodhisattva and Buddha veneration. Prior to Shinran's interpretation of Pure Land faith and practice, that is, there are no doctrinal or experiential parallels to his teaching of salvation by faith through absolute other-power alone. Shinran's reinterpretation of Pure Land faith and practice was completely original with him. Thus he pointed to his own experience of frustration and failure in achieving enlightenment through the self-powered practices of traditional Buddhist monasticism as a justification of his teachings-- experiences that he *read into,* not out of, the Pure Land tradition prior to his time. But after the death of the "second founder" of Jōdo Shinshū, Rennyo Shōnin (15th century). Shinran's doctrine of faith through other-power alone was gradually deemphasized by subsequent Pure Land teachers, partly because his views could not be easily reconciled with prior Buddhist tradition.

The Christian Way, however, has always stressed the otherness of God's gift of salvation by faith through grace alone. At least from a doctrinal point of view, as well as an experiential one, Christian teachings about faith and grace seem more highly evolved than comparable Buddhist teachings about faith and grace. I wish to be clear, however, that I am not claiming the superiority of the Christian Way over the Buddhist Way. But I am claiming that Buddhists in dialogue with normative Christian theological doctrines of faith and grace, such as Luther's or Calvin's or Augustine's, can creatively transform Shinran's teachings into categories more relevant for Buddhist experience in the modern world of religious and secular pluralism. For the experience of a gracious, compassionate, tran-

scendent sacred reality that Christians christologically experience, apprehend, and encounter in the
rough-and-tumble of historical existence has perhaps
engendered a higher degree of historical-social-
ethical-political consciousness among Christians than
is normal among Buddhists.

My point is not that Christian faith is superior to Buddhist faith, or that Buddhists are unaware
of history, or that Buddhists are ethically, socially,
or politically backward. Such is most certainly not
the case. My point is that normative Christian teaching stresses that the sacred reality it names "God" is
not only a transcendent object and source of faith, but
also a reality encountering human beings within the
limitations of finite, political-historical existence.
Thus, because the standards against which the
"rightness" of human action in the realm of history are
measured are the standards or "demands" that God continually reveals to humanity--for Christians finally in
the incarnation of God in the historical Jesus Christian teaching stresses the ethical practice of faith
within the ethical-social-political arena of human existence.

However, the Buddhist sense of the Sacred,
whether it is named the Dharma or Emptiness, strongly
deemphasizes history as the locus for encountering and
experiencing the Dharma. Meditative experience of the
eternal, transcendent Dharma (or Emptiness) is what
transforms an ordinary human being into a Buddha, and
this experience does not occur as a gift of grace. The
historical Gautama the Buddha, other Buddhas, and the

numerous Bodhisattvas of Mahayana tradition are finally models to imitate meditatively. One does not encounter the reality of the Dharma *through* these beings; one encounters the reality of the Dharma through one's own meditative apprehension of it within one's own experience.

So, the Sacred in Buddhist tradition is a-personal, ahistorical, and therefore not ethically or socially concerned with human community. In traditional Buddhist teaching, the Dharma is neither ethical, social, nor historical: the Dharma just "is" what "it" is at any moment of space-time. Therefore, Buddhist sensitivity to right and wrong, justice and compassion, derives from a transcendent Dharma that makes no demands that *we become* good, just, or compassionate. Appropriating John Cobb's observation, there appears to be no transcendent "principle of rightness" directing traditional Buddhist ethical practice or governing Buddhist historical consciousness.

Contemporary Pure Land faith and practice can, through dialogue with the most systematically evolved theological interpretations of faith and grace in Christian teaching, serve as a bridge for sharpening Buddhist consciousness of the gracious character of the Sacred as encountered within the conditions of historical-social-political existence. "Passing over" into this aspect of the Christian Way might possibly deepen an already existing tradition in the Buddhist Way, thereby enabling Buddhists to play more critical and relevant roles of social-ethical-political criticism in the contemporary "post modern" world.

Exactly how Buddhists should accomplish this transformation, or indeed whether it is even desirable to do so, remains ultimately up to faithful Buddhists. Christians can only remain available to be of service to Buddhists wishing to explore the possibilities.

A PERSONAL UNSCIENTIFIC POSTSCRIPT

Buddhist-Christian dialogue continues and, unless arbitrarily interrupted for whatever reasons, including lack of interest, will never reach completion. In a universe of processive becoming, nothing reaches final completion because there are no final endings, unless, perhaps, an entity dies. As a process, interreligious dialogue not only hastens the coming of death, the "objective immortality," of that which for whatever reason fails as a relevant vehicle for encountering the Sacred, however named; it also hastens the evolution of whatever emerges out of these "objectively immortal" religious forms and expressions. In other words, religious Ways "die," and are replaced by new religious Ways that incorporate and synthesize much of the older religious teachings and practices into a more comprehensive vision of the Sacred. This process proceeds, at times, very slowly, and may require thousands of years. At other times, the process is quite rapid, as when, for example, the Buddhist Way replaced the indigenous Bon tradition of Tibet even as it dialogically incorporated much of Bon shamanism into itself. A similar dialogical process occurred as the Christian Way replaced by incorporating much of the Greek mystery religions and some forms of gnosticism into its gospel. I suspect, although I cannot prove, that the process of interreligious dialogue is a particular example of processes mirroring more generic natural forces at present structuring existence in this present "cosmic epoch."

Accordingly, I believe it can be cogently argued that in the present post-Christian and Post-Buddhist pluralistic age, traditional Christian theological reflection and the Buddhist world view are presently at a dead end. Theologians and Buddhist teachers should now become self-conscious philosophers of religion concerned with analyzing, articulating, and proposing where the process of creative transformation might be leading relative to humanity's collective religious experience. Or in the language of Paul Tillich, Christian theologians and Buddhist teachers should resign themselves to stepping out of their respective "theological circles." Why should not the process of creative transformation now happening in the Christian Way, perhaps most rigorously and coherently in process theology, lead "beyond theology" in the present post-Christian age? Likewise, could not the similar processes now occurring in the Buddhist Way, as well as in the Jewish Way, and even in Islam, lead to their objective immortality as independent religious Ways as well?

If we actually do live in an age of religious and secular pluralism, should not any practicing religious person be concerned with transcending the limitations of the present boundaries of his or her particular religious Way in the conscious hope of discovering religious meaning more universal than any experienced before? Perhaps in another cosmic epoch the process of creative transformation through interreligious dialogue will energize the evolution of a more universal religious vision incorporating the insights of the Christian and Buddhist Ways, along with the Jewish and Islamic Ways, Yoga, and even the so-called "archaic" religious Ways of "pre-literate" cultures.

I do not intend these observations as a prediction of the future. But it should surprise no one if the processes now occurring in this present ages of religious and secular pluralism should be leading in this direction. Nor should anyone mourn the potential demise of the Christian or the Buddhist Ways into "objective immortality," or mourn their potential replacement by new religious Ways more universal and relevant to the needs of persons than either the Christian Way or the Buddhist Way can be in separation from one another. After all, the history of religions supplies good evidence for concluding that the Sacred, however named, cares very little about religious Ways, but cares very much about persons. Those religious teachings and practices failing to help persons achieve meaningful existence in this present age will die, just as they have died in the past for the same irrelevances. Not only because persons will "vote with their feet" and search for options apart from the traditional forms of religious faith and practice, but also because the Sacred continually expresses itself in ever new forms relevant to ever-changing human experience in a constantly becoming universe.

I consequently have a strong hunch that the evidence of the history of religions suggests that every religious Way, in differing degrees, represents traditions of human encounter with one sacred reality, named and experienced according to the particular historical-cultural contexts of each Way. I cannot, of course, "prove" this assertion, nor do I wish to defend the notion that "all paths lead to the same summit" or something like the older perennial philosophy of Aldous Huxley. But nevertheless, I do believe, in the sense of having a strongly held opinion, that the evidence of the history of religions supports my hunch. If so, interreligious dialogue itself becomes a form of religious *praxis* by which we open ourselves to fuller apprehension of the Sacred as the center around which the process of creative transformation now operating in the contemporary age of modern religious and secular pluralism revolves.

If, therefore, all religious Ways center on one transcendent sacred reality experienced and named differently in each Way, the purpose of dialogue becomes the relativization of the particular religious Ways of humanity in order to apprehend how the Sacred has been apprehended by others. For all religions experience, belief, and practice in *every* historic religious Way have been multifarious in the extreme. And while not every form of religious faith and practice is of equal value or importance, we should prepare ourselves to enter into dialogue with them all, with complete openness to learning what others may have to teach us about their particular experiences of the one sacred reality Christians call God and Buddhists call the Dharma, Emptiness, or Buddha Nature.

This, it appears to me, is what it means for Christians or Buddhists to relativize, rather than absolutize, their respective Ways of experiencing the one sacred reality in order to experience how It has been experienced by other religious persons. For Christians, but perhaps not all, *have* encountered the Sacred through Jesus as the Christ; Buddhists, but perhaps not all, *have* encountered the Sacred through the Dharma or Emptiness or the Buddha Nature in all things and events: Confucianists, but perhaps not all, *have* encountered the Sacred through *jen* or "humaneness"; Taoists, but perhaps not all, *have* encountered the Sacred through the Tao [Way]; Muslims, but perhaps not all, *have* encountered the Sacred through "surrender" or *'islam* to Allah, "the God"; Hindus, but perhaps not all, *have* encountered the Sacred through the infinite number of *avatar*-forms of Brahman. None of these encounters should be shunned. All should be critically and dialogically engaged by the earnest seeker of the Sacred.

NOTES

[1]F. L. Woodard and E. M. Hare trans., *The Book of Gradual Sayings [Aṅguttara-Nikāya]*, 4. vols. (London: Pali Text Society. 1961-70).

[2]For a discussion of the parallels between, and possible sources of Buddhist and biblical versions of the parable of the sower, see Roy C. Amore, *Two Masters, One Message* (Nashville: Abingdon Press. 1970), 83-85.

[3]The Roman Catholic and Protestant movements of liberation and feminist theology are, of course, exceptions to this dualistic separation of *theoria* and *praxis*. In fact, these traditions stress the unity of *theoria* and *praxis* within the political and economic contexts in which all persons, especially oppressed persons, must live their lives.

[4]The Soto Zen master Dogen's view of the unity of *theoria* and *praxis* is but a particular instance of the general Buddhist view; "Reading Zen sayings and *koans* and understanding the actions of Zen Masters of old to preach them to deluded people are all ultimately useless, either for one's own practice or for guiding others." Reiho Mastsunaga, trans., *A Primer of Soto Zen, A Translation of Dōgen's Shōbōgenzō Zuimonki* (Honolulu; East-West Center Press, 1971), 34. Also see Hee-jin Kim, *Dōgen Kigen, Mystical Realist* (Tucson: University of Arizona Press, 1975), chapter 3, and John C. Maraldo, " The hermeneutics of Practice in Dōgen and Francis of Assisi" *in Buddhist-Christian Dialogue, Mutual Renewal and Transformation*, ed. Paul O. Ingram and Frederic J. Streng (Honolulu: University of Hawaii Press. 1986), 53-72.

[5]William James, *The Varieties of Religious Experience* (New York: Longmans, Green, and Co., 1912), 485-527.

[6]The exceptions to this tradition are found in certain sectarian movements within the Nichiren Buddhist movement, most recently in Nichiren Shoshu Soka Gakkai [The Value Creation Society of the Orthodox School of Nichiren]. Rather than *upāya,* Sōka Gakkai practice centers on *shakubuku,* "to break and subdue,"

to achieve *kosen-rufu* or "world-wide conversion" to Nichiren Shoshu. For a splendid one-chapter analysis of Soka Gakkai, see H. Neill McFarland, *The Rush Hour of the Gods* (New York: Macmillan, 1967), chapt. 9.

[7]Cf. Agehananda Bharati, *The Light at the Center: Context and Pretext of Modern Mysticism* (Santa Barbara: Ross-Erickson. 1976), 84-100, 141-43; W. T. Stace, *Mysticism and Philosophy* (Philadelphia: J. B. Lippincott, 1960). pp. 88-111; William Johnson, *The Still Point* (New York: Harper and Row, 1971), 27-43; and David W. Linge, "Mysticism, Poverty, and Reason in the Thought of Meister Eckhart," *Journal of the American Academy of Religion,* 46 (1978): 465-88.

[8]John B.Cobb.Jr., *Beyond Dialogue* (Philadelphia: Fortress Press, 1982), 110-14.

[9]See John B. Cobb, Jr., "Buddhist Emptiness and the Christian God," *Journal of the american Academy of Religion* 45 (1977): 9-25.

[10]Ibid.

[11]Cobb, *Beyond dialogue,* 123-28.

[12]By "historical consciousness," I mean something similar to Langdon Gilkey's's analysis of the character of "modern historical consciousness": (1) all forms of individual and social existence are relative to their time and place, so that (2) human understanding of the forms of individual and social existence are relative to, and hence limited by, an individual's social, historical, cultural, and biological context. Therefore (3), all understanding is finite, limited, and conditioned by the context from which all judgments are made, so that (4) all truth claims are relative, never absolute. See Langdon Gilkey, *Reaping the Whirlwind, A Christian Interpretation of History* (New York: Seabury Press, 1981), 188-93.

[13]See my essay. "To John Cobb: Questions to Gladden the Atman in an Age of Pluralism," *Journal of the American Academy of Religion* 45 (1977): 722-24.

[14]For a comparative analysis of these distinctions in the form they assumed in Shinran's and Martin

Luther's teachings about faith and grace, see my essay
"Shinran Shōnin and Martin Luther: A Soteriological
Comparison," *Journal of the American Academy of Reli-
gion* 34 (1971): 430-47.

[15]*Kyōgyōshinshō* [Treatise on Teaching,
Practice, and Faith]. SSZ II, 59-60 and Mattō Shō
[Light in the Latter Days], Ibid.

SELECTED BIBLIOGRAPHY

BOOKS

Abbot, Walter M., S. J. *The Documents of Vatican II.* New York: Guild Press, 1966.

Akamatsu, Shunshu. *Kamakura no Bukkyo no Kenkyu* [Studies in Kamakura Buddhism]. Kyoto: Byorakuji Shoten, 1957.

Anderson, Dines, and Helmer Smith eds. *Suttanipata I: Pali Text Translation Series.* Oxford: Oxford University Press, 1913.

Anderson, J. N. P. *Christianity and Comparative Religion.* Downers Grove, Ill.: Intervarsity Press, 1977.

Andrews, Allan A. *The Teachings Essential for Rebirth.* Tokyo: Sophia University, 1973.

Aquinas, Thomas. *Summa Theologiae.* 22 vols. Translated by the English Dominicans. London and New York: 1912-1936.

Barth, Karl. *Against the Stream.* Edinburgh: Oliver and Boyd, 1956.

Berger, Peter L. *The Heretical Imperative.* Garden City, N.J.: Anchor Books, 1979.

Bharati, Agehananda. *The Light at the Center.* Santa Barbara: Ross-Erickson, 1976.

Bloom, Alfred. *Shinran's Gospel of Pure Grace.* Tucson: University of Arizona Press, 1965.

Bornkamm, Gunther. *Paul.* New York: Harper and Row, 1969.

Buddhaghoṣa. *Visuddhimaga* [Path of Purification]. Edited by Henry Clark Warren. Cambridge: Harvard University Press, 1950.

Bultmann, Rudolf. *Theology of the New Testament.* 2 vols. New York: Charles Scribner's Sons, 1951.

Capra, Fritjof. *The Tao of Physics.* Boulder,Colo.: Shambhala Publications, 1975.

Christian, William A. *An Interpretation of Whitehead's Metaphysics.* New Haven: Yale University Press, 1959.

Cobb, John B., Jr. *Beyond Dialogue.* Philadelphia: Fortress Press, 1982.

_____. *Christ in a Pluralistic Age.* Philadelphia: Westminster Press, 1975.

_____. *A Christian Natural Theology.* Philadelphia: Westminster Press, 1965.

_____. *God and the World.* Philadelphia: Westminster Press, 1969.

_____. *The Structure of Christian Existence.* Philadelphia: Westminster Press, 1967.

Cobb,John B., Jr. and David Ray Griffin. *Process Theology: An Introduction.* Philadelphia: Westminster Press, 1976.

Collcutt, Martin. *Five Mountains: The Rinzai Zen Monastic Institution in Medieval Japan.* Cambridge: Council on East Asian Studies, Harvard University, 1981.

Dasgupta, S. B. *An Introduction to Tantric Buddhism.* Calcutta: University of Calcutta Press, 1958.

Dawe, Donald G., and John B. Carman, eds. *Christian Faith in a Religiously Plural World.* Maryknoll, N. Y.: Orbis Books, 1978.

Drummond, Richard. *A History of Christianity in Japan.* Grand Rapids, Mich.: William B. Eerdmans Publishing Co., 1971.

Dumoulin, Heinrich. *Christianity Meets Buddhism.* Translated by John C. Maraldo. La Salle: Open Court Publishing Co. 1974.

Dunne, S. J. *The Way of All the Earth.* South Bend: University of Notre Dame Press, 1978.

Dutt, Nalinaksha. *Early Monastic Buddhism.* 2 vols. Calcutta: Calcutta Oriental Series, 1945.

Eliade, Mircea. *Cosmos and History.* Translated by William R. Trask. New York: Harper and Row, 1959.
_____. *Patterns of Comparative Religion.* Translated by Rosemary Sheed. New York: The Wald Publishing Co., 1963.

Eusden, John Dykstra. *Zen and Christianity.* New York: The Crossroad Publishing Publishing Co., 1981.

Fine, Paul, Johannes Behm, and Werner George Kummel. *Introduction to the New Testament.* Translated by A. J. Mattile. Nashville: Abingdon Press, 1966.

Fletcher, Joseph. *Situation Ethics.* Philadelphia: Westminster Press, 1966.

Gallagher, Louis J., S. J., trans. *China in the Sixteenth Century: The Journals of Matthew Ricci, 1583-1610.* New York: Random House, 1953.

Gilson, Etienne. *The Christian Philosophy of Saint Augustine.* New York: Random House, 1960.

_____. *The Christian Philosophy of St. Thomas Aquinas.* New York: Random House, 1956.

Graham, Aelred. *Zen Catholicism: A Suggestion.* London: Collins, 1969.

Griffin, David Ray, and Thomas J. J. Altizer, eds. *John Cobb's Theology in Process.* Philadelphia: Westminster Press, 1977.

Greene, Marjorie. *The Knower and the Known.* Berkeley and Los Angeles: University of California Press, 1974.

Guenther, H. V. *Tibetan Buddhism in Western Perspective.* Emeryville, Calif.: Dharma Publishing, 1977.

Hallencreuz, Carl F. *New Approaches to Men of Other Faiths.* Geneva: World Council of Churches, 1970.

Harvey, Van A. *The Historian and the Believer.* New York: The Macmillan Co., 1966.

Heick, Otto W. *A History of Christian Thought.* 2 vols. Philadelphia: Fortress Press, 1965.

Hick, John. *God and the Universe of Faiths.* London: Macmillan, 1973.

Hick, John, and Brian Hebblethwaite, eds. *Christianity and Other Religions.* Philadelphia: Fortress Press, 1980.

Ingram, Paul O. *The Dharma of Faith.* Washington, D.C.: University Press of America, 1977.

Ingram, Paul O., and Frederick J. Streng, eds. *Buddhist-Christian Dialogue: Mutual Renewal and Transformation.* Honolulu: University of Hawaii Press, 1986.

James, William. *The Varieties of Religious Experience.* New York: New American Library, 1958.

Johansson, Rune E. A. *The Psychology of Nirvana.* Garden City, N. J. Anchor Books, 1970.

Johnston, William. *Mysticism and Zen Masters.* New York: Harper and Row, 1974.

_____. *The Still Point.* New York: Harper and Row, 1971.

Kalupahana, David J. *Buddhist Philosophy, A Historical Analysis.* Honolulu: University of Hawaii Press, 1976.

Kim, Hee-jin. *Dōgen Kigen, Mystical Realist.* Tucson: The Association for Asian Studies, 1965.

Knowles, D. *Christian Monasticism.* New York: Mc Graw-Hill, 1969.

Küng, Hans. *On Being A Christian.* New York: Pocket Books, 1978.

Leith, John H. *Creeds of the Churches.* New York: Doubleday, 1963.

Labkowitz, Nicholas. *Theory and Practice.* South Bend: University of Notre Dame Press, 1967.

Mackintosh, Hugh Ross. *Types of Modern Technology* New York: Charles Schribner's Sons, 1937.

Matsunaga, Alicia. *The Buddhist Philosophy of Assimilation.* Tokyo: Charles E. Tuttle Co., 1969.

Matsunaga, Daigan and Alicia Matsunaga. *Foundations of Japanese Buddhism.* 2 vols. Tokyo: Buddhist Books International, 1974.

Merton, *Thomas. Mystics and Zen Masters.* New York: Dell, 1969.

Moltmann, Jürgen. *The Church in the Power of the Spirit.* New York: Harper and Row, 1975.

Morris, Ivan. *The World of the Shining Prince.* New York: Alfred A. Knopf, 1966.

Needhman, Joseph. *Science and Civilization in China.* 5 vols. Cambridge: At the University Press, 1961-1974.

Needleman, Jacob. *The New Religions.* Garden City, N. J.: Doubleday and Company, 1970.

Neill, Stephen. *Christian Faiths and Other Faiths.* New York: Oxford University Press, 1970.

Neville, Robert C. *The Tao and the Daimon.* Albany: State University of New York Press, 1982.

Niebuhr, H. Richard. *The Responsible Self.* New York: Harper and Row, 1963.

Oxtoby, Willard G., ed. *Religious Diversity: Essays by Wilfred Cantwell Smith*. New York: Harper and Row, 1976.

Panikkar, R. *The Interreligious Dialogue*. New York: Paulist Press, 1978.

Paul, Diana Y. *Women in Buddhism: Portraits of the Feminine in Mahayana*. Berkeley: Asian Humanities Press, 1978.

Perty, Ray C., ed. *Late Medieval Mysticism*. Vol. 13 of *The Library of Christian Classics*. Edited by John Ballie, John T. McNeill, and Henry Van Dusen. Philadelphia: Westminster Press, 1957.

Polanyi, Michael. *Personal Knowledge*. New York: Harper and Row, 1964.

Prebish, Charles S., ed. *Buddhism: A Modern Perspective*. University Park: Pennsylvania State University Press, 1975.

Rähner, Karl. *Theological Investigations*. Vols. 6 and 14. London: Darton. Longman, and Todd, 1966, 1976.

Rahula, Walpola. *What the Buddha Taught*. New York: Grove Press, 1962.

Ramsey, Paul. *Deeds and Rules in Christian Ethics*. New York: Charles Scribner's Sons, 1967.

Reischauer, Edwin O. and John K. Fairbank. *East Asia: The Great Tradition*. Boston: Houghton and Mifflin Company, 1960.

Ridderbos, Hermann. *Paul, An Outline of His Theology*. Grand Rapids, Mich.: Eerdmans Publishing Co., 1975.

Robinson, Richard H. and Willard L. Johnson. *The Buddhist Religion: A Historical Introduction*. Encino, Calif.: Dickenson Publishing Co., 1977.

Ross, Floyd H. *The Meaning of Life in Hinduism and Buddhism.* London: Routledge and Kegan Paul, 1952.

Sangharakshita, Bhiksu. *A Survey of Buddhism.* Bangalore: Indian Institute of World Culture, 1966.

Sansom, Sir George. *Japan: A Short Cultural History.* New York: Appleton, Century, and Crofts, 1962.

Schecter, Jerrold. *the New Face of the Buddha.* Tokyo: John Weatherhill, 1967.

Schillebeeckx, Edward. *Jesus, An Experiment in Christology.* Translated by Hurbert Haskins. New York: Crossroad Publishing Co., 1981.

Seeberg, Reinhold. *Textbook of the History of Doctrines.* 2 vols. Grand Rapids, Mich.: Baker Book House, 1964.

Sharpe, Eric J. *Comparative Religion: A History.* New York: Charles Schribner's Sons, 1975.

Sherburne, Donald W., ed. *A Key to Whitehead's Process and Reality.* Bloomington: Indiana University Press, 1966.

Shinshū Shōgyō Zenshō [Complete Works of Shinshu Teaching.] 5 vols. Kyōto: Kōkyō shōin, 1958.

de Silva, Lynn A. *The Problem of the Self in Buddhism and Christianity.* Colombo: Study Center for Religion and Society, 1975.

Smith, William Cantwell. *Belief and History.* Charlottesville: University Press of Virginia, 1977.

_____. *Faith and Belief.* Princeton: Princeton University Press, 1979.

_____. *The Faith of Other Men.* New York: New American Library, 1965.

_____. *The Meaning and End of Religion.* New York: New American Library, 1964.

_____. *Towards a World Theology: Faith and the Comparative History of Religion.* Philadelphia: Westminster Press, 1981.

Sontang, Frederick. *Love Beyond Pain: Mysticism Within Christianity.* New York: Paulist Press. 1977.

Spae, Joseph. *Buddhist-Christian Empathy.* Chicago: Institute of Theology and Culture, 1980.

Staal, Fritz. *Exploring Mysticism: A Methodological Essay.* Berkeley and Los Angeles: University of California Press, 1975.

Stace, W. T. *Mysticism and Philosophy.* Philadelphia: J. B. Lippincott and Co., 1960.

Streng, Frederick J. *Emptiness: A Study in Religious Meaning.* Nashville: Abingdon Press, 1967.

Swearer, Donald K. *Dialogue: The Key to Understanding Other Religions.* Philadelphia: Westminster Press, 1977.

Tillich, Paul. *The Courage to Be.* New Haven: Yale University Press, 1952.

_____. *Christianity and the Encounter With the World Religions.* New York: Columbia University Press, 1961.

_____. *Dynamics of Faith.* New York: Harper and Row, 1957.

Toulmin, Stephen. *An Examination of the Place of Reason in Ethics.* Cambridge: Cambridge University Press, 1950.

Takuwa, Shinji, trans. *Perfect Freedom in Buddhism.* Tokyo: The Hokuseido Press, 1968.

Toynbee, Arnold. *Christianity Among the Religions of the World.* New York: Charles Schribner's Sons. 1957.

Trenckner, V., and Lord Chalmers, eds. *Majjhima Nikāya: Pāli Text Society Translation Series.* Oxford: Oxford University Press, 1888.

Troeltsch, Ernst. *The Social Teachings of the Christian Churches.* 2 vols. Chicago: University of Chicago Press, 1981.

Turner, Victor. *The Ritual Process.* London: Routledge, 1969.

Walker, Williston. *A History of the Christian Church.* New York: Charles Schribner's Sons, 1959.

Watenabe, Shoko. *Nippon on Bukkyō* [Buddhism in Japan]. Tōkyō: Iwanami Shinso, 1964.

Welch, Holmes. *The Practice of Chinese Buddhism.* Cambridge: Harvard University Press, 1967.

Whitehead, Alfred North. *Adventures of Ideas.* New York: Free Press, 1967.

_____. *Process and Reality.* New York: Macmillan Company, 1967.

_____. *Religion in the Making.* New York: Meridian Books, 1961.

_____. *Science and the Modern World.* New York: Free Press, 1967.

Whitson, Robley Edward. *The Coming Convergence of World Religions.* New York: Newman Press, 1971.

Wharf, Benjamin Lee. *Language, thought, and Reality.* New York: John Wiley and Sons, 1956.

Wieman, Henry Nelson. *The Source of Human Good.* Carbondale: Southern Illinois University Press, 1946.

Yonker, Nicholas J. *God, Man, and the Planetary Age.* Corvallis: Oregon State University Press. 1978.

Zaehner, R. C. *Christianity and Other Religions.* New York: Hawthorne Books, 1964.

Zarnecki, George. *The Monastic* Achievement. New York: McGraw-Hill, 1973.

ARTICLES AND ESSAYS

Abe, Masao. "Hisamatsu's Philosophy of Awakening." *The Eastern Buddhist* 14 (Spring, 1981): 26-42.

_____. "The End of World Religion." *The Eastern Buddhist* 13 (Spring, 1980): 31-45.

Augustine, "The Spirit and the Letter" in *The Library of Christian Classics,* edited by John Burnaby, 8:182-250. Philadelphia: Westminster Press, 1955.

Berger, Peter L. "From Secularity to World Religions." *The Christian Century,* 97 (16 January 1980): 41-45.

Bolle, Kees W. "Reflections on the History of Religions and History." *History of Religions* (August-November 1980): 64-80.

Cobb, John B., Jr. "Buddhist Emptiness and the Christian God." *Journal of the American Academy of Religion* 45 (1977): 11-25.

_____. "Can a Christian Be a Buddhist, Too?" *Japanese Religions* 10 (December 1979): 1-20.

_____. Christianity and Eastern Wisdom" *Japanese Journal of Religious Studies* (December 1978): 285-98.

_____. "Whitehead's Philosophy and a Christian Doctrine of Man." *Journal of Bible and Religion* 32 (July 1964): 209-20.

"Cracking Down on the Big Ones," *Time,* 31 December 1979, 63.

Dumoulin, Heinrich. "Buddhism in Modern Japan." *Buddhism in the Modern World,* edited by Heinrich Dumoulin and John C. Maraldo, 125-276. New York: Macmillan, 1976.

Fenton, John Y. "Mystical Experience as a Bridge for Cross Cultural Philosophy of Religion: A Critique." *Journal of the American Academy of Religion* 49 (March 1981): 50-75.

Ford, Lewis S. "The Power of God and the Christ." In *Religious Experience and Process Theology*, edited by Harry James Cargas and Bernard Lee, 79-82. New York: Paulist Press, 1976.

Frankenberg, Nancy. "The Experiential Dimension of Religious Experience." *Process Studies* 8 (1978): 259-76.

Harrington, Ann M. "The Kakure Kirishitan and their Place in Japan's Religious Tradition." *Japanese Journal of Religious Studies* 7 (December 1980): 318-36.

Hartshrone, Charles. "The Compound Individual." In *Whitehead's Philosophy: Selected Essays, 1935-1970*, 41-61. Lincoln: University of Nebraska Press, 1972.

Hisamatsu, Shin'ichi. "On the Record of Rinzai." *The Eastern Buddhist* 14 (Spring 1981): 1-12.

Ingram, Paul O. "Hōnen's and Shinran's Justification of their Doctrine of Salvation by Faith through Other-Power." *Contemporary Religions in Japan* 9 (September 1969): 233-51.

_____. "Interfaith Dialogue as a Source of Buddhist-Christian Creative Transformation." In *Buddhist-Christian Dialogue: Mutual Renewal and Transformation*, edited by Paul O. Ingram and Frederick J. Streng, 79-94. Honolulu: University of Hawaii Press, 1986.

_____. "To John Cobb: Questions to Gladden the Ātman in an Age of Pluralism." *Journal of the American Academy of Religion* 45 (June 1977): 753-88.

Kitagawa, Joseph M. "The Career of Maitreya, With Special Reference to Japan. "*History of Religions* 21 (November 1981): 107-25.

Kitagawa, Joseph M. and Frank Reynolds. "Theravada Buddhism in the Twentieth Century." In *Buddhism in the Modern World*, edited by Heinrich Dumoulin and John C. Maraldo,43-64. New York: Macmillan 1976.

Kiyota, Minoru. "Buddhist Devotational Meditation: A Study of the *Sukhavativyuhopadesa.*" In *Mahayana Buddhist Meditation: Theory and Practice,* edited by Minoru Kiyota, 249-96. Honolulu: University Press of Hawaii, 1978.

Lai, Whalen W. "The Predocetic 'Finite Buddhakaya' in the *Lotus Sutra:* In Search of the Illusive Dharmakaya. *Journal of the American Academy of Religion* 49 (September 1981), 447-69.

McDaniel, Jay. "Zen and the Self." *Process Studies* 10 (Fall-Winter 1980): 110-19.

Nobo, Jorge Luis. "Whitehead's Principle of Relativity." *Process Studies* 8 (Spring 1978): 1-20.

Ocho, Enichi. "The Beginnings of Buddhist Text Classification in China." *The Eastern Buddhist* (Autumn 1981): 71-94.

Pittenger, Norman. "Process Theology: A Whiteheadian Version." In *Religious Experience and Process Theology,* edited by Harry James and Bernard Lee, 3-21. New York: Paulist Press, 1976.

Reynolds, Frank. "Contrary Modes of Action: A Comparative Study of Buddhist and Christian Ethics." *History of Religions* 20 (August November 1980): 128-146.

Slater, Robert Lawson. "The Coming Great Dialogue." In *Christianity: Some Non-Christian Appraisals,* edited by David. W. McKain, 1-16. Westport: Greenwood Press, 1964.

Swearer, Donald K. "Recent Developments in Buddhism." In *Buddhism in the Modern World,* edited by Heinrich Dumoulin and John C. Maraldo, 99-107. New York: Macmillan Company, 1976.

_____. "Reformist Buddhism in Thailand: The Case of Bhikkhu Buddhadasa." *Dialogue* 8 (January-December 1981): 27-42.

Swyngedouw, Jan. "Interfaith Dialogue: A Sociological Reflection." *Japanese Religions* 10 (July 1979): 7-26.

Thelle, Natto R. "Prospects and Problems of the Buddhist-Christian Dialogue: A Report." *Japanese Religions* 10 (July 1979): 51-65.

Welsh, Holmes. "Buddhism in China Today." In *Buddhism in the Modern World*, edited by Heinrich Dumoulin and John C. Maraldo, 164-78. New York: Macmillan Publishing Company, 1976.

Williamson, Clark M. "Process Hermeneutics and Christianity's Post-Holocaust Reinterpretation of Itself." *Process Studies* 12 (Summer 1982): 77-93.

INDEX

STUDIES IN COMPARATIVE RELIGIONS